THE BELIEF IN A LIFE AFTER DEATH

Publication Number 423

AMERICAN LECTURE SERIES®

A Monograph in

The BANNERSTONE DIVISION *of*

AMERICAN LECTURES IN PHILOSOPHY

Edited by

MARVIN FARBER, Ph.D.

Department of Philosophy

University of Buffalo

Buffalo, New York

The following books have appeared thus far in this Series:

Causality in Natural Science—V. F. Lenzen

Emotions and Reason—V. J. McGill

A Good and Bad Government According to the New Testament—Jean Hering

The Phenomenological Approach to Psychiatry—J. H. Van den Berg

Operationism—A. C. Benjamin

Psychoanalysis and Ethics—Lewis S ¯euer

Culture, Psychiatry, and Human Values—Marvin K. Opler

The Origins of Marxian Thought—Auguste Cornu

Metascientific Queries—Mario Bunge

Anthropology and Ethics—May and Abraham Edel

Naturalism and Subjectivism—Marvin Farber

The Language of Education—Israel Scheffler

A Critical Examination of

THE BELIEF IN A
LIFE AFTER DEATH

Second Printing

By

C. J. DUCASSE

Professor of Philosophy, Emeritus

Brown University

Providence, Rhode Island

CHARLES C THOMAS • PUBLISHER
Springfield • Illinois • U.S.A.

Published and Distributed Throughout the World by
CHARLES C THOMAS • PUBLISHER
Bannerstone House
301-327 East Lawrence Avenue, Springfield, Illinois, U.S.A.

(paper) ISBN 0-398-03037-5
Library of Congress Catalog Card Number: 60-12660

First Printing, 1961
Second Printing, 1974

*With THOMAS BOOKS careful attention is given to all details of
manufacturing and design. It is the Publisher's desire to present books that are
satisfactory as to their physical qualities and artistic possibilities and
appropriate for their particular use. THOMAS BOOKS will be true to those
laws of quality that assure a good name and good will.*

Printed in the United States of America
R-1

PREFACE

The question whether there is, or can be, or cannot be a life after death for the individual is seldom formulated unambiguously, or approached with a genuinely open mind, or discussed objectively on the basis of the relevant empirical or theoretical considerations. Persons in whom survival after death is an article of religious faith generally assume that it and other dogmas of their religion are, as such, authoritative; and hence that the point of engaging in discussions of the matter is not to try to find out whether or not survival is a fact, but only to convince others that it is a fact—or at least to show them that the reasons which lead them to doubt or to deny it are invalid.

Persons, on the other hand, who have had training in science, or at least those among them who do not lay aside their scientific habits of thought when subjects reputedly religious are concerned, commonly take it for granted today that the progress of physiological and behavioristic psychology has finally proved that the consciousness and personality of man is—as they are wont to phrase it—a function of the nervous system and of certain other constituents of the living human body; and hence that there cannot possibly be for the individual any life or consciousness after the body has died.

A position in some ways intermediate between the two just described is that of the Spiritists or Spiritualists. Survival of the personality after death is held by them to be not an article of faith but a matter of knowledge. That is, they hold it as something for the truth of which they have adequate empirical evidence in the communications, received through the persons they call mediums, that purport to emanate from the surviving spirits of the deceased. Thus, irrespective of whether or not that evidence really proves what it is alleged to prove, the fact that *empirical*—or more specifically *testimonial*—evidence is what Spiritualists appeal to for support of their belief means that, in so far, they conceive the question of survival as a scientific rather than as a religious one.

On the other hand, two factors have cooperated in making Spiritism or Spiritualism claim for itself also the status of a religion. One of these factors has been the need to protect the activities of mediums from the application of ordinances or laws against fortune-telling. The other has been that, because of the widespread vagueness as to what questions are or are not essentially religious, and because of the fact that most religions have asserted that there is for the individual a life after death, therefore belief or knowledge as to such life has uncritically been assumed to be religious *inherently*, rather than perhaps only instrumentally.

In the present book, the question as to the possibility, reality, or impossibility of a life after death is approached without commitment, explicit or implicit, to any one of the three positions concerning it just described. What the book attempts is a philosophical scrutiny of the idea of a life after death. That is, it attempts to set forth, as adequately as possible, the various questions which, on reflection, arise on the subject; to purge them both of ambiguity and of vagueness; to point out what connection the subject does, and does not, have with religion; to examine without prejudice the merits of the considerations—theological or scientific, empirical or theoretical—which have been alleged variously to make certain, or probable, or possible, or impossible, that the human personality survives bodily death; to state what kind of evidence would, if we should have it, conclusively prove that a human personality, or some specified component of it, has survived after death; and to consider the variety of forms which a life after death, if any, could with any plausibility be conceived to take.

Needless to say, this ambitious program is not likely to be carried through with complete success. Nor—in view of the prejudices and the wishful thinking either on the *pro* or on the *contra* side which infect the great majority of persons who take some interest in the question—is much of what will be said likely to be found agreeable by all readers; for the sacredness of a number of the "sacred cows" which have influenced the beliefs or disbeliefs entertained on the subject of survival after death will have to be questioned.

Moreover, at a few places, the issues to be considered cannot, by their very nature, be discussed with any prospect of deciding them in a responsible manner unless they are first formulated with greater precision, and their implications then developed more rigorously, than has usually been done in discussions of the question as to a life after death. But precision and rigor—even when utmost care is taken, as it will be, to make its literary form as psychologically painless as possible—entails the need on the reader's part of closer attention than many are willing to give. For it is much easier to jump to conclusions than to draw them responsibly—to jump to conclusions provided they be favorable, if one is moved by wish to believe; or to jump to conclusions provided they be adverse, if one is moved by wish to disbelieve.

The issues involved, however, are ultimately so important that wishful thinking, on either side, will, to the best of the author's ability, be excluded in this book from his consideration of their merits.

The author's obligations to the works of the various writers discussed or referred to in the text are indicated by the footnotes. Some portions of the text have appeared as articles in periodicals. Several Sections of Chapter XI formed part of a communication presented by the author at the 1957 Interamerican Congress of Philosophy, which later appeared in the journal, *Philosophy and Phenomenological Research,* as an article entitled "Life, Telism, and Mechanism." Chapter XVI borrows extensively from an address by the author at the celebration in 1956 of the Fiftieth Anniversary of the founding of the American Society for Psychical Research, which, with the other addresses, was published in the Society's journal. Chapters XX and XXV were published as articles, respectively in the *International Journal of Parapsychology,* and in the *Journal of the American Society for Psychical Research.* Grateful acknowledgement is here made to the editors of these periodicals for permission to incorporate into the text the materials mentioned.

C.J.D.

CONTENTS

Part II

The Key Concepts

Part III

The Relation Between Mind and Body

Part IV

Discarnate Life After Death and the Ostensibly Relevant Empirical Evidence For It

THE BELIEF IN A LIFE AFTER DEATH

PART I

Immortality, Religion, and Science

Chapter I

BELIEF AND DISBELIEF IN A LIFE AFTER DEATH

That there is for the human individual some sort of life after death has been and still is widely believed. To the majority of mankind, this idea has not seemed paradoxical nor a life after death difficult to imagine. It has often been conceived as lived in a body and surroundings nearly or quite as material as our present ones, though the future environment and the experiences to be had in it have generally been thought of as rather different, whether for the better or the worse, from those of life on earth.

1. **Life: physiological or psychological?** Persons, however, who find such a material conception of a future life incredible either because of its crudity or because of the destruction the body undeniably undergoes after it has died, are likely to think of survival in essentially psychological terms and therefore to mean by "personal survival" more or less what Dean W. R. Matthews does, to wit, "that the center of consciousness which was in existence before death does not cease to be in existence after death and that the experience of this center after death has the same kind of continuity with its experience before death as that of a man who sleeps for a while and wakes again."[1]

As we shall see eventually, a number of difficulties are implicit even in this seemingly clear statement. Yet, some meaning thus psychological rather than physiological has to be given to the word "life," if the hypothesis of a life after death is to have any of the personal and social interest it commonly has. For life in the merely biological sense of the word—the sense in which even the

---

[1]Psychical Research and Theology, The Sixth Myers Memorial Lecture, *Proc. Soc. for Psychical Research*, Vol. 46:15, 1940-41.

body of a man in coma, or a vegetable, has life—has, by itself, only an impersonal scientific interest for us. It acquires any other only if, or in so far as, an organism alive in this physiological sense is a necessary basis for life in the sense of conscious psychological experience. In these pages, therefore, the words, "life after death"—except at places where a different sense may be indicated specifically or by context—will be taken to mean at least conscious psychological experience of some sort, no matter how caused and whether incarnate or discarnate.

    2. **Survival, immortality, eternal life.** I shall refer to the belief that there is for the individual a life after death as belief in *survival* rather than as belief in *immortality;* for immortality, strictly speaking, is incapacity to die, which, as ascribed to a human consciousness, entails survival of it *forever* after bodily death. But survival for some indeterminate though considerable period, rather than specifically forever, is probably what most persons actually have in mind when they think of a life after death. Assurance of survival for a thousand years, or even a hundred, would, for those of us who desire survival, have virtually as much present psychological value as would assurance of survival forever: we should be troubled very little by the idea of individual extinction at so distant a time—even less troubled than is now a healthy and happy youth by the knowledge that he will die within fifty or sixty years.

    Persons, on the other hand, who are tired of life; or who have found it to have for them negative rather than positive value and believe this to be of its essence; or who, like Professor C. D. Broad would for some other reason welcome assurance of non-survival; would be more distressed by prospect of survival for a long period, and even more by prospect of survival forever, than by that of survival for only a short time.

    The expression *"eternal life"* is sometimes used to express, in a positive way, what "immortality"—distinguished from simply survival—expresses negatively. "Eternal" life, as so used, then generally means life that is everlasting *in the future*—life without end though not without beginning. Conceivably, however, life might be without beginning as well as without end. This is what theories such as that of metempsychosis assume, which regard not only the human body but also the human mind or consciousness or soul as an evolutionary product.

Similarly, when God's being is spoken of as "eternal" what is meant is sometimes that he is both without beginning and without end—that he always did and always will exist. Perhaps more often, however, what is meant is that God's consciousness is *timeless*. Eternal life, then, or consciousness of eternity, whether experienced by God inherently or by man on rare occasions, means a form of consciousness that does not include or that transcends consciousness of *time*.

For a person the content of whose consciousness were thus timeless, the question whether that content endured but a moment, or a thousand years, would have no meaning since he would have no consciousness either of duration or of change. Indeed, the question could not even present itself to him. But were external observation possible of the consciousness of such a person—for example, of a mystic in ecstasy—the observer could meaningfully say that the other experienced eternal life, or lived in eternity, for five minutes, or as the case might be, for fifteen, or for some other finite time, on a given occasion.

3. **Causes of belief in survival.** The first question which arises in connection with the idea that there is for the individual an after-death life is why the belief in it is so widespread.

The clue to the answer is to be found in the fact that each of us has always been alive and conscious as far back as he can remember. It is true, of course, that his body is sometimes sunk in deep sleep, or in a faint, or in coma from some injury or grave illness; or that the inhaling of ether or some other anaesthetic makes him unconscious of the surgical operation he then undergoes. But, even at those times a person does not experience unconsciousness, for to experience it would mean being conscious of being unconscious; and this, being a contradiction, is impossible. Indeed, at such times, he may be having vivid dreams; and these are one kind of consciousness. The only experience of unconsciousness a person ever has is, not of total unconsciousness, but of unconsciousness *of this or that;* as when he reports: "I am not conscious of any pain," or "of any difference between the color of this and of that," etc.

Nor do we ever experience as present in another person unconsciousness itself, but only the fact that, sometimes, some or all of the ordinary activities of his body, through which his being conscious previously manifested itself to us, cease to occur. That consciousness itself is extinguished at such times is only a hypothesis which we construct to account for certain changes in the behavior of another person's body; or to explain the eventual lack in him—or, as the case may be, in ourselves—of memories relating to the period during which the body—his or our own—was in an inert, unresponsive state.

Lack of present memory of having been conscious at a particular past time obviously is no proof at all that one was unconscious at that time; for if it were, then it would prove that one was unconscious during the first few years of one's life, and indeed during the vast majority of its days, since one has no memory whatever of one's experiences on any but a very small minority of one's past days. That we were conscious on the others is known to us not by memory of them, but only by inference from facts of various kinds.

The fact, then, is that each person has been alive and conscious at all times he can remember. Being alive and conscious has therefore become in him an ingrained habit; and habit automatically entails both tacit expectations and tacit belief that what is tacitly expected will occur.[2] Just as every step which finds ground underfoot builds up tacit belief that so will the subsequent steps, and every breath which finds air to breathe, tacit belief that so will the subsequent breaths, just so does the fact that every past day of one's life was found to have a morrow contribute to generate tacit expectation and belief that every day of one's life will have a living morrow. As J. B. Pratt has pointed out, the child takes the continuity of life for granted. It is the fact of death that has to be taught him. But when he has learned it, and the idea of a future life is then put explicitly before his mind, it seems to him the most natural thing in the world.[3]

---

[2] Cf. C. D. Broad: *The Mind and its Place in Nature*, p. 524.
[3] J. B. Pratt: *The Religious Consciousness*, Macmillan, New York, 1943, p. 225.

Such, undoubtedly, is the psychological origin of the wide-spread ingenuous belief that one's life and that of one's fellows does not end at death.

Another root of the idea and belief that persons who were known to us and have died continue to live—and hence that we too shall survive after death—is the fact that sometimes those persons, as well as persons who are still in the flesh, appear to us in dreams. Especially when the dream was both vivid and plausible, it easily suggests a view of the human personality which is rather common among primitive peoples and which has been held even by some educated and critical persons. It is that each person's body of flesh has a subtle counterpart or double, which can become detached from and function independently of that body; this separation being temporary as it occurs in periods of sleep during life, but permanent at the death of the body.

Evidently, such an idea of the constitution of man fits in very well with the ingenuous natural belief in life beyond death, for it provides concrete images in which to clothe the otherwise elusive abstract notion of a personality living on, discarnate.

Belief in a life after death, however, might conceivably originate in a given person in either one of two ways less ingenuous than those described in what precedes. One of these more critical ways would be out of attention to certain occurrences observed or reported, and then interpreted as empirical evidence of the survival of a deceased person. Communications purportedly from such a person and containing identifying details, received either through a "medium" or by oneself through automatic writing; or sight of an "apparition" of the dead person, would be examples of the kinds of experience in view.

The other possible kind of rational origin which belief in a life after death might have in a given person would be attention by him to arguments which, whether really or only seemingly cogent, purport to prove immortality on metaphysical grounds. It is safe to say, however, that the belief can have this origin only in a very few persons, and that those arguments, irrespective of their cogency or lack of it, function in fact for the majority of those who know and accept them, much rather only as rationalizations of a belief in immortality they had previously acquired either in the automatic manner described earlier, or out of wishful thinking, or out of uncritically accepted childhood teachings.

We shall eventually consider the merits of both of the above kinds—empirical and theoretical—of *prima facie* evidence for survival. At this point, however, what we must ask is why survival is desired by the many persons who do desire it; and what general connection obtains between desire and belief, lack of desire and lack of belief.

4. **Why a life after death is desired.** One does not actually desire valued things which one already has or assumes one has. They get desired only when loss of them occurs or threatens. This, which is true for instance of desire for air to breathe or for earth to stand on, is equally true of desire for continuation of life. It is not until the witnessing or the awareness of death thrusts upon the mind the question whether the life that was continues somehow, that actual desire for life beyond death arises. From then on, the desire operates automatically to bolster the shaken naive belief in survival, and the belief in so far becomes a "wishful belief."

The desire for survival of oneself and of other persons has its roots in a variety of more specific desires which death immediately frustrates, but satisfaction of which a life beyond death would make possible even if not automatically insure. In some persons, the chief of these is desire for reunion with persons dearly loved. In others, whose lives have been wretched, it is desire for another chance at the happiness they have missed. In others yet, it is desire for further opportunity to grow in ability, knowledge, character, wisdom; or to go on contributing significant achievements. Again, a future life for oneself and others is often desired in order that the redressing of the many injustices of the present life shall be possible.

Even in persons who believe that death means complete and final extinction of the individual's consciousness, the craving for continued existence is testified to by the comfort they often find in various substitute but assured forms of "survival." They may, for instance, dwell on the continuity of the individual's germ plasm in his descendants. Or they find solace in the thought that, the past being indestructible, the particular life they live will remain ever after an intrinsic part of the history of the world. Also—and more satisfying to the craving for personal importance— there is the fact that since the acts of one's life have effects, and these in turn further effects, and so on, therefore what one has done goes on forever influencing remotely, and sometimes greatly, the course of future events.

Gratifying to one's vanity, too, is the prospect that, if the achievements of one's life have been important or even only conspicuous, or one's benefactions or evil deeds notable, then one's name may be remembered not only by acquaintances and relatives for a little while, but may live on in recorded history.

Evidently, survival in any of these senses is but a consolation prize for the certainty of bodily death—a thin substitute for the continuation of conscious individual life, which may be disbelieved, but the natural craving for which nevertheless is evidenced by the comfort which the considerations just mentioned even then provide.

5. **Causes of disinterest or of disbelief in survival.** Lack of belief and even positive disbelief in survival are certainly more widespread now in Western countries than was the case in earlier times. Of the various causes which account for this, one of the chief is probably "the greater attractiveness of this world in our times and the increase of interests of all sorts which keep one's attention too firmly fastened here to allow of much thought being spent on the other world."[4]

As compared with earlier ages, the standard of living is now high for the large majority of the populations of Western countries. Leisure has greatly increased, and so have political liberties. Class distinctions no longer firmly stand, as formerly, in the way of personal ambition. And when there is pie at the baker's and money for it in one's pocket, "pie in the sky" is not thought of and hence not desired. It is when life is hard, joyless, and hopeless that one dreams of and longs for escape to another world

---

[4] J. B. Pratt: *The Religious Consciousness*, The Macmillan Co. N. Y. 1943, p. 238.

where those who on earth were the miserable last shall be the happy first.

Again, in the present Age of Science the spirit of critical inquiry, with its demand for proofs, has robbed the teachings of religion of the authority they had earlier. One consequence of this, and of the materialistic conception of the nature of man fostered by contemporary science, has been that the unplausibility—to use no stronger term—of the picturesque ideas of the life after death which had been traditional in the Western world has become glaring. And this in turn has deprived the idea of a future life of the support which desire for it had previously lent it; for, as Pratt pointedly remarks, "some sort of belief in at least the possibility of the object is a condition of any real desire for it."[5]

These are the chief factors which have caused substantial numbers of persons today to doubt or positively disbelieve that there is for the individual consciousness any life after the body's death; or at least to view the idea of it with little or no interest. These persons, however, although numerous, are probably still a rather small minority of the population; for death goes on frustrating of expression one's love of persons who were dear, and thereby thrusting upon the living the idea of a life after death, stimulating in them the desire that such life be a fact; and, through this desire, fostering the belief that it is a fact.

6. **Causes of, distinguished from grounds for, belief or disbelief.** It may not be amiss to stress here, however, that the arguments, the empirical facts, or the longings which suffice to *convince* some persons that a given idea is true, are not necessarily sufficient to prove or even to make objectively probable that the idea is true. For convincing is a psychological process where rhetoric and appeal to bias of various kinds are usually more efficacious than would be sound logic; and where automatic yielding to long-established habits of interpretation of appearances commonly takes the place of scrupulous verification.

It is only in exceptionally rational persons, or in exceptionally rational moments of the rest of us, or in circumstances where

---

[5] *Op. Cit.* p. 239.

nothing tempts us to jump to unwarranted conclusions, that only what suffices to prove suffices to convince; or, when the conclusion concerned is an unwelcome one, that what does suffice to prove or to establish a positive probability also suffices to convince.

However, since we are now emphasizing that many beliefs, for example belief in survival after death, can be and often are acquired uncritically, i.e., without adequate evidence or perhaps any evidence that the beliefs are true, impartiality requires us to stress also that the fact that a given belief has been acquired uncritically is not by itself positive evidence that the belief concerned is erroneous. What its having been so acquired does is only to put the burden of proof on the person who so acquired it, and who maintains that it is true.

Chapter II

RELIGION AND THE BELIEF IN A LIFE AFTER DEATH

Most religions have taught in one form or another that the "soul" or "spirit" of the individual does not perish when his body dies, but goes on living in another world where it meets conditions appropriate to its particular nature and deserts. Hence, before we turn to an exposition of the grounds on which contemporary natural science bases the case against the possibility of survival of man's consciousness after death, it will be well for us to consider the relation between religion and the belief in survival, and the grounds on which theologians—or more particularly Judaeo-Christian theologians—have affirmed that the belief is true.

1. **The belief in survival after death not inherently religious.** Although, as just noted, belief that the human personality survives bodily death has been inculcated by most religions, it is not in itself religious. If the survival hypothesis is purged of vagueness, is defined in a manner not involving contradictions or other demonstrable impossibilities, and is dissociated from the additional supposition commonly coupled with it that survival will be such as to bring reward or punishment to the surviving personalities according as they lived on earth virtuously or wickedly, then it is no more religious than would be the hypothesis that conscious beings live on Mars. In both cases alike the question is simply one of fact—however difficult it may be to get evidence adequate to settle it one way or the other.

If human personalities survive the body's death and do so discarnate, then—although their continued existence is normally as imperceptible to us as were bacteria before we had microscopes and as still are the subatomic entities of theoretical physics—those

14

discarnate personalities are just another part of the population of the world; and their abode—if the word still has significance in relation to them—is just another region or dimension of the universe, not as yet commonly accessible to us.

The supposition that there is an immaterial, or anyway a normally imperceptible realm of existence peopled by discarnate human consciousnesses is, moreover, quite independent logically of the supposition that a God or gods exist—as independent of it logically as is the fact that incarnate human consciousnesses now inhabit the earth: No contradiction at all would be involved either in supposing that one or more gods exist but that there is no *post mortem* human life, or in supposing that there is a life after death but no God or gods.

But although the belief in a life after death is thus not inherently religious, nevertheless a close connection between it and religion has obtained throughout the history of man. What I shall now attempt is to make clear the nature of this connection; that is, what it presupposes with regard to man's personality, and with regard to the relation between his life on earth and the *post mortem* life which the religions have taught he will have. For this purpose, what religion itself essentially is must first be considered briefly.

2. **Religion and religious beliefs.** Even a sketchy acquaintance with the history of religion suffices to show that the beliefs and practices which have been taught by the religions of mankind have been very diverse and in many cases irreconcilable. This entails that no possibility exists of conceiving the essense of religion in terms of some core of beliefs or/and practices common to all the religions—to the non-theistic as well as to the monotheistic, the polytheistic, and the pantheistic, and to the religions of primitive as well as of highly civilized peoples—for there is no such common core. Nor, of course, can the essence of religion be conceived responsibly as consisting of the teachings of some one particular religion, held to be the only "true" religion on the ground that its teachings are divine revelations; for the question would then remain as to whether the belief that *its* teachings are, and alone are, divine revelations is demonstrably true, or on the con-

trary is itself but one among other pious but groundless beliefs.

It follows that only a *functional* conception of religion can be comprehensive enough to apply to all the religions; a conception, that is to say, according to which religion is essentially a psychological instrument for the performance of certain functions ubiquitously important to human welfare, which are not otherwise performed adequately in any but a few exceptional cases—and which even religion has often performed none too well.

More specifically, this conception is that a religion is any set of beliefs that are matters of faith—together the observances, attitudes, injunctions, and feelings tied up with the beliefs—which, in so far as dominant in a person, tend to perform two functions, one social and the other personal.

The social function is to provide, for conduct held to be socially beneficial, a sanction that will operate on occasions where conflict exists between the private interest of the individual and the (real or fancied) social interest, and where neither the legal sanctions, nor those of public opinion, nor the individual's own moral impulses, would by themselves be enough to cause him to behave morally. In such cases, an additional and sometimes sufficient motivation for moral conduct is provided by religious beliefs, and in particular by a belief in a life after death if this belief is conjoined, as usually it has been, with a belief that, in that life, immoral conduct that escaped punishment on earth and moral conduct that went unrewarded each gets its just deserts through the inescapable operation of some personal or impersonal agency of cosmic justice.

To provide the motivation called for, the second of these two beliefs is of course necessary in addition to the first; for belief in a future life whose particular content were in no way dependent on the manner — virtuous or vicious — in which the individual lived on earth would exert no psychological leverage on him for virtuous conduct now. To exert this leverage is the function of the pictures of hells, heavens, paradises, purgatories, and other forms of reward or punishment, painted by the religions.

It is to be noted that, insofar as those two beliefs, acting jointly, cause the individual to behave morally, i.e., justly or altruistically, in cases where he otherwise would behave selfishly or maliciously, those beliefs foster in him the development of moral feelings and impulses; for as a person acts, so does he tend to feel and, on later occasions, tend to feel impelled from within to act again. The long-run effect of the harboring of beliefs religious in the sense stated could therefore be described as "education of the heart,"—arousal and cultivation in the individual of the feelings and impulses out of which, even at cost to himself, issues conduct beneficial or assumed beneficial to his fellows.

The individual, however, is likely to be much more directly aware of the value his religious beliefs have for him personally than of the value they have for society through the personal sacrifices they require of him for the social benefit. And what the individual's religious beliefs do for him personally in proportion to their depth and firmness and to the faithfulness with which he lives up to them is to give him a certain equanimity in the ups and downs of life—a certain freedom from anxiety in times of trouble, and from self-complacency in times of worldly good fortune. To the religious man, his religious beliefs can bring courage in adversity, hope in times of despair, and dignity in times of obloquy or frustration. Also, humility on occasions of pride, prudence in times of success, moderation and a sense of responsibility in the exercise of power; in brief, a degree of abiding serenity based on a conception of man's destiny and on the corresponding scale of values.

The belief in a life after death, in future compensation there for the injustices of earth, in future reunion with loved ones who have died, and in future opportunities for growth and happiness, undoubtedly operates to give persons who have it a measure of the equanimity they need wherewith to face the trials of this world, the death of those dear to them, and the prospect, near or distant, of their own death. But in order to operate psychologically in this way for the individual, and through him for the welfare of society in the way described before, the belief in survival and the other beliefs the religions have taught do not at all need to be in fact true, but only to be firmly *believed*. Nor do their contents need to be conceived clearly, but only believably. Indeed, the vagueness which commonly characterizes them is often a condition of their believability, for it insulates from detection the absurdities in some of them which would be evident if the beliefs were clear instead of vague. In order that the beliefs should *function,* what needs to be clear is only the sort of conduct and attitude they dictate.

The fact, then, that belief in a life after death has prominently figured in most religions and has with varying degrees of efficacy participated in performance there of the social and personal functions described above, constitutes no evidence at all that there is really for the individual some kind of life after death.

On the other hand, the psychological fact that what has operated towards performance of those functions is not *truth* of, but simply *belief* of, the idea of survival, constitutes no evidence at all that that idea is *untrue.* For here as elsewhere it is imperative to distinguish sharply between the question as to whether a given belief is true—which is a question *ad rem;* and questions as to how the given belief affects the persons who hold it, or as to how they came to hold it—which are questions *ad hominem,* i.e., biographical questions. That a given person came to believe or to disbelieve a given proposition does not entail anything concerning the truth or falsity of the proposition unless what caused him to believe or to disbelieve it consisted of *evidence adequate to prove,* or at least to make *objectively probable,* that the proposition is true, or as the case may be, that it is false. But if what induced the belief or disbelief did *not* consist of such evidence, then it leaves *wholly open* the question of truth or falsity of the proposition concerned.

3. **Grounds on which belief in survival is based in Christian theology.** The grounds on which Christian theologians have contended that the human personality survives after death are chiefly of two kinds—empirical, and moral.

The empirical argument consists in pointing at the resurrection of Jesus: That Jesus, having died, rose bodily from the dead proves, it is argued, that the human personality is not destroyed by death and that the human body admits of being resurrected after it has died. This proof of "immortality" has been accepted by millions of Christians and has been regarded as one of the most precious assurances brought to mankind by Jesus.

Yet the logic of the inference by which human immortality is deduced from the resurrection of Jesus is so fallacious that the argument has been characterized by Professor C. D. Broad as one of the world's worst. "In the first place," he writes, "if Christianity be true, though Jesus was human, He was *also* divine. No other human being resembles Him in this respect." Hence the resurrection of one so radically different from mere men is no evidence that they too survive the death of their bodies.

The fallacy of the reasoning which would infer the second from the first becomes glaring if one considers a reasoning of exactly the same form, but the particular terms of which are free from the biassing religious commitments that obtain for orthodox Christians in the case of the Resurrection: Obviously, from the fact that Tom Jones, who falls out of an airplane and has a parachute, survives the fall, it does not follow that John Smith, who falls out of the same plane *but has no parachute,* will also survive.

Moreover, Broad points out that the case of man is unlike that of Jesus in another respect also: "the body of Jesus did not decay in the tomb, but was transformed; whilst the body of every ordinary man rots and disintegrates soon after his death. Therefore, if men do survive the death of their bodies, the process must be utterly unlike that which took place when Jesus survived His death on the cross. Thus the analogy breaks down in every relevant respect, and so an argument from the resurrection of Jesus to the survival of bodily death by ordinary men is utterly worthless."[1]

But anyway, the facts concerning the resurrection of Jesus—taken as premise in that argument—are not known to us exactly, or in detail, or with certainty. The men to whom the passages of the New Testament bearing on the subject are (rightly or wrongly) ascribed, and the men who passed on from one generation to another their own account of what they had heard about the life, the death, and the resurrection of Jesus, were not dispassionate historians careful to check the objectivity of the reports which came to them and to record them accurately. Rather, they were essentially zealous propagandists of an inspiring message,

---

[1] *Religion, Philosophy, and Psychical Research,* Harcourt N. Y. 1953, pp. 236-7.

bent on spreading it and getting it accepted. As H. L. Willett points out, "the friends of Jesus were not interested in the writing of books. They were not writers, they were preachers. The Master himself was not a writer. He left no document from his own hand. The first disciples were too busy with the new problems and activities of the Christian society to give thought to the making of records."[2] The text of the Gospels was in process of getting formulated for several generations. Most of it did not reach the form in which we have it until some time near the middle of the second century A.D. Indeed, "the very oldest manuscript of the New Testament is as late as the fourth century A.D. All the originals, the autographs, perished at a very early date—even the first copies of the originals are utterly gone."[3]

These facts easily account for the discrepancies we find, for instance, between the several statements in the Gospels concerning the discovery of the empty tomb. Also, for the scantiness of the descriptions of the appearances of the "risen" Jesus during the weeks following his death. At the first of these appearances—to Mary Magdalene at the tomb—he is unaccountably mistaken by her, who had known him well, for the gardener (John 20 - 15); and later is similarly unrecognized at first by the disciples fishing in the sea of Tiberias (John 21 - 4). Nor is there any clear-cut statement that his appearances were touched as well as seen. For, at the tomb, he enjoins Mary not to touch him; and Thomas, when Jesus appeared to him and to the other disciples, apparently then felt no need to avail himself of the opportunity he had desired earlier to verify by touch the material reality of the visible appearance. And the statement in Matthew 28 - 9 that the two women, being met by Jesus on their way from the tomb, "took hold of his feet" may well mean only that, in reverence, they prostrated themselves at his feet.

That the body which the disciples and others repeatedly saw appearing and disappearing suddenly indoors irrespective of walls and closed doors, and likewise out of doors, was not the material

[2]*The Bible through the Centuries.* Willett, Clark & Colby, Chicago 1929, p. 220.
[3]Ernest R. Trattner: *Unravelling the Book of Books,* Ch. Scribner's Sons, N.Y. 1929, p. 244. Cf. Alfred Loisy: *The Birth of the Christian Religion,* preface by Gilbert Murray, Allen & Unwin, London 1948, pp. 41-53.

body of Jesus is further suggested by the accounts of his final disappearance; for the statement that he then "was taken up; and a cloud received him" out of the disciples' sight (Acts 1 - 9), or that, while blessing them, he "was carried up into heaven" (Luke 25 - 51) could be taken literally only in times when astronomical knowledge was so lacking as to permit the supposition that the earth is the center of the universe, and that heaven is some distance above the blue vault of the sky.

In the light of these considerations, and of the complete lack of facts as to what became of the material body of Jesus, the statements in the New Testament concerning the several appearances of Jesus after his death make sense only if interpreted as reports of what are commonly called "apparitions" or "phantasms" of the dead—an interpretation which, incidentally, is consonant with Paul's statement (I Corinthians 15 - 40/44) that the resurrection of the dead, which "is sown in a natural body; . . . . . is raised in a spiritual body. If there is a natural body, there is also a spiritual body," which Paul, in verse 44, calls also a "celestial" body and distinguishes from the "terrestrial."[4]

It is appropriate in this connection to note that apparitions of the dead (and occasionally of the living) are a type of phenomenon of which numerous well-attested and far more recent instances are on record;[5] and it is interesting to compare the earliest testimony we have for the *post mortem* appearances of Jesus— which was first reduced to writing some twenty-five years after the events; which reaches us through copies of copies of the original written record; and which concerns events dating back nearly two thousand years—with, for example, the testimony we have for the numerous appearances in Maine in the year 1800 of a woman, the first wife of a Captain Butler, after her death.

It is contained in a pamphlet now very rare, but of which there is an original in the New York Public Library and a photo-

---

[4]That the *post mortem* appearances of Jesus were not his physical body, but were "apparitions" in the sense of hallucinations telepathically induced by the then discarnate Jesus, is ably contended by the Rev. Michael C. Perry in a scholarly work, *The Easter Enigma*, Faber & Faber, London 1959, published since the present chapter was written.

[5]See for example G. N. M. Tyrrell: *Apparitions,* with a preface by Prof. H. H. Price, London, Duckworth & Co. Ltd., Rev. ed., 1953.

stat copy now before me. It was published in 1826 by the Rev. Abraham Cummings (1755-1827) A.B., A.M., Brown University, 1776. He was an itinerant Baptist minister who visited and preached in the small villages on the coast of Maine. The pamphlet, of 77 pages, is entitled *Immortality Proved by the Testimony of Sense.* It relates the apparitions of the deceased Mrs. George Butler at a village near Machiasport. "The Specter," as the Rev. Cummings terms her apparition, manifested itself not, as in most reports of apparitions, just once and to but one person, but many times over a period of some months and to groups numbering as many as forty persons together, both in and out of doors; and to Cummings himself in a field, on the occasion when, having been notified of its appearance, he was on his way to expose what he had thought must be a delusion or a fraud.

The "Specter" was both seen and heard; it delivered lengthy discourses to the persons present, and moved among them; it predicted births and deaths which came to pass; and on several occasions sharply intervened in the affairs of the village. Moreover, the Rev. Cummings had the rare good sense to obtain at the time over thirty affidavits—reproduced in the pamphlet—from some of the hundred or more persons who had heard and/or seen the "Specter."[6]

It is safe to say that most readers of the above summary account of the apparitions of the deceased Mrs. Butler will receive it with considerable skepticism. How much more skepticism, then, would on purely objective grounds be justified about a series of apparitions dating back nearly twenty centuries instead of only a hundred and fifty years, and concerning which we have none but remotely indirect evidence; whereas in the more recent series we have as evidence over thirty verbatim statements from as many of the very persons who observed the apparitions. Judging both cases objectively—in terms of the criteria applied in court to the weight of testimony—there is no doubt that the case for the his-

---

[6] A readily accessible, detailed account of this extraordinary affair can be found in William Oliver Stevens' *Unbidden Guests*, N.Y. 1945, Dodd, Mead & Co. pp. 261-9 where the essential facts recorded in the pamphlet are presented in more orderly manner than by Cummings, whose literary ability was low, and whose recital of the facts is encumbered by tedious theological reflections.

toricity of the appearances of Jesus is far weaker than that for the historicity of the appearances of Mrs. Butler. And yet, although we find the latter dubious and perhaps dismiss the account of it as "a mere ghost story," we—or anyway millions of Christians—accept on the contrary as literally true the traditional account of the appearances of Jesus.

The explanation of this irresponsibility is, of course, to be found in the great differences between the personalities concerned and between the historical setting and emotional import of the lives and deaths of the two. For the personality, the life, and the death of Mrs. Butler were commonplace and attracted no wide attention. The only thing that did so in her case was the series of her apparitions after death. On the contrary, the personality and the life and the death of Jesus were heroic and spectacular; and this, together with the inspiring nature of his message, gives great emotional interest to everything connected with him. This interest, the hunger to believe it begets, the implanting of the traditional stories in childhood, and the fact that it is easy to accept but hard to doubt what is believed and valued by everybody in one's environment—these are the psychological causes which account for the fact that most Christians to-day find it easy and natural to believe in the "resurrection," i.e., in the reappearance of Jesus after death, even when the weakness of the evidence for it is pointed out to them; but on the contrary find the reappearance of Mrs. Butler after her death difficult to believe even when the much greater strength of the evidence for it is brought to their attention.

4. **The moral arguments for the reality of a future life.** From the contention that the resurrection of Jesus assures man of life beyond death, we now turn to the so-called moral arguments also appealed to in support of the belief in personal survival.

The premise of these arguments is the goodness, justice, and might ascribed to God. Summarily put, the reasoning is that "if God is good and God is sufficiently powerful, how can such a God allow the values (potential or actual) bound up with individuals to become forever lost? . . . . . The world would be irrational if, after having brought into being human beings who aspire against so many almost overwhelming odds to achieve higher values, it should dash them into nothingness.'"[7]

Again, divine justice assures a future life to man, for, without one, the innumerable injustices of the present life would never be redressed. The wicked whose wickedness went unpunished on earth or perhaps even prospered them would at death be escaping punishment altogether; and the virtuous who made sacrifices in obedience to duty or out of regard for the welfare of others would at death be going finally unrewarded. If moral persons were not eventually to gain happiness, then morality, in the many cases where it brings no recompense on earth, would be just stupidity.

Such, in substance, are the moral arguments. Do they prove, or at least make probable, that there is for man a life after death?

Let us examine first the contention that it would be irrational to behave morally at present cost to oneself if such behavior is not eventually rewarded by happiness.

So to contend is tacitly to equate rationality in moral decisions with fostering of one's own distant welfare. The truth is, however, that to behave rationally is simply to behave in ways which one believes best promote attainment of one's ends, *such as these may be.* And the fact is that men do have not only egoistic but also altruistic ends: most men do genuinely care, in varying degrees, about the welfare of other human beings, or of certain ones among these, as well as about their own personal welfare. Hence, behavior designed to promote the welfare of another person whose welfare one happens to desire—and perhaps to desire more than one's own—is quite as rational as behavior intended and shaped to promote one's personal welfare. Thus, if a man's behavior towards others is motivated on the one hand by belief that the particular forms of behavior termed moral make for the welfare of such of his fellow beings as are affected by them, and on the other by the fact that he does desire their welfare enough to subordinate his own to theirs, then his behaving in the ways termed moral is perfectly rational. Indeed, so behaving is the essence of genuine love; that is, of love that prompts to action for the beloved's welfare; as distinguished from love merely senti-

[7]Vergilius Ferm: *First Chapters in Religious Philosophy,* Round Table Press, N.Y. 1937, p. 279.

mental which sees the loved one essentially as object that arouses beautiful love-feeling and which therefore uses the beloved as emotional candy, crippling him in the process if need be.

Moral behavior, on the other hand, is irrational or rather non-rational, when it consists only of uncomprehending, machine-like obedience to whatever code of behavior happens to have been psychologically planted in the mind during childhood years.

The bearing of these remarks on the contention that morality unrewarded on earth is irrational if not rewarded after death is that true morality is rooted in intelligent love and, for the person whose morality it is, constitutes self-expression and is self-rewarding. Being not investment but generous gift, it takes no thought of dividends whether on earth or in a future life.

As regards now the contention that if God is good and is sufficiently powerful, he cannot allow the actual and potential values bound up with individuals to become forever lost, its obvious weakness is that its premise is altogether "iffy": *if* there is a God, *if* he is good, *if* he is powerful enough to preserve the soul when the body dies, *if* the world is rational, *if* justice ultimately obtains, *then* there is for man a life after death! It may be that these *"ifs"* are true, but so long as they have not been proved true, neither has the reality of the future life, which their being true would entail, been proved.

And the fact is that their truth has never yet been proved nor even shown to be more probable than not. All the would-be proofs of the existence of an omnipotent, omniscient, and perfectly good creator of the world, which theologians and theologizing philosophers have elaborated in the course of the centuries have, on critical examination, turned out to be only ingenious pieces of wishful reasoning. Indeed, if a God *of that description* existed and had created the world, there could be no evil in it; for the endless sophistries which have been packed into the notion of "free will" for the purpose of eluding this ineludible conclusion have patently failed to do so. Hence, if the world was ever created, and if it was created by a God, then that God was finite whether in power or in goodness or in knowledge, or in two or in all of these respects. Even such a God, however, could be a powerful, wise and good friend, and as such well worth having.

In any case, that annihilation of the personality at death would be an evil—and hence that God would prevent it if he could—is far from evident. For there is ultimately no such thing as evil that nobody experiences; hence, if the individual is totally annihilated at death, the non-fulfilment of *his* desire for a *post mortem* life is not an evil experienced by him since, *ex hypothesi*, he then no longer exists and therefore does not experience disappointment or anything else. But, if *God* does not desire that man's desire for a life after death be fulfilled, and knows that it will not be, the non-fulfilment of man's desire for it is not a disappointment to God either, and is therefore not an evil at all. On the other hand, what *is* an evil—and this irrespective of whether there is or is not a life after death—is the distress experienced by the living due to doubt by them that they will, or that their deceased loved ones do, survive after death.

The remarks in this chapter concerning the nature and functions of religion, the alleged proofs of the existence of a God of the traditional kind, the nature of evil, and the implications of the fact that there is a vast amount of evil on earth, have perforce been much too brief to deal adequately with questions so heavily loaded with biassing emotion.[8] If those remarks are sound, however, they entail that neither religion nor theology really provides any evidence that there is for man a life after death.

But even if there is not, believing that there is does affect the believer's feelings, attitudes, and conduct; and to affect these in the valuable ways described earlier is the function of religion, which it has performed with varying degrees of success. The function, on the other hand, of the arguments on which theology bases its affirmative answer to the question as to a life after death, is to make the idea that there is such a life psychologically believable by the vast numbers of human beings who, for obvious reasons, turn to religion rather than to science or to philosophy for an answer to that momentous question.

---

[8]Readers who might wish to see what more elaborate defense of them the writer would give are referred to what he has written on the subject elsewhere. In particular, to Chapts. 8, 15, 16, and 17, respectively on What Religion is, Gods, The Problem of Evil, and Life after Death, of the author's *A Philosophical Scrutiny of Religion*, Ronald Press, New York, 1953.

That these arguments achieve this but nothing more, i.e., convince many of the persons to whom they are addressed notwithstanding that they really prove nothing, does not mean that those who propound them are not sincere. It means only that, except in the case of outstandingly rational persons, becoming convinced and convincing others is, as pointed out earlier, mostly a matter of rhetoric, of suggestion, of appeal to prejudices or to fears or hopes; whereas proving or establishing probabilities is a matter of logic or of empirical evidence.

Chapter III

THE CASE AGAINST THE POSSIBILITY
OF A LIFE AFTER DEATH

In Chapt. I we were occupied mainly with the variety of psychological factors which cause people to believe, or as the case may be to disbelieve, that there is or can be a life after death for the individual. As pointed out in Sec. 6 of that chapter and again at the end of Chapt. II, some considerations may induce belief, or disbelief, and yet constitute no evidence or insufficient evidence that what is believed is true or what is disbelieved false; for to convince is one thing, and to prove is another.

In the present chapter, on the other hand, what we shall consider are the grounds, empirical and theoretical, on which is based the now widespread belief that the Natural Sciences have by this time definitely proved that any life after death is an impossibility. As Professor J. B. Rhine notes in a recent article, "the continued advance of biology and psychology during the last half-century has . . . . made the spirit [survival] hypothesis appear increasingly more improbable to the scholarly mind. The mechanistic (or physicalistic) view of man has become the mental habit of the student of science; and with the wide popular influence of science, the effect on educated men is well-nigh universal."[1]

What then are, in some detail, the grounds on which the scholarly mind is maintaining that survival is impossible or at best improbable?

1. **Empirical facts that appear to rule out the possibility of survival.** There are a number of facts—some of common observation and others brought to light by the Natural Sciences—which, it has been contended, definitely show both that the existence of

---

[1]Research on Spirit Survival Reexamined *Journal of Parapsychology,* Vol. 20: 124, No. 2, June 1956.

consciousness is wholly dependent on that of a living organism, and—some of them—that the particular nature of the consciousness at given times likewise wholly depends on the particular state of the organism at those times.

a) For one, it is pointed out that nowhere except in living organisms are evidences of consciousness found.

b) Again, as observation passes from the lower to the higher animal organisms, the fact becomes evident that the more elaborately organized the body and especially the nervous system is, the greater, more subtle and more capable of fine discriminations is the consciousness associated with it.

c) Again, everyone knows that when the body dies, the familiar evidences of the consciousness it had possessed cease to occur; and that, even when the body is still living, a severe blow on the head or other injuries will, temporarily, have the same result.

d) The dependence of consciousness on the brain, moreover, is not only thus wholesale but obtains in some detail. Lesion, whether by external or by internal causes, of certain regions of the cortex of the brain eliminates or impairs particular mental capacities—for example, the capacity to understand written words; or as the case may be, spoken words; or the capacity to speak, or it may be to write, notwithstanding that the capacity to produce sounds or to move the hand and fingers is unimpaired.

Similarly, the capacity for the various kinds of sensations—visual, auditory, tactual, etc.—is connected in the case of each with a different region of the brain; and the capacity for voluntary motion of different parts of the body is dependent on different parts of the brain cortex, situated along the fissure of Rolando. ·The parts of the brain which govern these various sensory and motor capacities vary somewhat from person to person; and, in a given person, a capacity destroyed by lesion of the cortical center for it often returns gradually as, presumably, a different part of the cortex takes on the lost function. But the fact that the mental powers are dependent on the functioning of the brain remains.[2]

---

[2] Concerning the general plan of the nervous system, and the dependence of various mental capacities on particular regions of the brain, see for example pp. 24-35, and the diagrams there, in Warren & Carmichael's *Elements of Human Psychology*, Houghton Mifflin & Co. Boston, 1930.

e) The dependence is further demonstrated when certain regions of the brain are radically disconnected from the rest, as by the operation called prefrontal lobotomy; for marked changes in the personality then result.

f) Again, changes in the chemical composition of the body fluids affect the states of consciousness. The psychological effects of alcohol and of caffein are familiar to everybody. Various drugs —mescalin, lysergic acid diethylamide, sodium amytal, sodium pentothal, heroin, opium, benzedrin, etc.—affect in diverse remarkable ways the contents of consciousness, the impulses, dispositions, and attitudes. Consciousness is affected also by the quantity of oxygen, and of carbon dioxide, in the blood. And the retardation in bodily and mental development known as cretinism can be remedied by administration of thyroid extract.

g) To the same general effect is the fact that, by stimulating in appropriate ways the body's sense organs, corresponding states of consciousness, to wit, the several kinds of sensations, can be caused at will in a person; and, conversely, the capacity for them can be done away with by destroying the respective sense organs or cutting the sensory nerves.

h) Again, the typical differences between the male and the female personality are related to the differences between the sex functions of the body of man and those of the body of woman.

i) The facts of heredity show that the particular personality an individual develops depends in part on the aptitudes his body inherits from the germ plasm of his progenitors. And observation shows that the rest depends on the environmental conditions to which he is subjected from the time of birth onward. How important in particular these are during childhood is strikingly shown by such cases as that of the two "wolf children" of India, the older case of the "wild boy of Aveyron," and a few others where young children had somehow managed to maintain life and to grow up among animals without human contacts until later discovered and studied. They had developed various animal skills, and virtually lost the capacity to acquire the skills, e.g., for speech, which a child automatically picks up at a certain age when situated in a human environment.[3]

---

[3]*The Wild Boy of Aveyron,* by J-M-G Itard, The Century Co. London 1932

2. **Theoretical considerations that appear to preclude survival.** That continued existence of consciousness after death is impossible has been argued also on the basis of theoretical considerations.

j) It has been contended, for instance, that what we call states of consciousness—ideas, sensations, volitions, feelings, and so on—are in fact nothing but the minute chemical or physical events themselves, which take place in the tissues of the brain; for example, the chemical change we call a nerve current, which propagates itself from one end of a nerve fiber to the other, and then on to the dendrites of another fiber; the electrical phenomena, externally detectable by electroencephalography, which accompany nerve currents; the alterations which, at the synapse of two neurons, facilitate or inhibit the propagation of a nerve current from one to the other; and so on.

k) That these various brain processes must be the very processes themselves, which we ordinarily call mental, follows, it has been contended, from the fact that the alternative supposition—namely, that ideas, volitions, sensations, emotions, and other "mental" states are not physical events at all—would entail the absurdity that non-physical events can cause, and be caused by, physical events. For, it is asked, how could a non-physical volition or idea push or pull the physical molecules in the brain? Or, conversely, how could a motion of molecules in the brain cause a visual or auditory or other kind of sensation if sensations were not themselves physical events?

l) The possibility of it, one is told, is anyway ruled out *a priori* by the principle of the conservation of energy; for causation of a material event in the brain by a mental, i.e., by an immaterial event, would mean that some additional quantity of energy suddenly pops into the physical world out of nowhere; and causation of a mental event by a physical nerve current would mean dissipation of some quantity of energy out of the physical world.

(tr. from the 1894 French edition.) *Wolf Children of India*, by P. C. Squires, Am. J. of Psychol., 1927, No. 38, p. 313. *Wolf-Children and Feral Man*, by J. A. L. Singh and R. M. Zinng, Harper & Bros. New York 1942. *Wolf Child and Human Child*, by A. Gesell, Harper & Bros. New York 1941.

The conclusion is therefore drawn that the events we call "mental" cannot be either effects or causes of the molecular processes in the nerve cells of the brain, but must be those very processes themselves. And then, necessarily, cessation of these processes is cessation of consciousness.

m) Another conception of consciousness, which is more often met with today than the chemico-physical one just described, but which also implies that consciousness cannot possibly survive after bodily death, is that "consciousness" is the name by which we designate merely certain types of behavior—those, namely, which differentiate the animals from all other things in nature. According to this view, for example, an animal's *consciousness* of a difference between two objects *consists in* the difference of its behavior towards each. More explicitly, this means that the difference *of behavior* is what *consciousness* of difference between the two objects *is; not,* as commonly assumed, that the difference of behavior is only the behavioral *sign* that, in the animal, something not publicly observable and not physical—called "consciousness that the two objects are different"—is occurring.

Or again, consciousness of the typically human kind called "thought," is identified with the typically human sort of behavior called "speech;" and this, again not in the sense that speech *expresses* or *manifests* something different from itself, called "thought," but in the sense that speech—whether uttered or only whispered—*is* thought itself. And obviously if thought, or any mental activity, is thus but some mode of behavior of the living body, the mind or consciousness cannot possibly survive the body's death.

n) In support of the monistic conception of man which the foregoing facts and reflections point to as against the dualistic conception of material body-immaterial mind, the methodological principle known as the Law of Parsimony has also been invoked. This is done, for example, in the third chapter of a book, *The Illusion of Immortality*, which is probably the best recent statement *in extenso* of the case against the possibility of any life after death.[4] Dr. Lamont there states that the law of parsimony

---

[4]Corliss Lamont: *The Illusion of Immortality*, Philosophical Library, New York, 1950, Ch. III The Verdict of Science, pp. 114-16. Dr. Lamont states, erroneously,

"makes the dualist theory appear distinctly superfluous. It rules out dualism by making it unnecessary. In conjunction with the monistic alternative it pushes the separate and independent supernatural soul into the limbo of unneeded and unwanted hypotheses . . . . . the complexity of the cerebral cortex, together with the intricate structure of the rest of the nervous system and the mechanism of speech, makes any explanation of thought and consciousness in other than naturalistic terms wholly unnecessary. If some kind of supernatural soul or spirit is doing our thinking for us, then why did there evolve through numberless aeons an organ so well adapted for this purpose as the human brain?" (pp. 114-18)

3. **The contention that no plausible form of post mortem life is imaginable.** Another consideration still has been brought up, notably by Lamont in the book cited, as standing in the way of the possibility of a life after death. It is:

o) the difficulty of imagining at all plausibly what form a life could take that were discarnate and yet were not only personal but of the same person as the *ante mortem* one. For to suppose that a given personality survives is to suppose not simply persistence of consciousness, but persistence also of the individual's character, acquired knowledge, cultural skills and interests, habits, memories, and awareness of personal identity. Indeed, persistence merely of these would hardly constitute persistence of *life;* for, in the case of man anyway, to live is to go on meeting new situations and, by exerting oneself to deal with them, to enlarge one's experience, acquire new insights, develop one's latent capacities, and accomplish objectively significant tasks. But it is hard to

---

that the law of parsimony "was first formulated in the fourteenth century by . . . . . William of Occam, in the words: 'Entities (of explanation) are not to be multiplied beyond need.' " The fact, however, appears to be that the form *Entia non sunt multiplicanda praeter necessitatem,* to which Sir Wm. Hamilton in 1852 gave the name "Occam's razor," originated with John Ponce of Cork in 1639; and that the law of parsimony was formulated, prior to Occam, by his teacher Duns Scotus and some other mediaeval philosophers, in various forms; notably, *frustra fit per plura quod fieri potest per pauciora,* i.e., the more is in vain when the less will serve (to account for the facts to be explained.) See W. M. Thorburn, The Myth of Occam's Razor. *Mind,* XXVII (1927) pp. 345 ff.

imagine all this possible without a body and an environment for it, upon which to act and from which to receive impressions. On the other hand, if a body and an environment were supposed, but of some "etheric" or "spiritual" kind, i.e., of a kind radically different from bodies of flesh and their material environment, then it is paradoxical to suppose that, under such drastically different conditions, a personality could remain the same as before to an extent at all comparable to that of the sameness we now retain from day to day or even from year to year.

To take a crude but telling analogy, it is past belief that, if the body of any one of us were suddenly changed into that of a shark or an octopus and placed in the ocean, his personality could, for more than a very short time if at all, recognizably survive so radical a change of environment, of bodily form, of bodily needs, and of bodily capacities.

The considerations set forth in this chapter constitute the essentials of the basis for the contention that persistence of the individual's consciousness or personality after the death of his body is impossible. Such persistence, Lamont argues, is ruled out by the kind of relation between body and mind testified to by those considerations. The connection between mind and body is, he writes, "so exceedingly intimate that it becomes inconceivable how one could function properly without the other . . . . . . man is a unified whole of mind-body or personality-body so closely and completely integrated that dividing him up into two separate and more or less independent parts becomes impermissible and unintelligible."[5]

It should be noted, however, that both in the allegation that the considerations reviewed establish the impossibility of survival, and in the contention that those considerations on the contrary fail to establish this, certain key concepts are employed. Among the chief of these are "material," "mental," "body," "mind," "consciousness," "life," and a number of subsidiary others. Usually, in controversies regarding survival, little or no attempt is made to specify exactly the meaning those terms are taken to have, for all of them belong to the vocabulary of ordinary language and it is

---

[5]*The Illusion of Immortality.* Philosophical Library, New York 1950, pp. 89-113.

therefore natural to assume that they are well-understood. And so indeed they are—in the ingenuous manner, habit-begotten and unanalytical, that is adequate for ordinary conversational and literary purposes. But such understanding of them is far from precise enough to permit clear discernment of the issues in so special and elusive a question as that of the possibility or reality of a life after death for the individual.

The fact is that, so long as our understanding of those terms remains thus relatively vague, we do not even know just what it is we want to know when we ask that seemingly plain question—nor, *a fortiori*, do we then know what evidence, if we had it, would conclusively decide the question or at least establish a definite probability on one side or the other. Hence, if our eventual inquiry into the merits of the case outlined in this chapter against the possibility of survival is to have any prospect of reaching conclusions worthier of the name of knowledge than have been the findings of earlier inquirers, then we must first of all undertake an analysis of the pivotal concepts mentioned above. That analysis, moreover, must be not only precise enough to define sharply the issues to which those concepts are relevent, but must also be responsible in the sense of empirical, not arbitrarily prescriptive.

This is the task to which we shall address ourselves in Part II.

PART II

The Key Concepts

Chapter IV

WHAT IS "MATERIAL"; AND WHAT IS "LIVING"

Until the last years of the nineteenth century, physicists believed that the rocks, metals, water, wood, and all the other substances about us are ultimately composed of atoms of one or more of some seventy-eight kinds—those atoms, as the very word signifies, being indivisible, i.e., not themselves composed of more minute parts.

Since then, however, the progress of physics has revealed the sub-atomic electrons, protons, neutrons, positrons, mesons, etc. The sub-atomic "particles" are at distances from one another that are vast relatively to their own size, so that a material object, such as a table, turns out to consist mostly of space empty of anything more substantial than electric charges or electromagnetic fields.

This state of affairs is what is meant by the statement occasionally heard that modern physics has "dematerialized" matter—from which it is sometimes concluded that the traditionally sharp distinction between matter and mind, or material and mental, has been invalidated or at least undermined.

Yet, if in the dark one walks into a table, one does not pass through it but gets a bruise. Whatever may be the recondite sub-atomic constitution of the table and of other "solid" objects, they do anyway have the capacity to resist penetration by other such objects. Physics has not dematerialized matter in the sense of having shown that wood, water, air, living bodies, and other familiar substances do not really have the properties we perceive them to have. What physics has shown is that their familiar properties are very different indeed from those of their sub-atomic constituents.

1. **Two questions to be distinguished.** The allegation that physics has now shown that the things we call material are not really material rests only on a failure to distinguish between two quite different questions.

One of them is about the nature of the ultimate constituents of all material things and about the laws governing the relations of those constituents to one another. This is the question to which theoretical physics addresses itself. The task of answering it is long, highly technical, and still unfinished. And the answers, so far as they have yet been obtained, have no obvious bearing on the problem of the possibility or reality of a life after death.

The other question is on the contrary easy to answer; and the answer, as we shall eventually see, has bearing on the validity or invalidity of some of the considerations alleged to rule out survival. The only thing difficult about the second question is to realize that we already know perfectly well the answer to it, and that our failure to notice this is due only to the fact that we do not clearly distinguish the second question from the first.

For purposes of contrast, the first may be phrased: *What do physicists find* when they search for the ultimate constituents of the things we call "material?" On the other hand, the second but of course methodologically prior question is: *Which things are the ones called* "material?"

2. **Which things are "material?"** The answer to the second of these two questions obviously is that the things called "material" are the rocks, air, water, plants, animal bodies, and so on, about us; that is, comprehensively, the substances, processes, events, relations, characteristics, etc., *that are perceptually public or can be made so.*

No doubt is possible that, originally and fundamentally, these things are the ones denominated "material" or "physical;" i.e., that they are the ones *denoted—pointed at—*by these names. Moreover, unless the physicist already knew, thus *as a matter of linguistic usage,* that those things are the ones we refer to when we speak of "material" things, he would not even know *which things* are the ones whose ultimate constituents we are asking him to investigate and to reveal to us.

The point, then, which is here crucial is that the objects, events, etc., that are perceptually public are called "material" or "physical" *not* because technical research had detected as hidden in all of them some recondite peculiarity that constituted their materiality, but simply because some *name* was needed—and the name, "material," was adopted—by which to refer comprehensively to all perceptually public things.

The case with regard to these things and to our calling them "material" is thus parallel in all essentials to that of a given boy called George. He is not so called because scrutiny of him after birth disclosed to his parents presence in him of a peculiar characteristic, to wit, Georgeness. Rather, "George" is simply the *name* or *tag* assigned to him by his parents in order to be able to refer to him without actually pointing at him. Similarly, "material" or "physical" is simply the name or tag assigned by custom to the part of the world that is perceptually public or is capable of being made so.

Hence the question as to what recondite peculiarities are possessed by material things is intelligible at all and is capable at all of being empirically investigated, only *after* one knows *which things* are the ones to be examined in order to answer it; that is, knows which things are the ones *named* "material"—just as one can discover the recondite peculiarities of George only after one knows *which boy* is the one *named* George.

3. **"Material," derivatively vs. fundamentally.** Something, however, must now be added to the statement made above that, *originally and fundamentally,* what the expressions "the material world" or "the physical world" denote is the things, events, processes, characteristics, etc., that are or can be made perceptually public.

The addition called for is that, *secondly and derivatively,* those expressions denote also *the minute or otherwise unperceivable constituents* of whatever is or can be made perceptually public. The existence and the characteristics of these recondite constituents are discovered, not of course by perceptual observation of them since they are not perceptible; but by theoretical inference from certain perceived occurrences which turn out to be inexplicable and unpredictable except on the supposition that they are effects of certain processes among unperceivable constituents of the perceived things—constituents, namely, having the very properties in terms of which we define the nature of the "atoms," "electrons," etc., which we postulate exist. The reality of these is then confirmed empirically in so far as the postulating of them turns out to enable us to predict and sometimes to control occurrences that are capable of being perceived but that until then had remained unobserved or unexplained.

The title, then, of those recondite theoretical entities and events to be called "material" or "physical" is not, like that of trees, stones, water, etc., that they are perceptually public since they are not so; but that they are existentially implicit in the things that are perceptually public.

4. What is "living." In an article circulated to newspapers by the Associated Press early in December 1957, Dr. Selman Waksman, Nobel prize winner in biology, rightly points out that the question whether life after death is possible cannot be answered until its meaning has first been made clear. He then proceeds to define the meaning he attaches to "life" and to "death" by listing certain observable and measurable functions—growth, metabolism, respiration, reproduction, adaptation to environment, and intelligence—as being those which, together, differentiate living from non-living material and constitute the "life" of the former; and by defining "death" as termination of those functions.

After some technical biological elaboration, he comes to the conclusion that "any belief in life after death is in disagreement with all the accumulated wisdom and knowledge of modern biology"—a conclusion, however, which, notwithstanding its impressive allusion to biological science, then reduces to the mere truism that when the functions constituting life terminate they do not persist!

But, as we stated briefly at the beginning of Chapt. I, there are two senses in which a man may be said to "live." One is the *biological* sense, defined as by Dr. Waksman in terms of certain public, measurable processes. The other is the *psychological* sense. It is defined in terms of *occurrence of states of consciousness—*

occurrence of the sensations, images, feelings, emotions, attitudes, thoughts, desires, etc., privately experienced directly by each of us: that a man is "living" in the psychological sense means that ones and others of these keep occurring. Moreover life, in this psychological sense of the term, is what man essentially prizes and is usually what he means when he speaks of a "life" after the death and decay of the body.

A biologist would of course be likely to say that, anyway, states of consciousness are *effects* of certain of the processes going on in bodies that are biologically "living"; and hence that when these die the stream of states of consciousness necessarily terminates. But this does not logically follow from the known facts; for although the biologist knows that *some* states of consciousness are effects of bodily processes, he does not know but only piously postulates that all of them without exception are so. Moreover, he does not know that some at least of the states of consciousness which certain bodily processes cause might not possibly be causable also in some other way, and hence might not go on occurring after biological life terminates. In any case, the question as to whether they then can or do go on is not answered by the truism that when biological life terminates, it does not continue.

Dr. Waksman's conclusion that biological life after biological death is biologically impossible escapes vacuousness only if taken to refer specifically to the idea that "life after death" means *resurrection of the flesh;* that is, (a) *reconstitution* of the body after it has died and its material has been dispersed by decay or by worms, vultures, sharks, or cremation; and then, (b) *resumption* in the reconstituted body of the processes of growth, metabolism, respiration, etc., which constitute biological "life."

Such *reconstitution and resumption* is what indeed is "in disagreement with all the accumulated wisdom and knowledge of modern biology."

The distinction between biological and psychological life having now been made sharp, it is appropriate to notice that, in the case of either, being alive is not a matter of wholly or not at all. When the body is in coma, under anesthesia, in a faint, or in deep sleep, the processes of "vegetative" life still go on, but such bodily activities as eating, drinking, seeking food, hiding from or fighting enemies, etc., which are typical of the body's "animal" life, are in abeyance, as well as the bodily activities distinctive of "human" life—examples of which would be speaking, writing, reading, constructing instruments and operating them, trading, and the other "cultural" activities.

In the psychological life of human beings, various levels may likewise be distinguished. The neonate's psychological life comprises only sensations, feelings, emotions, and blind impulses. Memory, association of ideas, expectations, conscious purpose, do not yet enter into it. Soon, however, some states of consciousness come to function as *signs*—signs of events or facts other than themselves. At later stages of individual development, psychological life at a given time may consist only of uncontrolled dreaming, whether by day or night. At other times psychological life is on the contrary active—inventive, heuristic, critical, consciously purposive. And it is conceivable that, if there is any life in the psychological sense after biological death, such life may consist of only certain ones of these various kinds of psychological processes.

Chapter V

WHAT IS "MENTAL"

From the things, events, etc., called "physical" or "material," we now turn to those called "psychical" or "mental." With regard to these, the same two questions arise as did concerning the others. Stated here in their right methodological order, they are: (1) *Which events, processes, etc., are the ones named* "psychical" or "mental?" and (2) *What characteristic* does empirical examination *discover* as peculiar to all of them?

1. **Which occurrences are denominated "mental".** The answer to the first of those two questions is that, originally and fundamentally, the events, processes, etc. denoted by the terms "psychical" or "mental" are *the inherently private ones each person can, in himself and only in himself, attend to in the direct manner which*—whether felicitously or not—*is called Introspection.* "Mental" or "psychological" events are thus, fundamentally, the immediate experiences, familiar at first hand to each of us, of which the various species are called "thoughts," "ideas," "desires," "emotions," "cravings," "moods," "sensations," "mental images," "volitions," and so on; or comprehensively, "states or modes of consciousness."

What introspection discloses may to some extent be *published* by the person concerned, but is never *itself public.* To publish the fact that at a given time one's state of consciousness is of a certain kind consists in performing certain perceptually public acts—vocal, graphic, gestural, facial, or other—that are such as to cause the percipients of them to think of a state of consciousness of that kind and to believe that the state of consciousness of the performer of those acts is of that kind at the time. This is what, for example, utterance of the words "I am anxious," or "I wonder where I parked my car," or "I remember him," etc. ordinarily

45

causes to occur in the person who hears them. But the utterer's state of consciousness, which such words symbolized, is never *itself* public in the sense in which the sound of those words, or the written words, are public. That state of consciousness is inherently private to the particular person, of whose history alone it is an item—private in the sense that no other person can examine it, whereas each person can examine his own states of consciousness; can, for instance, compare directly the feeling he calls "anxiety" with the feeling he calls "wonder," etc.

2. **Introspection, Inspection, Intuition.** In the case of *sensations,* attention directly to them—vs. to what they may be signs of or to what they may be caused by—is termed by some writers *Inspection* rather than Introspection. Inspection in this technical sense, then, no less than Introspection, is attention directly to experiences that are inherently private; for, evidently, we cannot attend to another person's sensations themselves, but only to his appearance or behavior. Such knowledge as we have concerning his sensations results from our automatically interpreting certain modes of his behavior as signs that, in given situations, he is experiencing sensations similar to, or as the case may be, different from, those we are experiencing.

For example, we do not and cannot discover that another person is, say, color-blind to red-green, by inspecting the sensations *he* has when he looks at grass and at a poppy, and comparing them with the sensations *we* have when we look at the same objects. We discover it by attending to his perceptually public behavior on such occasions, by noticing that in certain ways it is consistently different from our own on the same occasions, and by taking this as signifying that his color-sensations correspondingly differ from ours.

For the direct kind of experience, whether attentive or inattentive, which when attentive is called specifically Introspection, or by some writers in the particular case of sensations, Inspection, a generic name is needed; but no such generic name less cumbersome than "State of consciousness, as such" appears to exist in ordinary language. I have therefore proposed for this elsewhere, in default of a better, the name *Intuition*—defining Intuition as occurrence of some state of consciousness, *as such,* i.e., as distinguished from what it may be consciousness *of,* in the sense of may signify.

Intuition, then, may be attentive (clear) or inattentive (dispersed, dim;) and, in so far as attentive, it is then inspective, or introspective, according as the state of consciousness attended to is a sensation, or is other than a sensation.

3. **"Content" vs. "object" of consciousness.** The second of the two questions mentioned at the outset, namely, what internal character is peculiar to all the events, processes, etc. that are intuitions as just defined, i.e., are "mental" or "psychical," is more technical than the first. Fortunately, it does not need to be gone into at any length for present purposes. I shall therefore say here, without attempting to argue the point, only that in the case of the events, processes, etc. in view and only in their case, existing consists solely in being experienced and being experienced constitutes the whole of existing. That is, in their case but only in their case, *esse est percipi.* This is the peculiarity that differentiates them from all other things, events, or processes. The term "Intuition" thus designates the experiencing of such an experience—*an* intuition standing to the intuiting thereof in the same kind of relation as, for example, a stroke being struck stands to the striking thereof (not, to the object struck;) that is, in both cases equally, as the "connate" or "internal" accusative of the activity concerned, as distinguished from the "alien" or "objective" accusative of it. Similarly, compare tasting a taste with tasting a substance, tasting bitter taste with tasting quinine, thinking a thought with thinking of New York, etc.

Introspection, then, and likewise "Inspection," is intuition attentive *to its own modality of the moment,* instead of, as normally, inattentive to it. Its particular modality at any moment I term the *content* of consciousness at the moment, as distinguished from the *object* of consciousness at the moment.[1]

In connection with the above account of states of conscious-

---

[1]The contentions and the terminological proposals sketched in this and the preceding two sections are explicated and defended in detail in Chapts. 12, 13, and 14 of my *Nature, Mind, and Death* Open Court Pub. Co. La Salle, Ill. 1951. See in particular pp. 230-40, 275-80, 293-5, 302.

ness, it will be appropriate to comment here briefly on the fact, of which much is being made these days, that we all possess a vocabulary, understood by our fellows, for mental states or states of consciousness. This, it is alleged, means that mental states cannot, as generally has been assumed and as asserted in the text above, be occurrences unobservable by other persons than the particular one in whom they occur, i.e., be inherently private.

Rather, it is contended, the denotation of the words which denote mental states must have been learned by us in the same manner as that of the words which denote physical objects and events; namely, by our hearing them applied by other persons to public occurrences which they and ourselves were witnessing—these, however, being denominated specifically "mental" when they consisted of modes of behavior of certain special kinds; e.g., anger-behavior, goal-seeking-behavior, listening-behavior, seeing-behavior, etc.

A crucial fact, however, is overlooked by this would-be-inclusive behavioristic account of the manner in which men have acquired a shared vocabulary for mental states notwithstanding the latter's inherent privacy. That crucial fact is that when the behavior, witnessed by another person, which moves him to employ one or another of the "mental" words in characterizing it, is *our own behavior*—e.g., when he says to us: "Now, don't be so *angry*," or "Don't you *see* that bird?" or "What were you *dreaming* just before I woke you?" or "You are *wondering* at my appearance today," etc.—then the words italicized do not denote *for us* our *behavior*, which the other person is attending to but *we* are not. Instead and automatically, they denote *for us* in each case *the mental state itself* which we are subjectively experiencing—feeling, intuiting, immediately apprehending—and which, irrespective of how in particular it may be *connected with* our behavior at the moment, is anyway *not that behavior itself* but something radically different and inherently private. In English, "anger-behavior" denotes one thing, which is public; and "anger" denotes another thing, which is publishable but never itself public. It is only in Behaviorese—the doctrinaire language of the creed of radical behaviorism—that "anger" denotes anger-behavior.

A recent widely discussed work, Gilbert Ryle's *The Concept of Mind,* appears largely based on its author's overlooking the crucial fact just mentioned. And one contention in it of which much has been made, to wit, that there are no acts of will or volitions, is based merely on failure to notice that although many voluntary acts indeed are not caused by any act of will, nevertheless certain other acts that are voluntary acts are in addition *willed acts,* i.e., are initiated *by deliberate volitions.*

4. **"Mental," derivatively vs. fundamentally.** There now remains to point out that, just as the expression "the material world" denotes not alone whatever events, processes, things, etc. are or can be made perceptually public, but also, *derivatively,* the imperceptible constituents of them; so likewise the events, processes, etc. denominated "psychical" or "mental" include not only those, such as mentioned above, that are introspectively or "inspectively" scrutinizable, but also, *derivatively,* certain others which are not accessible to "inspection" or introspection and are therefore termed "subconscious" or "unconscious" instead of "conscious."

These would comprise such items as the repressed wishes or impulses, the forgotten emotional experiences, the complexes, censors, etc. which psychoanalysts find themselves led to postulate as hidden constituents or activities of the human mind, in order to account for some otherwise inexplicable psychological peculiarities of some persons.

Such hidden constituents can sometimes be brought to consciousness under the direction of the psychoanalyst; but the exploration of these normally unintrospectable psychological factors is still in its infancy as compared with the exploration of the atomic and sub-atomic levels of materiality. The mere fact, however, now definitely known, that there are such things as unconscious, i.e., at the time unintrospectable, psychological processes, is, when taken together with even the limited knowledge of them so far obtained, of vast importance for assessment of the significance of certain of the phenomena alleged to constitute empirical evidence of survival of the personality after death.

Moreover, although the terms "the unconscious," "the subconscious," are commonly employed in connection with the factors brought to light in *therapeutic* psychoanalysis, nevertheless factors of the same kinds undoubtedly operate, but ordinarily in a non-pathological manner, in all of us.

Unconscious also, of course, are various assumptions under which a particular person happens to proceed, but which he does not realize he makes because he has never formulated them and nothing in his experience has happened that would have challenged their validity and thus made him conscious of them. Unconscious also at a given time are all those of his memories which he is not then remembering, and all those of his capacities or dispositions which he is not then exercising.

Chapter VI

WHAT IS "A MIND"

In a book cited earlier, Dr. Lamont defines mind as "the power of abstract reasoning," referring to the exercise of it as "the experience of thinking or having ideas," and stating that ideas "are non-material meanings expressing the relations between things and events."[1]

But although the power of abstract reasoning may well be what differentiates human minds from the minds of animals, and developed human minds from the minds of human infants, yet human minds comprise, besides the power of abstract reasoning, various others, wholly or partly independent of it. This power could at most be claimed to constitute the *intellectual* part of the mind of man; for minds, human as well as animal have also *affective* and *conative capacities,* the existence of which Lamont acknowledges but does not include in his definition of mind. His definition is therefore arbitrary and unrealistic.

1. **The traits in terms of which one describes particular minds.** When we are asked to state the characteristics in which a given person's mind differs from that of another, what we say is, for example, that he is patient whereas the other is irritable; intelligent, and the other stupid; widely informed, and the other ignorant; self-disciplined, and the other self-indulgent; and we add whatever else we happen to know about his particular tastes, opinions, habits, intellectual skills, attitudes, knowledge, personal memories, character, ideals, ambitions, and so on.

It is in terms of such traits that we spontaneously describe the particular nature of a particular mind. Correspondingly, the generic nature of the human mind would be described in terms

---

[1]*The Illusion of Immortality,* pp. 70, 100, 101.

of traits shared by all normal human minds. Examples of such generic traits would be the capacity to experience sensations—dizziness, thirst, warmth, pain, color, tone, etc.; the capacity to form mental images—visual, auditory, or other—as in dreams, in day-dreams, in memories, and in voluntary imagination; the capacity to experience emotions, moods, cravings, and impulses; the capacity to imagine and desire experiences or situations not at the moment occurring; and so on.

2. **What is a power, capacity, or disposition.** Lamont's definition of mind, however, although inadequate for the reason stated, is sound to the extent that it conceives minds in terms of "powers."

The term "power" is nowadays out of favor, as is its virtual synonym, "faculty," the utility of which was destroyed by misuse of it as answer to the question "Why?" The classical horrible example of such misuse is the *vis dormitiva* offered as answer to the question why opium puts people to sleep.

But a power, or faculty, or capacity, or ability, or—to use the term currently in fashion—a disposition, *is not an event* and therefore never can *itself* be a cause. A power or disposition is a more or less abiding *causal connection* between events of particular kinds.[2]

More specifically, that something T— whether T be a material thing or a mind—has a power, capacity, or disposition D means that T is such that *whenever* the state of affairs external or/and internal to T is of a particular kind S, then occurrence of change of a particular kind C in that state of affairs causes occurrence in it of a change of another particular kind E.

For example, solubility in water is a power, faculty, ability, capacity, or disposition of sugar. This means, *not* that the sugar's

---

[2]No need arises here to go into the question of the nature of causality itself. I shall therefore say only that a causal connection between events of specified kinds is a *causal law*, and that a causal law is a law of *causation* not in virtue of its being a law (since some empirical laws are not laws of causation) but in virtue of the fact that each of the particular sequences, of which the law is an inductive generalization, was, *in its own individual right*, a causal sequence. For the analysis of the nature of causality this assumes, interested readers are referred to Chs. 7, 8, and 9 of the writer's *Nature, Mind, and Death*, Open Court Pub. Co. La Salle, Ill. 1951.

solubility causes the sugar to dissolve when it is placed in water; but that sugar is such that (i.e., behaves according to the law that) whenever an *event* of the kind described as "placing the sugar in water" occurs, then, in ordinary circumstances, that event causes an event of a certain other kind, to wit, the kind described as "sugar's dissolving in water."

This illustration concerns a material thing—sugar. But the mental traits of persons are capacities or dispositions in exactly the same generic sense of these terms, defined above, as are the material traits of sugar and of other material things.

For example, that a person *possesses a memory of* certain personal experiences, or of some impersonal fact such as that Socrates died in 399 B.C., does not consist simply of occurrences in him, at some particular time, of mental images of those personal experiences, or of word-images formulating that impersonal fact, together with occurrence of what has been termed the feeling of familiarity. Rather, it consists in that person's being such that *whenever* a question or other "reminder" relating to those personal experiences or to that impersonal fact presents itself to his attention, *then,* provided that the circumstances in which he is at the time be not abnormal, the advent of the "reminder" causes those images, together with the feeling of familiarity, to arise in him.

Again, that a person is, say, irritable, does not mean that he is at the time experiencing the feeling called Irritation; but that he is such that events of kinds which in most other persons would not in ordinary circumstances cause the feeling of Irritation to arise in them do, in similar circumstances, regularly cause it to arise in him. And so on with the tastes, the skills, the gifts—intellectual, artistic, or other—the habits, etc., which a person possesses. All of them analyze as capacities or dispositions, i.e., as abiding causal connections in him between any event of some particular kind and an event of some other particular kind, under circumstances of some particular kind.

The term "dispositions", however, although currently in greater favor than "powers" or "capacities," is really less felicitous than these since it suffers from a certain ambiguity of which they are free and which easily leads to serious misconceptions.

For, besides the sense of "disposition" in which the word is syn-
onymous with "capacity" or with "power," it has another sense,
in which "a disposition" and the verb "being disposed to . . ."
designate an *event*, to wit, *occurrence of an impulse or inclination
to act* in some particular manner.

For example, that a given person is at the moment disposed
to forgive a certain injury that was done him means no more
than that, *at the moment,* an impulse or inclination to forgive
is present in him. This does not mean that he has, or is acquiring, "a forgiving disposition," i.e., that similar situations regularly
cause, or henceforth will regularly cause, the impulse to forgive
to arise in him.

3. **What a mind is.** The distinction essential in connection
with the immediately preceding paragraph is between the *nature*
of a given mind, and the *history* of that mind.

The history consists of *events*. Occurrence of some impulse,
occurrence of awareness of some situation, acquisition or loss of
some habit or capacity, etc., are events; each of them results from
exercise of some capacity, and each is an item in the history of a
mind. On the other hand, an account of the *nature* of a given
mind is an account of the *particular sort of mind* it is at the time,
i.e., of the particular set of dispositions, capacities, powers, or
abilities which are what as a matter of course we list when called
upon to describe that particular mind. The events that constitute
a mind's history doubtless are in large part responsible for that
mind's having come to be the particular sort of mind it is now.
But recital of them is no part of an account of what it now is.

The capacities that together constitute the nature of a mind
are of three comprehensive kinds. These may be denominated
psycho-psychical, psycho-physical, and *physico-psychical,* according,
respectively, as the cause-event and the effect-event entering in
the description of a given capacity are, both of them, psychical
events; or, the cause-event psychical but the effect-event physical;
or the cause-event physical but the effect-event psychical.

In all three cases the state of affairs, in which the cause-event
and the effect-event are changes, is *normally* in part somatic and
more specifically cerebral; and in part psychical. Whether this
is the case not only normally, but also invariably and necessarily,

is another question. Evidently, the possibility or impossibility of survival after death depends in part on the answer to it.

However, if a mind continues to function after the death of its body, its functioning would not then normally include exercise either of its physico-psychical or of its psycho-physical capacities. That is, such awareness, if any, as a discarnate mind had of physical events would be paranormal and more specifically, "clairvoyant", i.e., without the intermediary of the bodily sense organs; and such action, if any, as a discarnate mind exerted on physical objects would likewise be paranormal and more specifically "psycho-kinetic," i.e., without the intermediary of muscular apparatus.

It should be noticed that the various dispositions or capacities that enter into the nature of a mind constitute together a *system* rather than simply an aggregate. For one thing, as Professor Broad has pointed out, some dispositions are of a higher order than some others, in the sense that the former consist of capacities to acquire the latter.[3] An aptitude, as distinguished from e.g., a skill, is a capacity to acquire a capacity. Again, possession of certain capacities at a certain time is in some cases dependent on possession of certain other capacities at that time.

A mind, then, is a set of capacities of the three generic kinds mentioned, *qua* interrelated in the systematic manner which constitutes them a more or less thoroughly integrated personality; and the mind, of which we say that it "has" those capacities, *is not something existentially independent of them,* but "has" them in the sense in which a week has days or an automobile has a motor. That a mind *exists* during a certain period means that, during that period, ones or others of the capacities, which together define the particular sort of mind it is, *function.* That is, the *existing* of a mind of a particular description is the series of actual occurrences which, as causally related one to another, constitute *exercisings* of that mind's capacities. A mind's *existing* thus consists not just of its having a particular nature, but of its having in addition a *history.*

But further, just as a material object consists of various parts interrelated in some particular manner, each of which is itself a

---

[3] *Examination of McTaggart's Philosophy,* Vol. I: 264-278.

material object whose nature is analyzable into a set of capacities, though to a greater or less extent ones different from those of the whole; so likewise a mind has parts, normally connected with one another in a certain manner, each of which, like the whole, analyzes into some particular complex of capacities, though capacities to some extent different from those of the whole.

Moreover, in a mind as in a material object, some part of it may on occasion become dissociated from the rest and perhaps function independently, although then in a manner more or less different from that in which it functioned while integrated with and censored by the rest. As Professor H. H. Price has remarked somewhere, the unity of a mind is not a matter of all or none, but rather of more or less. Each of the parts of a mind is itself a mind, or mindkin, of sorts.

The foregoing account of what a mind is has revealed that a mind, and a physical substance such as sugar or a physical object such as a tree, ultimately analyze equally as complexes of systematically interrelated capacities. Had not the word "substance" so chequered a philosophical history, we could say that a mind is as truly a psychical substance as any material object is a physical substance. Let us, however, avoid the misunderstandings this might lead to, and say that a mind, no less than a tree or sugar, is a *substantive*—using this word as does W. E. Johnson for the kind of *entity* to which the part of speech called a "noun" corresponds.[4]

Evidently, the preceding analysis of the nature of a mind in terms of capacities or dispositions applies not only to the intellectual or cognitive powers sometimes specifically meant by the term "Mind," but also to the emotional, affective, and conative capacities sometimes more particularly in view when the terms "soul" or "spirit," instead of "mind," are used. In these pages, therefore, the term "mind" will be used in the broad sense comprehensive of "soul" and of "spirit," as well as of "intellect." That is, it will include whatever constituents of the human personality are other than material in the sense of this term defined in Chapt. V.

---

[4]*Logic*, Cambridge Univ. Press, 1921 Vol I:9. For a more elaborate account of the conception of what a mind is, outlined above, the interested reader is referred to Ch. 17 of the author's already cited *Nature, Mind, and Death*.

PART III

The Relation Between Mind and Body

Chapter VII

WHAT WOULD ESTABLISH THE POSSIBILITY OF SURVIVAL

The inquiry we undertook in Part II, as to what exactly the pivotal terms "material," "mental," "mind," and "life" denote, was unavoidably somewhat lengthy and technical. It may therefore be well to summarize its findings before we proceed, with their aid, to an exposition of the case for the possibility of survival.

1. **Summary of the findings of Part II.** The first question considered in Part II was: Which things—i.e., which objects, characteristics, events, processes, relations, etc.,—are denominated "material" or "physical." The answer reached was that, fundamentally, they are the things that are or can be made perceptually public; and in addition, derivatively, the minute or otherwise unperceivable existential constituents of those.

The next question was: Which things are denominated "alive" or "living." The answer was that the marks by which we distinguish them from the things called "dead," or "inorganic," are in general metabolism, growth, respiration, reproduction, and adaptation to environment; and that, more particularly in the case of human bodies, the minimal marks of their being "alive" not "dead" are breathing, heart beat, and maintenance of body temperature above a certain level.

The third question was: Which things—still taking this word in the comprehensive sense—are denominated "mental" or "psychical." We found the answer to be that, fundamentally, they are the ones capable of being introspectively observed; and in addition, derivatively, whatever unintrospectable processes, events, etc., are existentially implicit in those that are introspectable.

The fourth question was: What is "a mind." Distinguishing

between the *history* of a mind, which consists of a series of events, and the *nature* of a mind at a given time in its history, we found that its nature analyzes as a set of systematically interconnected "dispositions," i.e., capacities, powers, abilities; and that each of these consists in the more or less abiding sufficiency, or as the case may be, insufficiency, of change of some particular kind C in a state of affairs of a kind S, to cause change of another particular kind E in S immediately thereafter. For example, that a person is of a *patient* disposition means that kinds of occurrences that would in similar situations be sufficient to cause most other persons to feel irritation are in his case insufficient to cause this.

The dispositions, which together constitute the nature of a mind are, we further found, of three comprehensive kinds: psycho-psychical, physico-psychical, and psycho-physical, according as, respectively, the cause-event and the effect-event are both psychical, or the cause-event physical and the effect-event psychical, or the cause-event psychical and the effect event physical.

Lastly, we noticed that *existence* of a mind having a given nature consists, not in existence of something distinct from and "having" the set of dispositions that define that mind's nature, but in the series of actual occurrences which constitute *exercise* of ones or others of those dispositions; that is, constitute the historical individuation of a mind having that particular nature.

2. **Theoretical possibility, empirical possibility, and factuality.** In Chapt III, we set forth the considerations that constitute the basis—in common knowledge, in the knowledge possessed by the Natural Sciences, and in certain theoretical reflections—for the contention that survival of the individual's consciousness after the death of his body is impossible. The clarification of key concepts we achieved in Part II now puts us in position to judge whether or how far the items of the case against the possibility of survival are strong and cogent, or on the contrary weak or inept.

If and in so far as they turn out to have either of these defects, then and in so far they fail to establish the impossibility they are alleged to establish, and they therefore leave open the possibility of a life after death. That is, the case *for* the possibility (not automatically the reality) of survival consists of the case *against* the adequacy of the grounds on which survival is asserted to be impossible: That a life after death remains a *theoretical* possibility would mean that the *theoretical* grounds alleged to entail its impossibility are unsound; or, if sound in themselves, nevertheless do not really but only seemingly entail it. And, that survival remains an *empirical* possibility would mean that survival, notwithstanding possible appearances to the contrary, really is compatible with all the facts and laws of Nature so far truly ascertained by the sciences.

If critical examination of the merits of the case against the possibility of survival reveals that, notwithstanding the negative "verdict of science", a life after death remains both a theoretical and an empirical possibility, then certain questions will confront us.

The first will be as to what *prima facie* positive empirical evidence, if any, is available that survival is a fact. Next, we shall have to ask whether such evidence for it as our inquiry may turn up is really sufficient to establish survival or the probability of it. And, if this itself should be dubious, then the methodologically prior question will force itself upon us, as to what kind and quantity of evidence, if it should be or become available, would conclusively prove, or make conclusively more probable than not, that survival is a fact. Overarching of course these various problems, there is the question as to what forms survival, if it be a fact, can plausibly be conceived to take.

3. **The tacit theoretical premise of the empirical arguments against the possibility of survival.** One of the facts listed in Chapt. III as allegedly proving that consciousness cannot survive the body's death was that a severe blow on the head permanently or temporarily terminates all the evidences of consciousness which the body had until then been giving. This, it is alleged, and likewise the other empirical facts cited in that chapter, shows that a person's states of consciousness are direct products of the neural processes that normally take place in his brain; and hence that when, at death, these terminate, then consciousness necessarily lapses also.

This conclusion, however, is based not simply on the observed facts, but also on a certain theoretical premise, tacitly and in most cases unconsciously employed. The nature of it becomes evident if one considers the *prima facie* analogous empirical fact that smashing the receiver of a radio brings to an end all the evidences the instrument had until then been giving that a program was on the air, but that this does not in the least warrant concluding that the program was a *product* of the radio and therefore had automatically lapsed when the latter was smashed.

The hidden premise of the contention that the cessation at death of all evidences of consciousness entails that consciousness itself then necessarily ceases is, evidently, that the relation of brain activity to consciousness is always that of cause to effect, never that of effect to cause. But this hidden premise is not known to be true, and is not the only imaginable one consistent with the empirical facts listed in Chapt. III. Quite as consistent with them is the supposition, which was brought forth by William James, that the brain's function is that of intermediary between psychological states or activities, and the body's sense organs, muscles, and glands. That is, that the brain's function is that of receiver-transmitter—sometimes from body to mind and sometimes from mind to body.

These remarks are not intended to answer or to hint at a particular answer to the question of the nature of the relation between brain or body and mind; but only to make evident that the validity or invalidity of the conclusion, from the various empirical facts cited in Chapt. III, that man's consciousness cannot survive the death of his body, is *wholly dependent on what really is the relation between body and mind.*

Our task in the remaining chapters of Part III must therefore be to consider the various hypotheses which, in the history of thought, have been offered concerning the nature of that relation, and to decide which one among them best seems to accord with *all* the definitely known facts.

Chapter VIII

MIND CONCEIVED AS BODILY PROCESSES; MATTER CONCEIVED AS SETS OF IDEAS

Among the hypotheses concerning the relation between mind and body, one of the most ancient is the radically materialistic one. Let us consider it first; and then its polar opposite, the radically idealistic hypothesis.

1. **The contention that thought is a physical process.** The materialistic conception of mind is that "thoughts," "feelings," ideals," "mental processes," or, comprehensively, "states of con- sciousness," *are but other names* for material occurences of cer- tain kinds—more specifically, for molecular processes in the tissues of the brain; or for speech, vocal or sub-vocal; or for discrimina- tive and adaptive behavior. This, if true, would entail that the supposition that consciousness persists after death has terminated these material activities is absurd because then obviously self- contradictory.

But as Friedrich Paulsen long ago and others since have made quite clear, no evidence really ever has been or can be offered to support that materialistic conception of mind, for it constitutes in fact only an attempt unawares to force upon the words "thoughts," "ideas," "feelings," "desires," and so on, a *denotation* radically other than that which they actually have.

Paulsen writes: "The proposition, Thoughts are in reality nothing but movements in the brain, feelings are nothing but bodily processes in the vaso-motor system, is absolutely irrefuta- ble"; not, however, because it is true but because it is absurd. "The absurd has this advantage in common with truth, that it cannot be refuted. To say that thought is at bottom but a move- ment is to say that iron is at bottom made of wood. No argument avails here. All that can be said is this: I understand by a thought a thought and not a movement of brain molecules; and similarly, I designate with the words anger and fear, anger and fear themselves and not a contraction or dilation of blood vessels. Suppose the latter processes also occur, and suppose they always occur when the former occur, still they *are* not thoughts and feelings."[1]

Words such as "thought," "feeling," etc., have two possible functions. One is to *predicate* of something certain characters which the word connotes; the other is to *indicate*—point at, denote, tag, direct attention to—certain occurrences or entities. And the fact is that, just as our finger does point at whatever we point it at, or just as a tag does tag and identify whatever we tag with it, so do our words denote—name, tag, direct attention to—whatever we use them to denote. And what we use the words "thought," "feelings," etc., to denote are occurrences with which we are directly familiar, and which are patently quite different from those we denote by the words "molecular motions in the brain" or "modes of bodily behavior."

Hence, however much there may be that we do not know *about* states of consciousness or about bodily processes, however close and intimate may turn out to be the relation between them, and whatever the particular nature of that relation may be, it is at all events *not identity*.

2. **Connection to be distinguished from identity.** The point just made, although elementary, is crucial. Hence, even at the risk of laboring it, a few words will be added in order to render it unmistakable.

Let us consider the case, say, of the moon and the earth. They are connected and influence one another, but the moon and the earth are not one and the same thing. Hence it is possible to know much about one of them and little about the other. On the other hand, the *thing* which the words "the moon" denote is identically the same *thing* as that which the words "la lune," or the words "the earth's largest satellite," denote; and the *identity* entails that, although one might not know all three of these *names* of that single thing, nevertheless, whatever (other

---

[1] *Introduction to Philosophy*, transl. F. Thilly, Henry Holt and Co. N.Y. 1895, pp. 82-3.

than some of its names) one happened to know, or to be ignorant of, about the *thing* denoted by one of them, one would necessarily know it, or be ignorant of it, about the *thing* denoted by either of the other two names. For *one thing only* is concerned, not three.

Now, a parallel conclusion follows in the case of, say, the word "pain" and the words "a certain motion of the molecules of the nerve cells of the brain." If these two sets of words both denoted—i.e., were but two different *names* for—one single event, then any person who at a given moment knows pain, i.e., experiences the particular feeling which the word "pain" denotes, would necessarily know which particular motion of which particular things the words "a certain motion of molecules in the brain" denote at that moment; for, under the supposition, *one* event only would be occurring, but denoted equally by each of those two different names. But the patent fact is on the contrary that all men know directly and only too well *the event itself* which the word "pain" denotes. They know it in the sense of experiencing it, whether or not they happen to know also that it is called "pain"; whereas no man knows what particular molecular motion is occurring in the nerve cells of his brain at the time he feels pain; and only a few men know even that molecular motions occur there. Moreover, even this they know not empirically and directly as on the contrary every man knows pain, but know it only indirectly through theoretical inferences.

How one comes to learn that "pain" is the English name of the feeling he or someone else has on a given occasion is one question; but *what that feeling itself is* (and no matter what, if anything, it is called at the time) is another question. One learns what pain *is* by having pins stuck into him, and in various other manners that likewise cause it to occur. "Pain" is the name of the feeling caused in these various ways.

The concrete occurrences which the word "pain," and the words "thought," "ideas," "desires," "sensations," "mental states," etc., denote in English, are quite familiar at first hand to all of us, for they are directly experienced by us and open to our introspective attention; and what introspection reveals is, for example, that the event we denote by the word "pain" when we say "I have a pain" *does not in the least resemble*—to say nothing of being identically—what attention to perceptually public facts reveals when directed perhaps to the cutting or burning of the skin, or to the writhing or shrinking behavior or to the groans on such an occasion; or to the words "I have a pain," or to the (postulated, not observed) molecular motions in the brain.

All these are material events, and no doubt are *connected* with the mental event called "pain," which occurs when they occur. But *connection is one thing and identity is wholly another.*

This simple fact, which becomes patent if only one attends strictly to the *denotation* of the "material" and of the "mental" terms, strangely eludes some of the writers who express themselves on the subject of the mind-body relation. Dr. C. S. Myers, for example, in his L. T. Hobhouse Memorial Lecture for 1932 entitled "The Absurdity of any Mind-Body Relation," writes:

"The conclusion which I have at length reached is that the notion of any *relation* between mind and body is absurd—because mental activity and living bodily activity are *identical.* The most highly specialized forms of these two activities are, respectively, conscious processes and the processes of living brain matter." (p.6)

But obviously what is absurd is to do, as these statements do, both of the following things: On the one hand, to mention *two* activities, to wit, the activity called "mental" and the activity called "living bodily activity"—both of which are observable and when observed are found to be each patently unlike the other; and yet, on the other hand, to assert that these *two* utterly dissimilar activities are *identically one and the same!*

Farther on, we shall consider specifically another contention which is often confused with this and which—however otherwise open to criticism—is anyway not absurd; namely, the contention that mental activity and living bodily activity are two *aspects* of one same process.

In conclusion, then, since connection is one thing and identity wholly another, the fact that the events which the expression "mental events" denotes, and certain of the events which the expression "material events" denotes (specifically, certain neural or behavioral events) are perhaps so connected as to form a "psychophysical unity"—this fact does *not* entail, as Lamont and others have alleged, that the unity is *indissoluble;* but only that, *so long as the connection remains what it has been,* the two series of quite dissimilar events—the mental and the bodily—continue . . . . to form "a psychophysical unity"!

What cessation of the connection may entail as regards continuance, or not, either of the bodily series or of the mental one, depends on the specific nature of the connection, and cannot be inferred simply from the fact that during the life of the body, the two were in *some* way united, i.e., closely connected.

3. **Disguised assertions about the word "thought" mistaken for assertions about thought.** Some additional remarks are called for at this point in order to account for the fact that such statements as that thought is really a motion of molecules in the brain, or is really a particular mode of bodily behavior, have been made by some intelligent persons and have been considered by them penetrating instead of absurd as in fact they are.

The first thing to note is that of course anybody can devise and use language that differs from the common language in that certain words of the common language—for example, the words "thoughts," "ideas," "feelings," "desires," "mental states"—are employed in the devised language to denote certain things—for example, brain states of certain kinds—which are radically other than the things they denote in the common language.

Moreover, a person who is using such a subverted language may be unaware that he is doing so and may assume, as naturally will his hearers, that when, for instance, he makes the statement that "thought is really a motion of molecules in the brain," he is using the common language.

That statement, however, when taken as made in the common language, is so paradoxical that hearers of it are likely to assume—humbly though in fact gratuitously—that somehow it must express a truth which the utterer of it perceives, but which the hearer is as yet unable to apprehend. And the utterer too— but proudly instead of humbly—is likely to assume this.

On the other hand, if one allows neither humility nor pride to becloud one's judgment, then what one perceives is that the statement "thought is really a motion of molecules in the brain" is in fact not worded in the common language; and that to make that statement is on the contrary to perform an act of subversion of the common language.

That is, one perceives that the statement is in fact not an assertion about thought itself and molecular motion itself, but only about the *words* "thought" and "molecular motion;" and that, in that assertion, the word, "really," expresses not at all an insight, but only the utterer's naive preference for language as in so far subverted!

The case is thus exactly parallel, except in one irrelevant respect, to a case where a Frenchman who, using English but holding with naive pride that French is the one "real" language, were to say: "A dog is really *un chien*." He would appear to himself and to others to be talking about dogs, but he would in fact be talking only about the *word* "dog" and claiming that it would be preferable to use instead the word "chien." The minor and only difference between the two cases is that "dog" and "chien" belong to two independent languages but have the same denotation in each; whereas both the word "thought" and the words "molecular motion in brain cells" belong to the same language, to wit, English, but, in it, do *not* have the same denotation. They would have it only in (materialistically) subverted English.

The statement that thought is really a motion of molecules in the brain thus operates as do the statements in which communists—sometimes perhaps equally sincerely but then naively—use "liberation" to denote enslavement and "democracy" to denote tyranny: Such statements only befuddle both the persons who make them honestly and the persons who accept them uncritically.

4. **The radically idealistic conception of material objects.** Only a few words will now be needed to make evident that the radically idealistic conception of material objects is invalidated by the same kind of absurdity which we have seen invalidates the radically materialistic conception of mind.

Paulsen, it will be remembered, rightly insists that feelings, sensations, or thoughts themselves, which are introspectively known to all of us, *are* what the words "feelings," "sensations," or "thoughts" denote, and *not* the very different things denoted on the contrary by such expressions as "motions of molecules in in the brain" or "modes of bodily behavior."

Now, conversely here, we must insist that when we use the latter expressions, or the broader expression "material events and objects," we denote by them material events and objects themselves, or motions of molecules or modes of behavior themselves and *not,* as Berkeley would have it, certain groups of systematically associated sensations; for these are something very different indeed. They are elements in the process of *perceiving* material objects, but not in the material objects themselves, which exist independently of whether they are or are not being perceived.

The contention of a radical idealism would be on the contrary that what the words "material objects" denote is, *identically,* the same as what the words "perceivings of material objects" denote; namely the particular kind of state of consciousness which such perceiving constitutes. As in the case of the analogous radical materialistic claim, this radical idealistic claim too cannot be refuted; and this, again not because it is true but because it is absurd. It can and need be met only by flat denial: The words "the object perceived" do not, in English as distinguished from Idealese, denote the same thing as the words "the perceiving of an object;" and words *do* denote what we employ them to denote. To assert that the two expressions denote one and the same thing, instead of each something different, is not to set forth a novel truth but only here again to subvert the English language and thereby to muddle oneself and possibly one's hearers or readers. What specifically the relation is between the material object perceived and the psychological events—sensations and others—that enter into the process of perceiving the object is a most interesting but intricate question, into which fortunately we do not need to go for present purposes. What need be said is only that, whatever may be the relation between the two it is anyway *not identity.*

Chapter IX

TWO VERSIONS OF PSYCHO-PHYSICAL PARALLELISM

In the present chapter, we turn from the radically materialistic and radically idealistic conceptions of the body-mind relation, which we have now seen to be untenable, and pass to an examination of two versions of the conception of it termed Psycho-physical Parallelism.

1. **Mind and body as in "pre-established harmony."** The "pre-established harmony" conception of the connection between the series of mental events and the series of bodily events goes back to Leibnitz. According to him, only "monads" exist—simple, unextended "substances" whose essence consists in the power of action and whose exercise of this power consists in having ideas. A substance, however, is conceived by him as well as by others in his day as something wholly self-dependent and therefore as incapable of influencing or of being influenced by the activities of other substances. Hence the monads "have no windows" through which anything might come in or go out. The sequence of their ideas proceeds solely out of their own internal, i.e., psychological activity. The material world consists of masses of monads, whose aggregations, separations, and motions are determined, not like the internal states of each monad by mental causes, but solely by mechanical ones. Yet, harmony obtains between the succession of ideas in a given monad, and the motions of it and of the other monads associated with it in what we call its body. On this view, the correlations which obtain between a man's mental states and his bodily states—for example, that a pin prick and pain, or that volition to move the arm and motion of the arm regularly go together notwithstanding that neither causes the other—is

analogous to the correlation which obtains between the motions of the hands of two clocks notwithstanding that neither clock causes the other to behave as it does.

The explanation of the harmony between the behavior of the two is of course that it was preestablished by the maker of the clocks, who so constructed and so set them that.they would keep time to each other. Similarly, on the Leibnitzian view, the harmony which obtains between the series of a man's bodily states and the series of his mental states is due to its having been preestablished by man's maker, God.

It is perhaps unnecessary to comment on this quaint conception beyond saying that no evidence at all exists that body and mind are each inherently incapable of influencing the other; nor is there any evidence that the harmony which obtains between them was preestablished by a cosmic clock maker.

But even if this should somehow happen to be the case, nothing at all could be inferred from it as to whether or not mental life continues after the body dies. For inferences as to this could be drawn only if one knew—whereas in fact one does not—first that such a divine "clockmaker" as postulated by the preestablished harmony conception exists; and only if one knew in addition what his will is as to survival, or not, of man's or of some men's minds after death.

On the other hand, if one supposes the connection—or more properly then simply the correlation—between the bodily and the mental series of events to be a purely *de facto* parallelism; that is, one neither due to causation of the events of either series by those of the other, *nor* due to causation of both series by some one same cause distinct from both as in the preestablished harmony conception; then, *ex hypothesi,* termination of either series would have no effect at all on the other. Termination of the bodily series might, or might not, *de facto,* be paralleled by termination also of the mental series. From purely *de facto* parallelism in the past and present, nothing at all can be inferred as to the future.

2. **Mind and body as two aspects of one same thing.** Still another conception of the connection between mind and body is of the type envisaged by Spinoza, but divorced in the writings of

contemporary biologists and psychologists that accept it from the theological hypothesis in terms of which Spinoza phrased it.

The connection in view is of the so-called "double aspect" kind, analogous to that which obtains, for example, between the two sides of a sheet of paper. There, a creasing of the sheet appears as a ridge on one side, and automatically and simultaneously as a valley on the other side, although the ridge does not cause the valley nor the valley the ridge.

If the paper analogy is used at all, however, its additional features also must be considered; for example, the fact that a spot of color on one side is not necessarily matched by a difference of any kind on the other side. The implication of the paper analogy as regards the "double aspect" conception of the connection between body and mind is then that one cannot tell whether the difference on the material side, which cessation of the body's life constitutes, is or is not automatically matched on the other side by cessation of consciousness, unless one knows *independently* what the entity or substance is, of which body and mind are alleged to be two "aspects;" and knows what properties it, as distinguished from either of its aspects, has. For only such knowledge would enable one to judge whether the body's death is analogous to, say, the ridging of one side of the paper—which, because of the properties of the paper sheet, is automatically matched by a valleying of the other side—or is analogous on the contrary to the staining of one side—which, again because of the properties of the paper sheet, is *not* automatically matched by any change on the other side.

In short, the supposition that body and mind are two "aspects" of one same thing is *wholly metaphorical;* and unless and until the metaphor has been translated into literal terms identifying for us the entity or substance itself, of which brain and mind are supposed to be two "aspects," *nothing* can be inferred as to whether the material change—death of the brain—is or is not automatically matched by death of the mind.

But no substance or thing having body and mind as two aspects has ever yet been exhibited, both aspects of which could be so experimented upon that one might discover what kinds of changes, if any, and of which aspect, are or are not automatically paralleled by changes of the other aspect.

Moreover, if it were suggested, as occasionally it is, that the body itself or the brain is that substance, and that mental activity *is* brain activity, but "viewed from within"—from the inside instead of the outside—then the appropriate comment would obviously be that the word "inside" as so used really means nothing at all. For, if one wishes to observe what goes on *literally* inside the brain, what one must do is simply to *open it up and look.* Such an operation might, in a then facetiously etymological sense of the word, be termed "Introspection," but would anyway be something radically different from what in fact is denominated Introspection.

Thus, although the "double-aspect" description of the connection between mind and brain or mind and body has found favor with a number of biologists and psychologists, it turns out on examination to be nothing but a vacuous metaphor, from which nothing at all follows as to whether or not mental life can continue after death.

4. **Mental activity as a function of cerebral activity.** A statement currently much in vogue is that mental activity is a function of the activity of the brain and nervous system.

The word "function," (from L. *fungere,* to perform) has a variety of meanings, some of which are not wholly distinct from certain of the others. Most broadly, when two things, A and B, each of which admits of variations, vary concomitantly, i.e., in such manner that variation of kind or/and magnitude V (a) of A, and variation of kind or/and magnitude V (b) of B, occur regularly together, then the two sets of variations are said to be functionally related; and either can be said to be a function of the other.

If, however, the variations given, or instituted, are, say, those of A, and the variations then observed those of B, then B is termed the dependent variable and A the independent variable.

If the variations of one of the two functionally related variables, say, those of B, occur *after* the variations of A of which they are functions, then ordinarily the dependence of the variations of B upon those of A is *causal dependence,* direct or indirect. This, apparently, is the meaning which "dependent upon" is intended to have in Webster's definition of one of the senses of "function of" as: "any quality, trait or fact so related to another that it is dependent upon and varies with that other." This sense is usually the one in which thought, or mental activity, is said to be a function of brain activity; and in which it is said that the specific function of the brain is to "perform" the various mental activities—thinking, perceiving, remembering, etc.

In the light of these remarks, it is evident that to speak of mental activity as a function of brain activity is not to offer a new description of the connection between the two, different from all those already mentioned; for each of these asserts that brain states and mental states are functionally related: If the functional dependence is causal, and of mental activity on brain activity, then this is the type of connection, i.e., of function, which *epiphenomenalism* describes. If the dependence is causal, but is of brain activity on mental activity, then this type of functional relation would be describable as *hypophenomenalism*—the exact converse of epiphenomenalism. If the functional dependence is causal, but not exclusively either of mental upon cerebral states, or of cerebral upon mental states, then what we have is psycho-physical *interactionism.* Lastly, if the functional dependence is *not* causal, then it constitutes *parallelism* of one or another of the types described in what precedes, from which, as we have seen, nothing can be inferred as to whether survival of the mind after death is or is not possible.

We shall now consider in turn epiphenomenalism, hypophenomenalism, and interactionism.

Chapter X

MIND AS "THE HALO OVER THE SAINT"

When a person who has leaned to the purely physicalistic conception of mind sees that it presupposes the absurdity that certain of our words do not denote what we do denote by them, he is likely to adopt in its place the less radically materialistic conception which the late Professor G. S. Fullerton picturesquely termed the "halo over the saint" theory of the mind's relation to the body.

1. **Epiphenomenalism.** That theory asserts that mental events have to brain events much the same sort of relation which the saint's traditional halo supposedly has to him: the halo is an automatic *effect* of his saintliness, but does *not itself cause* or contribute at all to it. This is the relation which, as between brain events and mental events, is technically termed *epiphenomenalism* (from the Greek *epi* = beside, above + *phainomai* = to appear): the mental events are conceived to be an epiphenomenon of, i.e., a phenomenon beside or above certain of the physical events occurring in the brain; and to be a by-product, and hence an automatic accompaniment, of cerebral activity; but never themselves to cause or affect the latter.

This conception is not, like the radically physicalistic one, open to the charge of absurdity since, unlike the latter, it admits that the term "mental events" denotes events that are other than those denominated "physical" and more specifically "cerebral." Epiphenomenalism is thus not strictly a physicalistic monism. But virtually, i.e., for all practical purposes, it is both a monism and a physicalistic one, for it holds that the only occurences that ultimately count in determining behavior are bodily ones and therefore physical. And this means that if it were possible to do away altogether with a person's mental states without in any way altering his brain and nervous system, he would go on behaving exactly as usual, and nobody could tell that he no longer had a mind.

Now, obviously, if it is true as epiphenomenalism asserts that all mental states actually are effects of cerebral states, and also that no mental states could be caused otherwise than directly by cerebral states, then it follows that mental states and activities cannot possibly continue after the life of the brain has ceased.

2. Metaphorical character of the epiphenomenalistic thesis. Let us, however, now examine critically the epiphenomenalistic conception of the body-mind relation.

It is associated chiefly with the names of T. H. Huxley and of Shadworth Hodgson. As defined by the latter, it is the doctrine that "the states of consciousness, the feelings, are effects of the nature, sequence, and combination, of the nerve states, without being themselves causes either of one another or of changes in the nerve states which support them."[1] Huxley, similarly, writes: "It seems to me that in men, as in brutes, there is no proof that any state of consciousness is the cause of change in the motion of the matter of the organism . . . . . our mental conditions are simply the symbols in consciousness of the changes which take place automatically in the organism; and that . . . . . the feeling we call volition is not the cause of a voluntary act, but the symbol of that state of the brain which is the immediate cause of that act."[2]

In so stating, however, Huxley ignores the fact that symbolizing is not a physical but a psychological relation: That S is a symbol of something T means that *consciousness* of S in a mind M that is in a state of kind K, regularly causes M to *think of* T.[3] Other metaphors used by epiphenomenalists to characterize the relation between brain states and states of consciousness are that consciousness is but "a spark thrown off by an engine," or (by Hodgson) "the foam thrown up by and floating on a wave . . . . a

---

[1]*Theory of Practice*, London, Longmans, Green, 1870 Vol. I:336.
[2]*Collected Essays*, Appleton, New York, 1893, Vol. I:244.
[3]Cf. the writer's Symbols, Signs, and Signals, *Jl. of Symbolic Logic*, Vol. 4:41-43, No. 2, June 1939.

mere foam, aura, or melody arising from the brain, but without reaction upon it."[4]

The spark and the foam in these metaphors are indeed by-products in the sense that they do not react—or more strictly, only to a negligibly minute extent—upon their producers. But—and this is the crucial point—they are themselves, like their producers, *purely physical;* whereas states of consciousness, as we have seen and indeed as maintained by epiphenomenalists, are *non-physical* events, irreducible to terms of matter and motion. The analogy those metaphors postulate is therefore lacking in the very respect that is essential: If states of consciousness are effects of brain activity, they are not so in the sense in which occurrence of the spark or the foam is an effect of the activity of the machine or of the water under the then existing conditions; for the spark and the foam are *fragments* of the machine and of the wave, but states of consciousness are not fragments of cerebral tissue.

Hence, if mental events are effects of cerebral events, they are so in the quite different sense that *changes* in the state of the brain cause *changes* — modifications, modulations, alterations — in the state of the mind; the mind thus being conceived in as *substantive* a manner as is the brain itself, i.e., as something likewise capable of a variety of states, and of changes from one to another in response to the action of certain causes.

3. Arbitrariness of the epiphenomenalistic contention as to causality between cerebral and mental events. This brings us to another respect in which the epiphenomenalistic account of the mind-body relation is indefensible, namely, its arbitrariness in asserting that although cerebral events cause mental events, mental events on the contrary never cause cerebral events nor even other mental events.

That assertion is arbitrary because if, as epiphenomenalism

---

[4]*Time and Space,* London, Longmans Green, 1865, p. 279. The wave-and-foam metaphor is used by Hodgson in this book to characterize a theory of the mind-body relation which he there *attacks.* But in his *Theory of Practice,* published five years later, he *embraces* the (epiphenomenalistic) theory he had attacked in the earlier book, and declares entirely erroneous the "double aspect" theory he had opposed to it there (p. 283). The "wave-and-foam" metaphor is therefore true to the radically epiphenomenalistic conception of the mind-body relation formulated in the passage quoted previously from the later book.

contends, causation can occur between events as radically different in kind as, on the one hand, motions of molecules or of other physical particles in the brain and, on the other, mental events, then no theoretical reason remains at all why causation should not be equally possible and should not actually occur in the converse direction; that is, causation of brain events by mental events.

The paradoxical character of the contention that states of consciousness never determine or in the least direct the activities of the body is perhaps most glaring when, as Ruyer points out, one considers on the one hand painful states of consciousness and desire to prevent them and, on the other, man's invention and employment of anaesthetics: "The invention of anaesthetics by man supposes that disagreeable states of consciousness have incited man to seek means to suppress such states of consciousness. If, according to the (epiphenomenalistic) hypothesis, disagreeable consciousness is inefficacious, how, on the one hand, can it originate an action? On the other hand, how can a chain of pure causality (as between brain events) so manage as not to 'become' such as to get accompanied by disagreeable consciousness?"[5]

As a matter of fact, the *empirical* evidence one has for concluding that occurrence, for example, of the mental event consisting of decision to raise one's arm *causes* the physical rising of the arm, is of exactly the same form as the empirical evidence one has for concluding—as the epiphenomenalist so readily does—that the physical event consisting of burning the skin,—or, more directly, the brain event thereby induced—*causes* the mental event called pain. If either the conception of causality which the so-called "method" of Single Difference defines, or the regularity-of-sequence conception of causality, warrants the latter conclusion, then, since the one or the other is likewise the conception of causality through which the former conclusion is reached, that conclusion is equally warranted.

On the other hand, if the supposition that a volition or idea or other mental event can push or pull or somehow otherwise move a physical molecule were rejected, either on the ground of its being absurd or on the ground that it would constitute a vio-

---

[5]Raymond Ruyer: *Néofinalisme,* Presses Universitaires de France, Paris 1952, p. 24.

lation of the principle of the conservation of energy, then the supposition that motion of a physical molecule in the brain can cause a mental, i.e., a nonphysical event, would have to be rejected also, since it would involve the converse absurdity or would involve violation of that same principle.

Again, if it is argued that mutilations of the brain, whether experimental or accidental, are known to cause alterations of specific kinds in the mental states and activities connected with that brain, it must then be pointed out that, as psychosomatic medicine now recognizes, mental states of certain kinds generate corresponding somatic defects; so that here too causation is sometimes from mind to body, as well as sometimes from body to mind.

The preceding considerations, then, make amply evident that the epiphenomenalistic theory of the relation between body and mind is altogether arbitrary in holding that causation as between brain and mind is always from brain to mind and never from mind to brain.

Furthermore, it is arbitrary also in holding that *all* mental states are effects of brain states; for this is not known, but only that *some* mental states—of which sensations are the most obvious examples—are so. Moreover, observation, as distinguished from epiphenomenalistic dogma, testifies that, in any case of association of ideas, occurrence of the first is what causes occurrence of the second. Nor do we know that mental states of certain kinds, which normally have physical causes, might not—although perhaps with more or less different specific content—be caused otherwise than physically. This possibility is suggested by the occurrence of visions, apparitions, dreams, and other forms of hallucination; for in all such cases mental states indistinguishable at the time from sensations are caused somehow otherwise than, as normally, by stimulation of the sense organs.[6] That even then those states are *always* and *wholly* effects of cerebral states is not a matter of knowledge but only of faithfully epiphenomenalistic speculative extrapolation.

Moreover, if the capacity of mescalin or of lysergic acid diethylamide to induce hallucinations by physical means should

---

[6] See, for instance, the remarkable case of a waking hallucination reported in Vol. XVIII of the *Proc. of the Society for Psychial Research*, pp. 308-322.

be cited, the comment would then have to be that what needs to be accounted for is not only *that* hallucinations then occur, but also *what* specifically their content—which in fact varies greatly—happens to be. That is, do these drugs cause *what* they cause one to see in a sense comparable to that in which a painter's action causes *the picture* he paints and sees; or, on the contrary, do they cause one only *to see* what one then sees, in a manner analogous to that in which the raising of the blind of a window on a train causes a passenger in the train to see the landscape which happens to be outside at the time?

These remarks are not offered as an argument that, since we do not know that the specific content of hallucinations has cerebral causes, therefore probably its causes are non-cerebral; for so to argue would be to become guilty of the fallacy *argumentum ad ignorantiam.* They are offered only to underline that this very fallacy infects the contention that, if, as in fact is the case we do *not* know that *only some* mental states are cerebrally caused, then probably *all* of them are so caused.

That all mental states have exclusively cerebral causes is thus *only postulated;* and—notwithstanding the contrary empirical evidence we cited—postulated only out of pious wish to have an at least virtual physicalistic monism, since a strict physicalistic one is ruled out by the absurdity pointed out in Ch. VIII, which it involves. What the epiphenomenalist does is to erect tacitly into a creed as to the nature of all reality what in fact is only the program of the sciences dedicated to the study of the material world—the program, namely, of explaining in terms of physical causes everything that happens to be capable of being so explained.

The upshot is then that the epiphenomenalistic conception of the relation between brain and mind not only is not known to be true, but even arbitrarily disregards positive empirical facts which appear to invalidate it. Hence the consequence that would follow if that conception were true—namely that no mental activities or experiences can occur after the brain has died—is itself not known to be true. That is, so far as goes anything that epiphenomenalists have shown to the contrary, after-death mental life—at least of certain kinds—remains both a theoretical and an empirical possibility.

Chapter XI

HYPOPHENOMENALISM: THE LIFE OF ORGANISMS AS PRODUCT OF MIND

There is a conception of the relation between mind and body which is in a certain respect the converse of the epiphenomenalistic and which might therefore be termed Hypophenomenalism (Gr. *hypo* = under + *phainomai* = to appear.) It is, in brief, that the living body is a hypophenomenon of the soul or mind or of some constituent of it—an effect or product or dependent of it, instead of the converse of this as epipheomenalism asserts.

Conceptions of this type have appeared several times in the history of thought, but they have been presented as parts or corollaries of certain cosmological speculations rather than as conclusions suggested by the results of observation.

1. **Two hypophenomenalistic conceptions.** In Plotinus, for example, who conceived the universe as arising from the ineffable One, God, by a series of emanations, the soul is the penultimate of these, two degrees below God; and the lowest is matter. Thus, the soul is not in the body, but the body is in, and dependent upon, the soul, which both precedes and survives it, and whose forces give form and organization to the matter of which the body is composed.

Schopenhauer's conception of the relation between body and "soul" is somewhat similar to this, but he does not speak here of soul or of mind but more specifically of "will," which he does not regard as a part of the psyche. Except in cases where the will has kindled to itself the light we call intellect, that impersonal will is blind as to what specifically it craves but nonetheless creates. Schopenhauer accordingly conceives the body, or more exactly the body's organization, as objectification of the will-to-live; the hand, for example, being an objectification of the

81

unconscious will to be able to grasp. He writes that "what objectively is matter is subjectively will. . . .our body is just the visibility, objectivity of our will, and so also every body is the objectivity of the will at some one of its grades."[1] And elsewhere he speaks of a certain part of the body, to wit, the brain, as "the objectified will to know."[2]

2. **Biological hypophenomenalism distinguished from cosmological.** In philosophical discussions of the mind-body relation, the type of theory of which two classical examples have just been cited, and for which the name Hypophenomenalism is here proposed, has received relatively little attention as compared with epiphenomenalism, materialism, idealism, parallelism, or interactionism. We shall therefore have to provide here ourselves the formulation of it that would seem most defensible. It will unavoidably have to be fuller than in the case of the familiar other theories of the mind-body relation.

The first thing we must do is to distinguish between what may be termed, respectively, *cosmological* and *biological* hypophenomenalism. Cosmological hypophenomenalism would contend that not only the living body, but also all other material objects are hypophenomena of minds, i.e., are products or objectifications of psychical activity or, as Schopenhauer had it, of Will.

Biological hypophenomenalism, on the other hand, concerns itself only with the material objects we term "living," and contends only that the *life*, which differentiates living things from dead or inorganic things, is a product, effect, or manifestation of psychic activity and more particularly of conation. This is the hypophenomenalism which alone we shall have in view, for it is the one directly relevant to the central problem of the present work, namely, that of the relation between the individual's mind and the life and the death of his body. This relation is different both from the ontological relation between mind and matter in general and from the epistemological relation between them, which constitutes mind's knowledge of matter.

---

[1]*The World as Will and Idea,* Supplements to Bk II, Ch. XXIV p. 52. Haldane and Kemp Transl. Vol. 3. Kegan Paul, Trench, Trübner & Co. London 1906.

[2]*The Will in Nature,* tr. Mme. Karl Hillebrand, London, George Bell and Sons, 1897, p. 237.

Biological hypophenomenalism does not occupy itself with the question whether matter in general, or in particular the matter of the body as distinguished from its life, is a product or objectification of mind. It has to do only with the relation between the *life* of the body and its mind; but whereas epiphenomenalism maintains that both the occurrence at all of consciousness and the particular states of it at particular times are products of the living brain's activity, biological hypophenomenalism on the contrary maintains *that the life of the body and of its brain is an effect or manifestation of psychic activities and in particular of conations*—these being what "animate" living organisms.

3. **The life processes apparently purposive.** The fact from which hypophenomenalism starts is that not only the distinctively human life activities and the life activities typical of animals, but even the vegetative activities—where life is at its minimum—seem to be definitely purposive. And hypophenomenalism, on the basis of an analysis of the notion of purposiveness more careful than the common ones, contends that the life activities, even at the vegetative level, do not just seem to be purposive but really are so.

Most biologists, however, are averse to employment of the notion of purpose on the ground that it is a subjective, phychological one, inadmissible in a biology that strives to be as wholly objective as are physics and chemistry. They therefore speak instead of the "directiveness," or of the "equifinality" of biological processes or, as does Driesch in the formulation of his Vitalism, of an "entelechy" which, however, is not psychic but only "psychoid." But the question is whether, *if these terms are not just would-be-respectable-sounding aliases for purposiveness*, what they then designate is ultimately capable of accounting for the facts it is invoked to explain. For the sake of concreteness, let us therefore advert to some examples of those facts.

The peculiarities that differentiate living things from inanimate objects include not only the fairly obvious characteristics —metabolism, growth, reproduction, adaptability to environment —by which we ordinarily identify the things we term "living"; but also various more recondite facts. An example would be that "when. . .one of the first two cells of a tiny salamander embryo is destroyed, the remaining one grows into a whole individual, not a half, as one might expect." Again, that "two fertilized eggs induced to fuse by artificial means were found to produce one animal instead of two." The facts of regeneration similarly challenge explanation: "The leg of a tadpole, snipped off, may be restored, or the eye of a crustacean"; and so on. In sum, "if the organism is prevented from reaching its norm of 'goal' in the ordinary way, it is resourceful and will attain it by a different method."[3]

Facts such as these strongly suggest that the life processes are purposive. But that a process or activity is "purposive" is commonly taken to mean that it is incited and shaped by the presence together of three factors in the agent: (a) the *idea* of an as yet non-existent state of affairs; (b) a *desire* that that state of affairs should eventually come to exist; and (c) *knowledge* of diverse modes of action respectively adequate in different circumstances to bring about the desiderated state of affairs. And, obviously, such an explanation of the biological occurrences in view is open to several *prima facie* serious objections. These, even when they have been merely felt rather than explicitly formulated, have been responsible for the reluctance of biologists and physicists to accept a teleological explanation of the facts cited, notwithstanding the difficulty, which they have also felt, of doing altogether without it. Let us now state and examine each of those objections.

4. **Objections to a teleological explanation of life processes.** (a) The first objection is that it is scientifically illegitimate to ascribe processes which, like those in view, are *material*, to the operation of factors which, like thought, desire, and intelligence, are *mental*.

The sufficient reply to this objection, however, is that, as David Hume made clear long ago, only experience can tell us what in fact is or is not capable of causing what. The Causality relation presupposes nothing at all as to the ontological nature— whether material, mental, or other—of the events that function as its terms. That a material event can be caused only by an event also itself material is not a known fact but merely a metaphysical dogma. To *look for* a material explanation of every material

---

[3] E. W. Sinnott: *Cell and Psyche, the Biology of Purpose,* Univ. of North Carolina Press, 1950, pp. 6, 29, 33.

event is of course a legitimate research program and one which has yielded many valuable fruits; but to assume that, even when the search yields no material explanation of a given material event, nevertheless the explanation of it *cannot be* other than a material one is, illegitimately, to erect that legitimate research program into a metaphysical creed—the creed, namely, of pious ontological materialism.

(b) The second objection is that a teleological explanation of biological processes is superfluous because all their peculiarities can be adequately accounted for by ascribing them to the existence and operation, in the organism we call "living," of various servo-mechanisms; that is, of mechanisms whose attainment and maintenance of certain results (to wit, growth of the organism to a normal form, restoration of it when it gets damaged, preservation of a normal equilibrium between its internal processes and the changes in its environment, etc.) is due to guidance of the mechanism's activity at each moment by elaborate feed-back. channels that are constituents of the mechanism itself.

The reply to this objection is that, although some servo-mechanisms are known to exist in the organism, and although the existence and operation of additional servo-mechanisms would indeed be theoretically capable of accounting for those results, nevertheless servo-mechanisms that would be specifically such as to insure *all those particular results* are not in fact independently known to exist in organisms. Hence, unless and until their existence is established by observation *of them,* or by observational verification of predictions deduced from the supposition that they exist and are *of specifically such and such descriptions,* invocation of them to account for *all* biological processes is nothing but invocation of a *deus ex machina.*

This means that the possibility of a teleological explanation of biological processes is as yet left entirely open; and in turn, this underlines the general requirement that, for an explanation to be acceptable, the cause it invokes must be of a kind not just postulated *ad hoc,* but independently *known to exist;* and further, *known to be capable* in some cases of causing effects similar to those which it is invoked to account for in the case of biological processes.

Moreover, the fact that *some* servo-mechanisms—though not ones adequate to explain all the particular facts in view—are known to exist in living organisms leaves the existence there of these known servo-mechanisms themselves to be accounted for. And, to explain their existence as being the end-product of the operation of some "more fundamental" servo-mechanism is not really to explain it at all unless the existence of the latter is not just postulated but is independently known, *and itself then somehow explained.*

(c) The third objection to the ascribing of purposiveness to biological processes is that presence of the three factors of purposiveness mentioned—an *idea* of an as yet non-existent form or state of the organism, a *desire* for its existence, and *knowledge* of what means would, under varying circumstances, bring it into existence—is dependent on presence of a highly developed brain and nervous system; which, however, is altogether absent at the biological level of the processes here in view.

To this objection, the reply is that conjunction of those three factors is characteristic not of *all* purposive activity, but only of certain kinds and levels of it. More specifically, it is characteristic of purposive activity that is both consciously and skillfully heterotelic, but not of purposive activity that is blind, as in the case of the vegetative life activities.

5. **The nature, kinds, and levels of purposive activity.** But the force and the implications of the above reply to the third of the objections considered can become fully evident only in the light of an analysis of purposive activity and of its various kinds and levels. The branch of philosophy which occupies itself thus with the *theory of purposive activity* has no current name but might be called *Prothesiology* (from Gr. πρόθεσις = purpose, resolve, design.) Kant's discussion of the teleological judgment, in Part II of his *Critique of Judgment,* would belong to it. In his discussion, however, he considers chiefly man's *judgments* of purposiveness in Nature rather than the nature, kinds, and levels of purposive activity itself.

Moreover, the "mechanism" he contrasts with purposiveness is mechanism conceived in terms only of motion of material objects or particles, and thus leaves out of consideration such psychological processes as are not purposive but mechanical, i.e., automatic. Also, he erroneously conceives teleology as a different kind *of causality* instead of, properly, as causality in cases where the *cause-event* (not the causality relation) is of a special kind. Kant's discussion of teleology therefore does not furnish us with the analysis and conspectus we need at this point. We shall introduce it by considering first a concrete case of purposive activity of the type in which the three factors mentioned above operate— say, the case of our shaking an apple tree for the purpose of getting one of the apples it bears. In this activity, we discern the following five elements:

1) The *idea* we have, of our as yet non-existent possession of one of the apples.

2) Our *desire* that possession of one by us shall come to exist.

3) Our *knowledge,* gained from past experience, that shaking the tree would cause apples to fall into our possession.

4) *Causation* in us—by the joint presence to our mind of that idea, that desire, and that knowledge—of the act of shaking the tree.

5) *Causation* in turn, by this act, of the imagined and desired eventual fall of apples into our possession.

This analysis of the example is enough to make evident already that, contrary to what is sometimes alleged, purposive activity involves no such paradox as would be constituted by causation of a present action by a future state of affairs. For obviously what causes the act of shaking the tree is not the as yet non-existent *possession* by us of an apple; but is, together, our *present thought* of our future possession of one, our *present desire* for such future possession, and our *present knowledge* of how to cause it to occur. By the very definition of Causality, the cause, here as necessarily everywhere else, is prior in time to its effect.

6. **Conation: "blind" vs. accompanied by awareness of its conatum.** Let us, however pursue the analysis of purposiveness by considering next the various respects in which examples of purposiveness may, without ceasing to be such, depart from the type of the example analyzed above.

One possibility is that factor (1) in that analysis—to wit, an *idea* of the state of affairs to be brought about—should be absent.

In such a case, factor (2) would properly be describable not as a *desire,* but only as a *blind conation* or craving—blind as to what sort of state of affairs would satisfy it. A new-born infant's craving for milk would be an example of this. "Desire," then, is *conation conjoined with an idea of its conatum;* whereas "blind conation" is *conation unaccompanied by any idea of its conatum.*

The activity incited by blind conation is even then purposive, but *not consciously* purposive; and it is: (a) relatively *random* and therefore successful, i.e., satisfying, only by chance; or (b) *regulated automatically* (within a certain range of conditions) by some somatic of psychosomatic servo-mechanism and therefore successful notwithstanding variations that do not go beyond that range, as for example web building by spiders; or (c) *stereotyped* irrespective of its appropriateness or inappropriateness to the special circumstances that may be present in the particular case— as when, for example, the hungry neonate *cries,* irrespective of whether anybody is there to hear him or not.

7. **Desire, and ignorance or knowledge of how to satisfy it.** When the inciting conation is a desire, i.e., is coupled with awareness of the nature of its conatum—then termed its desideratum— knowledge of a form of action that would bring about occurrence of the desideratum may either be lacking or be possessed. If it is lacking, the purposive activity incited is then of the *consciously exploratory,* "trial-and-error," type. If on the contrary that knowledge is possessed, the activity it incites is then not only consciously purposive but in addition *skilled,* or *informed,* according as the knowledge shaping it is present in the form of "know-how," or in conceptualized form.

8. **Autotelism and heterotelism.** Purposive activity—whether induced by a blind conation or by a conation conjoined with awareness of the nature of its conatum—may be *autotelic,* instead of *heterotelic* as in the example analyzed. That is, what satisfies the conation may be *the very performing* of the activity, not some ulterior effect caused by the performing of it. Examples of purposive activity that is thus autotelic would be sneezing, coughing, yawning, stretching; and, at a more elaborate level, the various play activities. In all such cases, what we crave is to *do* these very

things. The doing of them of course has effects, but the activities are not, like the heterotelic ones, performed for the sake of those effects, but for their own sakes.

9. **What ultimately differentiates purposiveness from mechanism.** The foregoing survey of a number of ways in which telic activity may depart from the type illustrated by the example of the shaking of the apple tree makes evident that the one factor essential, i.e., necessary and sufficient, to purposiveness in an activity, is that what *directly* incites the activity should be either wholly or in part *a conation.*

It then becomes evident that causation of an activity or of any other event is on the contrary "mechanical" if and only if the *direct* cause of it does *not* consist, either wholly or in part, of a conation. Moreover, this analysis of the essence of "mechanical" causation applies irrespective of whether the activity or event caused be a physical or a psychical one. Much of what goes on in our minds occurs not purposively but mechanically; for example, occurrence of ideas that had become associated with others by contiguity or by similarity; rote recollections; orderly mental activities so habitual as to have become automatic; etc. The mechanical character of such psychological processes, and similarly of some psychosomatic and of some somatic processes, holds if what *directly* incites them is *not* a conation; and holds even if a mechanism being directly caused to function at a given time by something that is not a conation, came itself to exist as endproduct of a purposive activity that aimed to construct it. (One's knowledge of the multiplication table would be an example of a psychological mechanism that was so instituted.)

10. **Servo-mechanisms.** A servo-mechanism is a mechanism so provided with feed-backs that the functioning of its does, notwithstanding disturbances of certain kinds and magnitudes, automatically insure attainment or maintenance within certain limits of a certain effect. A simple instance of a servo-mechanism is an oil-burning furnace controlled by a thermostat which maintains the house temperature within specific limits.

The point essential here to bear in mind in connection with servo-mechanisms is that although, to an observer struck by the similarity of their *behavior* to that of the *behavior* of a man actuated by a purpose, their behavior seems purposive too, nevertheless it is *wholly mechanical*. The purpose which the observer infers from his observation of the servo-mechanism's behavior is not entertained *by the servo-mechanism itself*, but is the purpose which the *constructor* of the mechanism intended that it should be capable of serving, and which the *user* of the mechanism is employing it to serve: the thermostat's action, which turns the furnace burner on or off, is not caused by a craving or desire *in the thermostat* to maintain the room temperature within certain limits. Although the *existence* of the thermostatically controlled furnace is artificial, i.e., came about through somebody's purposive constructional activity, nevertheless once the mechanism has come to exist, its operation is just as wholly mechanical as is operation of the increase or decrease of the quantity of water pouring over the natural spillway of a natural mountain lake, in maintaining the level of the lake constant within certain limits.

But although the action of the thermostat in turning the burner on or off is not *itself* purposive, it is nevertheless *purpose-serving*—the purpose served being of course the householder's purpose of maintaining the house temperature approximately constant. On the other hand, as the case of the mountain lake shows, an activity, in order to be capable of serving somebody's purpose, does not need either to be the activity of a purposive agent, or to be the activity of a purposively constructed mechanism.

11. **Creative vs. only activative conations.** In the various types of telism considered up to this point, the effect of the conations involved was to activate some preexisting psychological or psychosomatic mechanism; either, autotelically, for the sake of its very activity; or, heterotelically, for the sake of an ulterior effect which the mechanism's activity automatically causes.

What we must notice next is that, instead of or in addition to being thus activative, a conation may be both *creative*, and *blind* as to the determinate nature of that whose creation would satisfy the conation.

An example would be the imaginative creation of the poem, drama, or musical or pictorial composition which issues out of the composer's "inspiration," i.e., which is "breathed into" his consciousness by the specific conation operating in him at the time. The creative process is here usually a step-by-step one, in which ideas of portions or features of the composition are spontaneously *generated* by the conation; these ideas, when they turn out to be such as to satisfy it, being then embodied by the composer in perceptible material—words, tones, colors, etc., as the case may be.

Other examples would be those constituted by *discovery* of the solution of some intellectual problem; for instance the problem of discovering a proof that no cube can be the sum of two cubes. The correct solution, if it comes, is—like the incorrect ones that come—generated spontaneously by the intense conation to solve the problem; which conation, however, is satisfied only by advent of the correct solution and awareness that it is correct.

Another category is that of instances where what the conation generates is a psychological or psychosomatic servo-mechanism such that possession of it constitutes possession of a *skill*. Instances of this are of special interest in the present connection because part of what is then created is an elaborate set of connections among neurons in the brain and the cerebellum; and the fact that the conation to acquire a skill thus has a creative *somatic* effect lends plausibility to the supposition that the somatic phenomena of organic growth to a normal form, of regeneration, of adaptation, etc., are similarly manifestations of conations that are somatically creative, but are autotelic and blind as to what will satisfy them. This would mean that the tadpole's new leg, restored after the original one had been snipped off—and indeed the original one too—is, as Schopenhauer would have put it, an "objectification" of, i.e., a spontaneous somatic construction by, the blind conation for capacity to swim; and the crustacean's restored eye similarly a spontaneous construction by the conation for capacity to see.

12. **The question as to how conation organizes matter.** It might perhaps be objected, however, that anyway we do not understand *how* a conation manages to organize or to shape matter. If so, the pertinent reply would be that the puzzle is a wholly supposititious one. For wherever, as in this case and in many others, what is in view is *not remote but proximate* causation, i.e., causation of one event by another *not through causation of intermedi-*

ary other events but *directly and immediately,* then the question as to the "how" of the causation is strictly absurd. It is absurd because in any such case it loses the only meaning it ever has, which is: *"Through what intermediary causal steps does* A *cause* B?" and hence to ask this, i.e., to ask "how," in cases of *direct* causation, is to ask what the intermediary causal steps are *in cases where there are none!*

13. **Telism ultimately the only type of explanation in sight for the life processes.** The supposition formulated above—of organization as direct effect of conation—has the merit that it invokes a kind of cause, to wit, conation, of which—by introspective attention to our psychological experience—we know that some cases exist; a kind of cause, moreover, which we know to be sometimes creative; and indeed sometimes somatically creative.

On the other hand, our examination of the objections to teleological explanation of the life processes showed that each of the three objections is without force. Moreover, no explanation of those processes, other than a teleological one, is in sight; for to speak (as do E. S. Russell, R. S. Lillie, and others) of the "directiveness" of the life processes; or (as does Driesch) of an "entelechy" that is not psychic but "psychoid"; or (as does von Bertalanffy) of the "equifinality" of the life processes; and so on, is either to bring in purposiveness itself, under an alias; or else it is to invoke the operation of servo-mechanisms whose existence, however, even if it were observed instead of only postulated, *would itself stand in need of explanation.* That the explanation could ultimately be only in terms of purposiveness follows from two considerations.

One is that since what differentiates living material, *even in its most elementary forms,* from non-living material is the *prima facie* purposive character of its processes, this character of *all* living material cannot be accounted for by the hypothesis of chance variations or mutations *in living material,* and of survival of those fittest to survive.

The other consideration is that the adequacy of that hypothesis to account even for the differentiation of species within already living material is to-day seriously questioned by a number of biologists for several reasons. One is: (a) that mutations are "rare, isolated, occurring in but one out of thousands or tens of thousands of individuals, and hence have but infinitesimal chances to propagate themselves and to persist in such a population." Moreover, (b) mutation "does not recur sequentially in the same form, and hence cannot be cumulative" and thus cannot produce the continuous and harmonious change which the hypothesis of progressive evolution depicts. Besides, (c) "by the very laws, which govern crossings in sexual reproduction, mutants have but infinitesimal chances to survive and to propagate their type." Furthermore, (d) "mutation is almost always a depreciative, noxious, or pathological phenomenon." Again, (e) "mutation never affects any but relatively minute details, and never traverses the limits of the species. . . . In brief, mutation is at the most a factor of variation within a species . . . it certainly cannot transform the existing species into novel ones."[4]

14. **Conation in the vegetative, the animal, and the human activities.** The eminent author from whose chapter on "Evolutionism: An illusory science" the preceding observations are quoted considers in another chapter entitled, "Do cells have a soul?", the neo-finalism of Ruyer, and criticizes it.

According to Ruyer, the apparent preordination of biological processes to specific ends is owing to a dominating, essentially active and dynamic "primary organic consciousness," whose sole intent, or ideal, consists of the forms and capacities of the organs it constructs. This primary organic consciousness would thus be concerned basically with the vegetative processes of living things; and the processes of animal and of typically human life would be eventual derivatives from it.

Ruyer contends in addition, however, that a similar consciousness, though at more elementary levels, operates also in individual molecules and atoms, since they are not mere aggregates but are systems. His hypophenomenalism would thus be not bio-

---

[4]Louis Bounoure: *Déterminisme et Finalité,* Flammarion, Paris, 1957, Ch. II, pp. 70-72. Note also Raymond Ruyer: *Néofinalisme,* Presses Universitaires de France, Paris, 1952; especially chs. IV, V, XVI, XVII. Also, H. Graham Cannon: *The Evolution of Living Things,* Thomas, Springfield, Ill. 1958, and *Lamarck and Modern Genetics,* Manchester Univ. Press, 1958—See, however, E. Schroedinger: *Mind and Matter,* Cambridge Univ. Press, 1959—Ch. 2.

logical only but cosmological. But—leaving aside that additional contention of his—the "primary organic consciousness" he invokes to account for the apparent purposiveness of biological processes would seem to be much the same thing in essence if not perhaps in its details, as the conations which we found to be the constituent alone indispensable and therefore essential in the only actions whose purposiveness is, not inferred, but directly and intimately observable by us. These are, of course, our own purposive actions, whose motivation we can scrutinize introspectively; whereas external perception, as we pointed out earlier, has no way to distinguish between action really purposive, and action automatically regulated by servo-mechanisms.

Bounoure criticizes Ruyer's hypothesis, by emphasizing that the processes that go on in living organisms are triggered at every stage by determining conditions—chemical stimuli, mitogenetic causes, etc., of which he describes various interesting examples in some detail.

This determinism, however, which is beyond question, does not account for the organism's *inherent capacity* to respond to those determinants and to variations in them in a manner so adaptable as to attain a fixed result. Possession of such capacity is the characteristic of servo-mechanisms, *but it does not account for its own existence*. Indeed, Bounoure himself points this out when he writes that "finality is *implicate* in organisms, but implication does not constitute explanation. What needs to be accounted for is not organization already existent, but the activity that constructs and organizes life" (p. 216). Immediately after, however, he dismisses as futile and anthropomorphic Ruyer's postulated immanent agent-consciousness.

What then does Bounoure himself ultimately offer us instead? Unfortunately, only a statement that, in the organism, "the preordination of phenomena and. . .the vital value of their concatenation" are *"marvellous* characteristics of life;" or a reference to the "essential mystery of life;" or an "acknowledgment, in the organism's development of a veritable marvel." In effect, nothing but virtuously emphatic avowals that he has no explanation whatever to offer!

As we shall see in the next chapter, however, some biologists no less distinguished, among them H. S. Jennings, whose observations on the behavior of paramecium Bounoure has occasion to cite—have not shared Bounoure's metaphysical prejudice against the possibility of psycho-physical causation.

15. **Hypophenomenalism vs. epiphenomenalism.** How now do the merits of the hypophenomenalism we have formulated compare with those of epiphenomenalism?

Epiphenomenalism as we saw, has two defects. One is that although it acknowledges that states of consciousness *are not material events,* nevertheless it describes their relation to brain activity—which activity it alleges generates them—only in terms of the in fact non-analogous relation between an activity of a material object and generation by it of *another material* object.

The biological hypophenomenalism we have described, on the other hand, does not suffer from any corresponding defect, for it does not contend—as would a cosmological hypophenomenalism —that purposive mental activity, i.e., conation, generates the *matter* of which the body consists, but only that it "animates" or "enlivens" this matter, i.e., organizes it purposefully.

Again, epiphenomenalism is, we pointed out, altogether arbitrary in its dogma that causation as between consciousness and brain is always from brain states to states of consciousness, but never causation of brain states by states of consciousness. In the contentions of hypophenomenalism, on the contrary, there is nothing to preclude causation of particular changes in the state of the living brain by particular changes in the state of consciousness; nor is there anything to preclude causation in the converse direction. The biological hypophenomenalism we have described is hospitable equally to both possibilities; for the causality relation does not require that both its cause-term and its effect-term be material events, nor indeed that either of them be so; and what unprejudiced observation reveals is not only instances of physico-physical causation, but also instances of psycho-physical, of physico-psychical, and of psycho-psychical causation. This, however, brings up interactionism, which will be the subject of the next chapter.

16. **Hypophenomenalism and experimentation.** Each per-

son whose body is functioning normally is in position to make perceptual observations of it and of the bodies of others; to act physically upon it and upon them; to observe introspectively in his own case the psychological effects of physical stimuli on his body, and, in the case of other human bodies, to infer the psychological effects of such stimuli more or less well from the behavior of those bodies. Also, situated as we are, each of us is in position as occasion arises to observe human bodies unconscious as well as conscious, dead as well as alive, and being born as well as dying. It is because we have been in position to make these and related observations of human bodies and of other physical objects and events, that we have been able to gain such knowledge as we have of physico-physical causation in general, and of physico-physical causation upon, by, and within the human body. These last facts of causation are what in particular has invited, and has been used as an empirical and experimental springboard for, the speculative leap of epiphenomenalism, which, as we saw, goes far beyond those facts.

For the sake of healthy philosophical perspective, it is necessary now to point out the respects in which our situation would need to be different from what it is during life, in order that it should provide us with an analogous empirical and experimental springboard for the hypophenomenalistic speculative leap.

In order to have such a springboard for this, we would need to be *discarnate minds,* instead of as now minds possessed of and confined to a physical body. We would need, as discarnate minds, to be able to communicate with and act upon other discarnate minds *directly,* i.e., without, as now, physical bodies as intermediaries; perhaps also, to some extent and exceptionally, to be able to communicate with and act upon some incarnate minds likewise directly. We would need to be able to observe the "spirit birth" of a mind, i.e., its advent, at bodily death, into the world of discarnate minds; and conceivably also its "spirit death", if bodily birth should happen to consist of incarnation of an already existing "spirit" or "germ of a mind."

The situation of a discarnate mind as just depicted is of course more or less what Spiritualists believe to be that of the minds of persons whose bodies have died. They speak, however, of "spirits" rather than of discarnate minds—apparently meaning by a "spirit" a mind or "soul" which although discarnate is clothed with a "spiritual," more subtle kind of body. Spiritualists hold that such discarnate minds can on exceptional occasions describe to us, in terms of the observations and experiments which minds are able to make when discarnate, a mind-body relation which, although not labelled by them hypophenomenalistic, is yet essentially this; those occasions being the rare ones on which, purportedly, a discarnate spirit borrows for the moment the body or part of the body of an entranced "medium," and by its means communicates with us whether vocally, or by automatic writing, or typtologically. Such paranormal incursions by a discarnate mind into the world of living bodies would be the analogues of the paranormal incursions of incarnate minds into the world of spirits, which Swedenborg and some other psychics have claimed to have made.

It is interesting to note in this connection that if, at or after death, a then discarnate spirit should lose the memories of the incarnate life he left at death, he would then probably be just as skeptical of reports as to the existence of an earth world and of physical human bodies as now we, who have no memories of a spirit world, are skeptical as to the existence of one and as to our having had, or being eventually to have, a life in one!

These remarks are of course not intended to prejudge the question of survival after death; but only to make clear why the hypophenomenalistic speculative leap cannot, *our minds being situated as now they are in a physical body,* be made from an empirical and experimental springboard analogous to that which, *situated as they now are,* they can use in making the epiphenomenalistic leap.

Attention to beliefs such as those of Spiritualism, which seem to us queer or even paradoxical, can have the value of freeing to some extent our imagination from the unconscious parochialism of its outlook, which naively terms "unrealistic," or "contrary to commonsense," or perhaps "unscientific," anything that clashes with our existing habits of thought.

Of course, readiness to consider paradoxical ideas must not generate readiness to accept them without adequate evidence;

but readiness to consider them can well turn out to generate awareness that some of the ideas currently orthodox whether in science or elsewhere are being accepted without adequate evidence.

Chapter XII

MIND AND BODY AS ACTING EACH ON THE OTHER

The contention considered in the preceding chapter was that the processes constituting the living body's minimal, i.e., vegetative, *life* are autotelic objective expressions of blind cravings of mind or minds to organize matter. Such of these blind cravings as are present in the human mind might be termed its vegetative conations, as distinguished from its distinctively animal and human ones.

The hypophenomenalistic contention was of interest to us primarily because of the superiority, in the respects we noticed, of the alternative it provides to the contention that the life of living things is a purely physico-chemical process and that a mind and its various conations and states are mere epiphenomena of those processes in the living brain. We shall not, however, need to occupy ourselves further with hypophenomenalism since the question to which it is an answer is different from the question central for us in these pages.

The latter question has to do with the nature of the relation between two terms. One of them is a *living* human body— no matter whether its being "alive" be a physico-chemical epiphenomenon or be a hypophenomenon of some primitive conations. The other term of the relation is constituted by existence and exercise of the animal and especially of the typically human capacities or "dispositions" in a person's total mind conceived in the manner set forth in Chapter VI. Man's living material body is of course a necessary, even if not a sufficient, factor in the development of his mind from the rudimentary state in which it is at the birth of his body. But our problem is whether on the one hand a person's living body, and on the other the part of that person's mind consisting of the distinctively human capacities peculiar to him, are so related that, once those capacities have been acquired by him, they, or some of them, can continue to exist and to function after that body dies.

Interactionism, as conceived in these pages, answers that no impossibility—either theoretical or empirical—is involved in so supposing. Let us, however, first consider the classical account of mind-body interaction.

1. **Interaction as conceived by Descartes.** The contention that the human mind and the living human body can, and to some extent do, act each on the other is associated chiefly with the name of Descartes. His account of their interaction, however, is burdened with difficulties that are not inherent in interactionism but arise only out of some of the peculiarities of his formulation of it.

The most troublesome of these is that mind and body are conceived by Descartes as each a "substance" in the sense that, aside from the dependence of each on God, each is wholly self-sufficient. This entails that changes in the state of either cannot without inconsistency be supposed to cause changes in the state of the other. Descartes, in one of his letters, acknowledges this.[1] Nevertheless he asserts that such causation does occur: "That the spirit, which is incorporeal, is able to move the body, no reasoning or comparison from other things can teach this to us. Nevertheless, we cannot doubt it, for experiments too certain and too evident make us clearly aware of it every day; and one must well notice that this is one of the things that are known of themselves [une des choses qui sont connues par elles mêmes] and that we obscure them every time we would explain them by others."[2]

Yet, as if to mitigate the illegitimacy which, on Descartes' conception of substance, attaches to interaction, he insists that it occurs only at one place. This is at the center of the brain, in the pineal gland, which he holds is the principal "seat" of the soul. The deflections of it by the "animal spirits," Descartes says, cause perceptions in the soul; and, conversely, the soul's volitions

---

[1]Letter of June 28, 1643, to Elizabeth. *Descartes' Correspondence*, ed. Adam & Milhaud, Vol. 5:324.

[2]Letter VI, Vol. 2:31.

deflect the pineal gland and thereby the "animal spirits," whose course to the muscles causes the body's voluntary movements.

But to pack into the meaning of the word "substance" the provision that one substance cannot interact with another is— here as in the historical precedents—quite arbitrary; for no theoretical need exists to postulate any substance as so defined; nor is the term, as so defined, applicable to anything actually known to exist. As ordinarily used, the term denotes such things as water and salt, steel and wood, nitric acid and copper, which can and on occasion do interact. Indeed, all the dispositions (except internal ones) in terms of which the nature of any substance analyzes consist of capacities of the substance concerned to affect or to be affected by some other substance.

Thus, the paradox Descartes finds in the interaction which he anyway acknowledges occurs between body and mind, arises only out of his gratuitously degrading to the status of "modes" the things ordinarily called "substances"—which do interact—and, equally gratuitously, defining "substances" as incapable of interacting.

2. **Interaction and the heterogeneity of mind and body.** What causes Descartes to find paradoxical the interaction of mind and body and yet to find no difficulty in the interaction of substances such as steel and wood, etc., is that, in the latter cases, the two substances concerned, being both of them material, are ontologically homogeneous; whereas body and mind—being one of them *res extensa* and the other *res cogitans*—are ontologically heterogeneous.

But the supposed paradox of interaction between them evaporates as soon as one realizes that the causality relation is wholly indifferent to the ontological homogeneity or heterogeneity of the events figuring in it as cause and as effect. This indifference or neutrality holds no matter whether causality be defined, as later by Hume, as consisting in *de facto* regularity of sequence; or more defensibly, as in experimental procedure, in terms of a state of affairs within which only two changes occur—one, called "cause," occurring at a given moment, and the other, occurring immediately thereafter, called "effect." All that the causality relation presupposes as to the nature of its cause-term and its effect-term is that both be *events,* i.e., occurrences in time. Hence, as Hume eventually pointed out and as we have insisted, an event, of no matter what kind, can, without contradiction or incongruity, be conceived to cause an event of no matter what other kind. Only experience can tell us what in fact can or cannot cause what. That, as experiment testifies, volition to raise one's arm normally causes it to rise, and burning the skin normally causes pain, is not in the least paradoxical.

3. **H. S. Jennings on interaction between mind and body.** The interactionist views of the eminent biologist, H. S. Jennings, are free from the artificial difficulty present in those of Descartes, and are far clearer and more critical than those of most of the biologists who have expressed themselves on the subject of the relation between body and mind.

In an address, *Some Implications of Emergent Evolution,* which he delivered in 1926 as retiring chairman of the Zoological Section of the American Association for the Advancement of Science, and later in a book, *The Universe and Life,*[3] Jennings sharply distinguishes two conceptions of determinism. He calls them respectively "radically experimental determinism" and "mechanistic determinism." The latter is the one commonly entertained by scientists, and is to the effect that whatever occurs in the universe, whether novel or not, is theoretically explicable in terms of the properties and relations of the elementary constituents of matter; and hence that even radical novelties such as the advent of life in an until then lifeless world are the inherently predictable necessary or probable effects of certain collocations— that is, are predictable in principle even if not in fact by us at a given time for lack of the required empirical data. This—except for the substitution of probabilities for necessities at the subatomic level in consequence of the state of affairs recognized in Heisenberg's principle of indeterminacy—is essentially determinism as conceived in Laplace's famous statement we have quoted earlier, that "an intelligence knowing, at a given instant of time,

---

*Yale Univ. Press, New Haven, 1933. The address appeared in *Science,* Jan. 14, 1927, and was reprinted with corrections the same year by the Sociological Press, Minneapolis.

all forces acting in nature, as well as the momentary positions of all things of which the universe consists, would be able to comprehend the motions of the largest bodies of the world and those of the smallest atoms in one single formula, provided it [i.e., that intelligence] were sufficiently powerful to subject all data to analysis; to it, nothing would be uncertain, both future and past would be present before its eyes."[4]

Obviously, however, such a *physico-chemical* determinism is in fact only a metaphysical creed; for it vastly outruns what theoretical physics and physical chemistry are actually able to predict. What has occurred is that something which in reality was but a program—namely to explain in physico-chemical terms *whatever turns out to be capable of explanation in such terms*—has unawares been transformed into the *a priori* creed that *whatever does occur* is ultimately capable of being explained in such terms. Doubtless, the enthusiasm resulting from the truly remarkable discoveries which have been made under that program is what has brought about the unconscious metamorphosing of the latter into a creed, i.e., into a belief piously held without adequate warrant both by scientists and by laymen awed by the vast achievements of science.

On the other hand, the determinism Jennings terms "radically experimental determinism" does not assume, as physico-chemical determinism gratuitously does, that only physical or chemical events can really cause or explain anything. Rather, it holds, as did David Hume, that only experience can reveal to us what in fact can or cannot cause what; and holds further as does the present writer, that, ultimately, the only sort of experience that can reveal what can or cannot cause what is experience *of the outcome of an experiment:* "The only test as to whether one phenomenon affects another is experiment . . . . the test is: remove severally each preceding condition, and observe whether this alters the later phenomena. If it does, this is what we mean by saying that one condition affects another; that one determines another. Such experimental determinism is not concerned with likenesses or differences in kind, as between mental and physical,

---

Théorie Analytique des Probabilités, Paris, 3d. edition, 1820.

nor with the conceivability or inconceivability of causal relations between them; it is purely a matter of experiment."[5]

Jennings goes on to point out that "if we rely solely upon experiment, the production of mental diversities by preceding diversities in physical conditions is the commonest experience of mankind; a brick dropped on the foot yields other mental results than from a feather so dropped." But "experimental determinism also holds for the production of physical diversities by preceding mental diversities; for experimental determinism of the physical by the mental. One result follows when a certain mental state precedes; another when another mental state precedes . . . . No ground based on experimental analysis can be alleged for the assertion that the mental does not affect the physical; this is a purely *a priori* notion. According therefore to radical experimentalism, consciousness does make a difference to what happens . . . . . the mental determines what happens as does any other determiner . . . . Among the determining factors for the happenings in nature are those that we call mental. Thought, purpose, ideals, conscience, do alter what happens."[6]

4. **What interactionism essentially contends.** The interactionism that seems to the present writer to constitute the true account of the relation between the human mind and the living human body contends, as does Jennings, that each of the two acts at times on the other. Certain brain events, caused by environmental stimuli upon the external sense organs or by internal bodily conditions, cause certain mental events—notably, sensations of the various familiar kinds. On the other hand, mental events of various kinds (and no matter how themselves caused) cause certain brain events—those, namely, which themselves in turn

---

[5]*Some Implications of Emergent Evolution,* p. 9 of the reprint. Cf. the present writer's own analysis of Causality in his *Causation and the Types of Necessity* Univ. of Washington Press, Seattle, 1924, pp. 55-6, and in his later *Nature, Mind, and Death* Open Court Pub. Co. La Salle, 1951, Ch. 8, Sec. 3, where he insists that Causality is the relationship, which an *experiment* exhibits, between a state of affairs, an only change in it at a time T, and an immediately sequent only other change in it; and that causal laws are generalizations obtained by attention to the similarities that turn out to exist between two or more experiments each of which, *in its own individual right,* revealed a case of causation.

[6]Ibid. p. 10. Cf. *The Universe and Life,* pp. 33-48.

cause or inhibit contractions of muscles or secretions of glands. But that mind and body thus interact does not entail that each cannot, or does not at times, function by itself, i.e., without acting on the other or being acted upon by it. Certainly, many of man's bodily activities—at the least the vegetative activities—can and do at times go on in the absence of conscious mental activity or without being affected by such as may be going on at the time. On the other hand, at times during which the mind is engaged in reflection, meditation, or reminiscence, and is thus in a state of what is properly called "abstraction" (from sensory stimulations and from voluntary bodily actions,) the thoughts, desires, images, and feelings that occur are directly determined by others of themselves together with the acquired dispositions or habits of the particular mind concerned.

5. **Which human body is one's own.** In connection with the interactionist thesis, it is of particular interest to raise a question which at first sight seems silly, but the answer to which turns out to be decisive in favor of interactionism. That question is, How do we know which one of the many human bodies we perceive is *our own?*

We might answer that it is the only human body whose nose we always see if it is illuminated when we see anything else; or that we call that human body our own, the back of whose head we never can see directly, etc. But this answer would not be ultimately adequate; for if a human body, the back of whose head we do see directly, were such that when and only when *it* is pricked with a pin or otherwise injured, *we* feel pain; such that when and only when *we* decide to open the door, *it* walks to the door and opens it; such that when and only when *we* feel shame, *it* blushes; and so on, *invariably;* then *that body* would be the one properly called our own! And the body, the back of whose head we never see directly—but whose injuries cause *us* no pain, and over whose movements *our* will has no direct control—would be for us the body *of someone else,* notwithstanding the peculiarity that we never manage to see the back of its head directly.

Thus when, in the question: What is the relation between a mind and its body? we substitute for "its body" what we have just found to be the meaning of that expression, then the question turns out to have implicitly contained its own answer, for it then reads: What is the relation between a mind and the only body with which its relation is that of direct interaction? That is, that the mind-body relation is the particular relation which interactionism describes is analytically true.

Let us, however, now examine a consideration that has been alleged to rule out the possibility of interaction between mind and body.

6. **Interaction and the conservation of energy.** It has often been contended that the principle of the conservation of energy precludes causation of a mental event by a material one, or of a material event by a mental one; for such causation would mean that, on such occasions, a certain quantity of energy respectively vanishes from, or is introduced into, the material world; and this would constitute a violation of that conservation principle.

Prof. C. D. Broad, however, has pointed out that no violation of the principle would be involved if, each time energy vanished from the material world at one point, an equal quantity of it automatically came into it at another point. Also that, even if all physico-physical causation involves transfer of energy, no evidence exists that such transfer occurs also in physico-psychical or psycho-physical causation.[7]

To this it may be added that if by "energy" is meant something experimentally measurable, and not just a theoretical construct, then the fact is *not* that causation is ascertainable only by observing that energy has been transferred, but on the contrary that "transfer of energy" is ultimately definable only in terms of causation as experimentally ascertainable. That is, even if it should happen to be true that energy is transferred whenever causation occurs, nevertheless transfer of energy is not what we notice and mean when we observe and assert that a certain event *C* caused a certain other event *E*. For, obviously, correct judgments of causation have been made every day for thousands of years by millions of persons who not only did not base them on

[7]*The Mind and its Place in Nature,* Harcourt, Brace & Co. New York, 1929, pp. 103, ff.

measurements of energy, but the immense majority of whom did not have the least conception of what physicists mean by "energy." Everyone of the verbs of causation in the common language—to kill, to cure, to break, to bend, to irritate, to remind, to crush, to displace, etc.—acquired its meaning out of common perceptual experiences, not out of laboratory measurements of energy. The Toms, Dicks, and Harrys who have witnessed the impact of a brick on a bottle and the immediately sequent collapse of the bottle judged that the striking brick *broke* the bottle, i.e., *caused* its collapse. And they so judged because the impact of the brick was *prima facie* the only change that occurred in the immediate environment of the bottle immediately before the latter's collapse.

Anyway, as Prof. M. T. Keeton has pointed out, the proposition that energy is conserved in the material world is not known, either *a priori* or empirically, to be true without exception. The "principle" of conservation of energy, or of mass-energy, is in fact only a *postulate*—a condition which the material world must satisfy *if* it is to be a wholly closed, isolated system. And, when interaction between mind and body is asserted to be impossible on the ground that it would violate the "principle" of the conservation of energy, the very point at issue is of course whether the material world *is* in fact a *wholly* closed, isolated system.[8]

Thus, the ground just considered, on which the interactionist conception has been attacked, quite fails to invalidate it. Nor does the fact that, up to the time of the brain's death the *shaping* of the mind has been due in part to interaction between mind and brain, entail that the conscious and subconscious mind—such as it has become by the time the body dies—cannot after this continue to exist and to carry on some at least of its processes.

Interactionism leaves the possibility of this open, but does not in itself supply evidence that such survival is a fact. Lamont, however, argues at length in the book cited earlier against any dualistic conception of the nature of body and mind. Examination in some detail of the considerations alleged by him to rule out dualism must therefore be the subject of our next chapter.

---

[8]Some Ambiguities in the Theory of the Conservation of Energy, *Philosophy of Science*, Vol. 8, No. 3, July 1941.

Chapter XIII

LAMONT'S ATTACK ON MIND-BODY
DUALISM

Most of the items, which in Chapter III were cited as together constituting the essentials of the case against the possibility that the mind survives the body's death, are presented in considerable detail by Lamont in his book, *The Illusion of Immortality.*[1] As he proceeds, he points out various difficulties which he regards as insuperably standing in the way of a dualistic conception of the mind-body relation, and as dictating instead a monistic and naturalistic conception of it. Let us now consider some of the chief of his remarks both concerning the dualism he attacks and concerning the monism which he contends constitutes "the verdict of science."

1. **Dualism and supernaturalism.** A few words are in order to begin with concerning the relation assumed by Lamont to exist between dualism and supernaturalism. Again and again in his characterization of the other-than-bodily constituent of man, which dualism envisages, we find Lamont referring to that constituent as a "supernatural soul" (e.g., p. 116.). He alludes to "the notion that a supernatural soul enters the body from on high, already endowed with a pure and beautiful conscience . . ." (p. 95); also to the idea that "a transcendental self or a supernatural soul holds sway behind the empirical curtain;" again, to the supposition that "some kind of supernatural soul or spirit is doing our thinking for us . . ." (p. 117); to the notion of "an agent soul or mind somehow attached to the body and somehow doing man's thinking for him" (p. 124); and to the idea that "the personalities of human beings . . . . enter ready made into this world" (p. 93). In the same vein, he speaks of dualism as paying homage to the human faculty of reason "by elevating it

---

[1]Philosophical Library New York, 1950.

to a superhuman and supernatural plane" (p. 100); and by conceiving ideas as "existing independently in some separate realm" (p. 100).

All that need be said concerning the use of such expressions in characterizing dualism is that—whether or not they be faithful to certain of the speculations which some theologians or theologizing philosophers have put forward on the subject of the constitution of man—those expressions of Lamont's are nothing but smear words if alleged to apply to dualism as such. For they then gratuitously load upon it vagaries that are as foreign to its essence as they are to Lamont's would-be monism.

They can, of course, be inserted into dualism, but they do not constitute an intrinsic part of its conception of mind, any more than, for instance, do atoms as conceived by Democritus constitute an intrinsic part of materialism's conception of matter.

Nor does the hypothesis of survival after death—whatever merits it may otherwise have or lack—have to be formulated in terms of Lamont's "supernatural soul." To attack dualism as painted by him in the expressions quoted is to attack but the freak offspring of an irresponsible affair between dualism and theology.

2. **Naturalism and materialism.** Lamont's belief that psychophysical dualism is inherently supernaturalistic is only a corollary of his wholly arbitrary equating of naturalism and materialistic monism.

The fact is that a dualism can be just as naturalistic as a monism unless by "naturalism" one tacitly means *ontological materialism* (or, of course, ontological idealism;) for Nature is simply the realm of events that are effects of other events and that in turn cause further events; and a responsible dualism insists that mental events and processes are nowise "supernatural" but exactly as natural in the sense just stated as are the material events and processes of the human body.

Lamont writes that "ideas . . . . are not apart from but are *a part of* Nature" (p. 101); and the responsible dualist too, of course, contends exactly this, but does not, like Lamont, base the contention on the tacit and quite arbitrary equation of Nature and the material world, and hence of Naturalism with ontological

materialism. The dualist bases it on the fact that the events denominated "mental" or "psychological" and more specifically "occurrences of ideas" are not anarchistic any more than are those
denominated "material" and more specifically "physiological."
Both alike are causally determined by some anterior events and
in turn causally determine posterior ones—which means that both
alike are wholly natural.

3. **The senses in which ideas respectively are, and are not,
ultimately private.** At this point, something must be said concerning Lamont's comments on the connection between dualism
and the privacy of ideas, as contrasted with the public character
of material events. He writes that although "for the individual
who is thinking to himself ideas are private and to that extent
subjective . . . ideas are also objective in that human beings can
communicate them to one another . . ." And he goes on to say
that "the objectivity and non-materiality of ideas has been a strong
factor in impelling philosophers of a dualist bent to set up a
realm of ideas or mind apart from and above Nature" (p. 101).

As regards the last words of this statement, we have pointed
out in what precedes that ideas are not "apart from and above
Nature" unless one arbitrarily equates Nature with the material
world as Lamont tacitly does; and does inconsistently with the
fact that occurrence of an idea is an event, which has causes and
effects, and yet which according to Lamont's own declaration is
not a material event. For he tells us that "ideas, which are non-
material meanings expressing the relations between things and
events, occur in human thought" (p. 100).

Concerning, however, Lamont's assertion that ideas can be
communicated and hence are not inherently private, it is obvious
that his assertion altogether ignores the differences between an
idea's being *published* and its being *public*. The analysis of it we
supplied in Sec. 1 of Ch. V need not be repeated here. But it is
worth while to notice that Lamont's failure to distinguish between
the sense in which "ideas" are, and that in which they are not,
inherently private arises out of the ambiguity of the blessed word,
"meanings," in his definition of ideas as "non-material meanings
expressing [in a sense he does not specify] the relations between
things and events."

The point is that the word "meanings" may designate occurrences of the *meaning activity,* or may designate the *objects meant.* This is the distinction between the *idea itself* and what the idea *is of;* or, to put it in still other terms, the distinction is between the psychological *act of objective reference* and the *object referred to* by it. The former is the *idea itself,* is a psychological event, and is inherently private. The object meant, on the other hand, is *the idea's referent,* and can be anything whether material or mental. Two persons may each have an idea of the same object, but the idea of it one of them is having is not only existentially distinct from the idea of it the other is having—which is the case likewise with their bodily movements; but, unlike their movements, which are public, their ideas, being psychological events, remain unalterably private; i.e., accessible only to the introspection of each. What is communicated, when anything is, is *what object is meant,* not the idea itself, which has it as object. And the communicating of what object is meant consists, on the one hand, in the communicator's "coding" the object's nature into public symbols, usually words, i.e., in his "describing" it; and, on the auditor's part, in then "decoding" the symbols, i.e., "understanding" what object they designate.[2]

4. Lamont's position actually an ontological dualism. Let us, however, return to the monism which Lamont tells us is the verdict of science concerning the nature of the mind-body relation.

On examination this monism turns out to be of a very queer sort indeed; for Lamont expressly states, as we have seen, that ideas "are non-material meanings," and endorses the "non-materiality of ideas" (pp. 100/1). In so doing he is, of course, automatically — although seemingly unawares — declaring himself an *ontological dualist,* since those words of his expressly acknowledge, in addition to the material world, a *non-material* realm of being that comprises ideas at least, to say nothing of other mental states and processes.

Moreover the ontological dualism automatically embraced

---

[2] The privacy of mental events has been attacked also by Gilbert Ryle in his book, *The Concept of Mind.* For a pointed criticism of his attack, see a paper by Arthur Pap, Semantic Analysis and Psycho-physical Dualism, in *Mind,* Vol. LXI: 209-221, No. 242, April, 1952.

when one declares that not only material events but also non-material ideas occur is not in the least done away with or impaired by the particular manner in which mental activities on the one hand, and on the other bodily or more specifically cortical activities, may turn out to be related—for instance by the extent, if any, to which the two may happen to be, or not to be, independent or separable. For the point here crucial is that, unless the relation between them be *strict identity*, not just "connection" or "conjunction" of some sort, what one then has is not an ontological monism but an ontological dualism. Thus, Lamont's statement that "the experience of thinking or having ideas is *distinguishable* from man's other actvities, but not existentially *separable*" (p. 101) does not save the monism for which he is arguing. That ideas may be so *connected with* certain bodily processes as to be existentially inseparable from them is a possibility nowise inconsistent with ontological dualism. Only if the existential inseparability consisted not in connection but in strict *identity* would dualism be excluded.

More generally, if two things, activities, or experiences are *distinct* from each other in the sense that neither of them is a constituent *part* of the other, (as on the contrary an angle is a constituent part of a triangle or a motor a constituent part of an automobile,) then the two are not only distinguishable but also *theoretically* separable. That is, they are separable in the sense that to suppose either to exist without the other implies no contradiction. Then the question arises as to whether, or how far, they are in addition separable *existentially*, i.e., separable *in fact* not only in theory. But *this* question cannot be settled, as in Lamont's quoted statement concerning thinking and bodily activities, by dogmatic negation; nor by declaring, as in the statements quoted from his chapter, that the connection between mind and body is "so exceedingly intimate that it becomes inconceivable how one could function properly without the other," or that "man is a unified whole of mind-body or personality-body so closely and completely integrated that dividing him up into two separate and more or less independent parts becomes impermissible and unintelligible" (pp. 89, 113).

Rather, the only way to settle the question as to the existential separability, in whole or in part, of body and mind is—aside from the experimental way which would consist in shooting oneself in order to observe whether one's mental activity survives that drastic laboratory procedure—the only way, I repeat, is to consider, as we have done in the preceding chapters of Part III, what various types of connection or union between the two are conceivable; and what grounds there may be for concluding that the union of body and mind is of a type that entails or permits, or of one that precludes, their partial or perhaps total existential separability.

In the absence of such an inquiry as basis for the quoted assertions of inseparability, those assertions are merely pseudo-scientific dogmatism.

5. **The mind as a "productive function" of the body.** But, as we shall now see, the strangeness of the monism Lamont professes in the name of science is not exhausted by the fact that it describes the mind-body relation in dualistic terms.

Lamont contends that the mind is a "productive function" of the body; declaring, for example, that "when ideas, which are non-material meanings expressing the relations between things and events, occur in human thought, they always do so as functions or accompaniments of action patterns in the cerebral cortex of a thoroughly material brain" (pp. 100/101). Again, he tells us that the findings of the sciences that deal with man "have inexorably led to the proposition that mind or personality is a function of the body; and that this function is . . . productive and not merely transmissive" (p. 113).

To make clear that what he means by a "productive" function is a function in whose case one of the variables stands to the other as effect stands to cause, Lamont offers as example that "steam is a productive function of the tea-kettle and light of the electric circuit, because the kettle and the circuit actually create these effects" (p. 102).

According to these explicit statements, therefore, when Lamont asserts unqualifiedly that the mental and emotional life of man is always a productive function of "action patterns in the cerebral cortex of a thoroughly material brain" (p. 101), what he means is that the latter stand to the former *as creative cause stands to created effect.*

The facts Lamont refers to as basis for this contention are:

(a) That "the power and versatility of living things increase concomitantly with the development and complexity of their bodies in general and their nervous systems in particular."

(b) That the genes or other factors from the germ cells of the parents determine the individual's inherent physical characteristic and inherent mental capacities."

(c) That, during the course of life, "the mind and personality grow and change, always in conjunction with environmental influences, as the body grows and changes."

(d) "That specific alterations in the physical structure and condition of the body, especially in the brain and cerebral cortex, bring about specific alterations in the mental and emotional life of a man."

(e) And, "conversely that specific alterations in his mental and emotional life result in specific alterations in his bodily condition" (p. 114).

Taken by themselves, the facts under the (a), (b), (c), and (d) headings would support the unqualified contention that man's mental and emotional life is a productive function in the sense stated above, of the activities of his body. But the facts which come under the (e) heading, and on which Lamont dwells at some length, clearly testify that, contrary to that unqualified contention, the causal relationship in *their* case is in the opposite direction; i.e., that, in *their* case, it is *the bodily state which is a productive function of the mental and emotional state!*

Indeed, Lamont writes that his "citation of facts showing how physical states affect the personality and its mental life does not in the least imply that mental states do not affect physical" (p. 87). As examples of the latter, he mentions that we are "constantly altering our bodily motions according to the dictates of mental decisions." Also, he cites "the far-reaching results that optimism or worry, happiness or sadness, good humor or anger, may have on the condition of the body;" also the remarkable bodily effects which can be caused by auto suggestion or by suggestion under hypnosis; and, most striking, the fact that in the case of St. Francis and of a number of other saints or mystics, long meditation by them on the wounds of the crucified Jesus causes corresponding wounds to appear on their own bodies.

It is interesting to note in this connection that Lamont feels called upon to add that "modern psychologists believe that the phenomenon of the stigmata can be explained in entirely naturalistic terms and that it is due to as yet undiscovered mechanisms of the subconscious or unconscious" (p. 89). But what does he mean here by explanation in *naturalistic* terms? Does he mean in terms of *material causes*? Or does he mean that stigmatization, like every other event in Nature, is caused by some anterior event —here by the *mental* event he himself has mentioned, namely, "prolonged meditation upon the passion and crucifixion of Jesus"?

When Lamont considers the stigmata of St. Francis and the other facts he mentions in the same connection, he apparently realizes that they render indefensible the unqualified statement that man's mental and emotional life is a productive function, i.e., a creation, of his bodily states. Accordingly, his then much less radical contention is only that those facts point "to a connection between the two so exceedingly intimate that it becomes inconceivable how the one could function properly without the other" (p. 89). Or again that "as between the body and personality, the body *seems to be* the prior and more constant entity"; and hence that "it has been *customary* to regard the body as primary and to call the personality its function rather than the converse" (pp. 113/4). (Italics mine.)

But, as if to mitigate departure even to this extent from his would-be monistic naturalism, Lamont—like the murderer who sought to diminish the heinousness of his deed by observing that the man he had killed was only a small one—Lamont observes at one place that anyway "many of the mental states that exercise an influence on the condition of the body are set up in the first place by phenomena primarily physical" (p. 89).

This is true enough. But it is equally true, as shown by the facts he himself cites, that many of the bodily states that exercise an influence on the condition of the mind are set up in the first place by phenomena primarily mental. For example, among other facts now recognized by psychosomatic medicine, that the painful physical phenomenon of stomach ulcers is in some cases set up in the first place by such mental states as anxiety, tension, and worry. Anyway, just how would Lamont propose to decide in any given case which place constitutes "the first place"?

The upshot of the comments in the present section is that when Lamont attends not only to the facts which come under the (a) to (d) headings of his list, but also to those which come under the (e) heading, the purported monistic psychology of science turns out actually to be an *interactionistic dualism!* An *interactionistic dualism*, it is true, that involves no "supernatural soul" but only, besides processes in a material body, various non-material ideas and other mental occurrences. The "supernatural soul" however, which functions as the Devil in Lamont's would-be monistic creed, may well be left to such employment; for a responsible interactionism has no need of it.

6. A supposititious puzzle. As we have just seen, Lamont is definitely committed to psycho-physical interactionism by such statements as that on the one hand "physical states affect the personality and its mental life" (p. 87), and on the other that, conversely, "specific alterations in [man's] mental and emotional life result in specific alterations in his bodily condition" (p. 114). It is therefore surprising that, when considering "certain fundamental difficulties that have always characterized the dualistic psychology," he should assert, as constituting one of them, that "it is impossible to understand how an immaterial soul can act upon and control a material body" (p. 102). To the same effect, he speaks of "the insoluble riddle of how the immaterial can be associated with and work together with the material . . ." (p. 104).

Two comments on this supposititious riddle immediately suggest themselves. The first is that, as we pointed out in an earlier chapter, the Causality relation is wholly neutral as regards the ontological nature of the events that enter into it. Hence no paradox is involved in the supposition that a mental, i.e., non-material, event causes a material event in the brain cortex; any more than is involved (or apparently found by Lamont) in the fact, which he asserts, that bodily events produce or affect mental ones.

The second comment is that to understand "how" an event C causes another event E never has any other meaning than to know *what the intermediary causal steps are*, through which C eventually causes E. Hence, where, as in the case of a mental and of the corresponding cortical event, *proximate* not *remote* causation is what one has in view, the question as to the "how" of causation loses the only meaning it ever has. That is, the question becomes literally nonsensical, and to ask it is absurd *because of this, not* because mental and material events are ontologically heterogeneous; for the absurdity of asking for the "how" of *proximate* causation remains the same no matter whether the two events in view be one of them mental and the other material, or both of them mental, or both of them material.[3]

7. **"Verdict of Science?"** or **"Turning aversions into disproofs?"** We have now examined in some detail Lamont's attack on psychophysical dualism, and have seen, (a) that he tacitly and gratuitously equates naturalism and materialistic monism, and hence, (b) gratuitously assumes dualism to be inherently supernaturalistic; (c) that he misconstrues the communicability of the referents of ideas as entailing that ideas themselves are communicable and hence not inherently private; (d) that, besides material objects and events, he acknowledges also the occurrence of ideas, which he explicitly declares to be non-material; (e) hence that, notwithstanding the monism he proclaims, what he actually sets forth is a dualism; (f) that, having declared without qualification that the mental life of man is a product of his bodily activities, he nevertheless contends—citing facts in support—that not only do bodily states affect mental, but mental states too affect

---

[3]Lamont is of course not alone in overlooking the absurdity just pointed out. Prof. Ryle too among others, does so. He assumes that if mind and matter should be two species of existents instead of merely "existing" in two different senses (as the behaviorism he espouses requires him dogmatically to assert), then interaction between mind and matter would be "completely mysterious;" for one would then have to ask: "How can a mental process, such as willing, cause spatial movements like the movements of the tongue? How can a physical change in the optic nerve have among its effects a mind's perception of a flash of light?" (*The Concept of Mind*, pp. 23, 52, 19.) As we have just seen, however, the "how" of causation is capable either of being mysterious or of being known only where remote not proximate causation is concerned. Hence, to ask "how?" concerning the latter is to be guilty of a "category mistake." But there is no room here to consider the various strange assertions concerning mind, dictated in that book by the caricaturing of contentions attacked, which is employed there as a method.

physical; (g) that this entails that actually, what he contends for under the misnomer of "monistic psychology" is an interaction-istic dualism; (h) and this notwithstanding that the action of mind on body, which he explicitly declares occurs, is with equal explicitness declared by him to be an insoluble riddle, impossible to understand, that rules out dualism!

What then is to be said concerning the chapter of Lamont's *The Illusion of Immortality* in which the above mass of incon-sistencies and *non-sequitur* is to be found? Suggestion for an appropriate characterization of it may be found in the title which, in a later chapter, he gives to a section where he cites pointed ex-amples of a procedure to which protagonists of immortality are addicted. The title of that section is: "Turning wishes into proofs." I submit that, correspondingly, the appropriate title for the chapter Lamont entitles "The verdict of science" would have been: "Turning aversions into disproofs!"

PART IV

Discarnate Life After Death and the Ostensibly Relevant Empirical Evidence For It

Chapter XIV

VARIOUS SENSES OF THE QUESTION REGARDING SURVIVAL AFTER DEATH

Does the human personality survive bodily death? This question, phrased thus in the terms F. W. H. Myers used in the title of his famous work,[1] seems to most of the persons who ask it simple and direct enough to admit of a "Yes" or "No" answer— the only difficulty being to find out which of the two it should be.

As will become evident in what follows, however, the question is in fact highly ambiguous. Hence, in order to be in position to judge intelligently what bearing on it given items of *prima facie* evidence of survival may really have, the first step must be to distinguish clearly the several senses which the expression "survival of the personality after death," can have.

1. **The bodily component of a personality.** When we reflect on what makes up a human personality, we find first a physical or more specifically a biological component. It comprises the particular facial features, the build and marks of the body, its weight, gait, carriage, voice, and so on. The body's dissolution following death automatically destroys all this. That the physical part of the personality does not survive is definitely known. A closely similar body might conceivably some time miraculously arise again, as the doctrine of the "resurrection of the flesh" contemplates; and this would not require that it should be composed of identically the same material particles which constituted the body at death, for the materials of it anyway change from day to day to some extent, and more or less completely over a period of some years, without the body's ceasing to be recognizably the same. But, aside from the occasional reports—many of them

---

[1]*Human Personality and its Survival of Bodily Death*, 1903.

dubious—of materializations for a few minutes of a replica of the body of some deceased person, no evidence at all exists that a person survives after death in the sense that his body gets reassembled and revived, and continues then to live a life somewhere, in the sense in which his now decayed body lived a life on earth between its birth and its death.

2. Survival—of just what parts of the psychological component. As pointed out already in Chapt. 1, what the question of survival essentially concerns is not the physical but the psychological component of the human personality. We saw in Chapt. VI that it consists of various "dispositions, i.e., capacities or abilities—some of them psycho-psychical, some psycho-physical, and some physico-psychical.

Now, some of these might survive and others not. For example, the capacity to remember past experiences might survive, being then perhaps more extensive, or less so, than it was during incarnate life; and yet the capacity for intellectual initiative, critical judgment, or inventiveness might perish. Or again, what survived might be only a person's aptitudes; that is, the capacities he has, to acquire under suitable circumstances various kinds of more determinate capacities such as skills, habits, or knowledge constitute.

But certain of the capacities of a person are organized in particular groups relevant each to one of the chief roles which life calls upon him to play. Each of these groups constitutes what may be called a particular "role-self," which has interests, purposes, beliefs, and impulses more or less different from those of the others. Examples would be the "father" role, the "husband" role, the vocational roles of, for instance, "physician," or "teacher," or "policeman," or "inventor," or "bookkeeper," or "business executive." Any of these roles is in turn different from that of "religious devotee," of "sex hunter," of "bully," of "predator," and so on. A man is thus a society of various "role-selves" all using the same body, and getting along with one another harmoniously or not in various degrees, much as do men in social groups. At certain times, some one of these role-selves is in charge of the body's behavior. Sometimes, two or more of them compete for, or cooperate in, command of it—the predator perhaps competing with the would-be saint; or the latter cooperating perhaps with the father in repressing the would-be Casanova or the thief which the circumstances of the moment would tempt out.

Normally, these various role-selves function together somewhat as a committee, whose eventual action represents the balance of the claims, weak or strong, of the various parties having interests affected by the committee's decisions. But under abnormal circumstances, some one of these role-selves may get strong enough to get temporary dictatorial command uncensorable by the others. This is what occurs in the cases of split personalities, of which the Beauchamp case described by Dr. Morton Prince, the Doris Fischer case described by Dr. W. F. Prince, and recently that of "The Three Faces of Eve," described by Drs. C. H. Thigpen and H. M. Cleckley, are examples.

These cases bring up the interesting question as to which ones of the role-selves, which together make up the total personality of the living man, might or might not survive the death of his body; and also the question as to the nature and the strength or weakness of the connection that could remain between such of them as did survive, once the bond constituted by their joint association with the one body had been destroyed by the latter's death. Survival of the "father" role-self, or as the case might be, of the "mother," or "daughter," or "son," or "friend," etc., role-self would be what the relatives or personal friends of the deceased would automatically look for; but evidences of survival of *it* would be far from being evidence that the whole or a major part of the psychological component of the personality of the deceased had survived.

Aside from this, the kind of evidence one happens to have, in support of the hypothesis that a particular part of the psychological component of the personality of a deceased person survives, could itself impose limits, minimal or maximal, on the content of the hypothesis. If, for example, the evidence consisted of identificatory facts communicated purportedly by the surviving spirit of the deceased *directly "possessing"* temporarily the vocal organs or the hand of an entranced medium and expressing itself through them, then this would require survival of *the psychophysical capacity* which the mind of the deceased had, to cause speech or writing movements in a living body with which it was suitably related. But this would not be a required part of the hypothesis if the identifying facts were communicated not thus through direct possession of the entranced medium's organs of expression, but indirectly, through telepathic "rapport" between the medium's subconscious mind and the surviving part of the mind of the deceased. In this case, on the other hand, capacity for such telepathic rapport would be part of the equipment required to be possessed by the hypothetically surviving part of the personality of the deceased.

3. **Survival—for how long.** Were survival to be for only an hour, or a week, or even a year, then empirical evidence that such survival is a fact would have relatively little interest for most persons. If on the other hand the evidence were that survival is normally for a much longer period—at least for one similar in length to that of a person's normal life on earth—then it would be of considerable interest to most men, and the prospect of its eventual ending at such a distant time would now probably not trouble them much.

But anyway the question, "survival for how long?" necessarily raises the prior one of how length of time after death is to be measured if, as the survival hypothesis usually contemplates, the surviving personality does not have a physical body—the body one revolution of which around the axis of the earth defines "one day"; and around the sun, "one year."

The answer would have to be in terms of hypothetically possible communication by us with that discarnate personality: If (assuming availability of a medium) communication with that personality remained possible during, say, one year, or n years, of earth time after the death of that personality's body, then specifically this would be what it would mean to say that that personality had survived one year, or n years, after death. Of survival forever, which is what "eternal" life is usually taken to mean, there could of course be no empirical test.

4. **"Sameness" in what sense, of a mind at two times.** The personality of each of us changes gradually as the months and the years pass; but, notwithstanding our acquisition of new capacities

and loss of some we possessed earlier, each of us is to himself and to others, in some sense admitting of more and less, the "same" person at different ages. The question now before us is, in what sense or senses of "sameness" or "personal identity" this is true.

We noted earlier that the human personality includes various bodily traits as well as psychological ones and that, since death destroys the body, the psychological components are the ones directly relevant to the possibility of survival. But the question as to what it means, to say of something existing at a certain time that it is, or is not, "the same" as something existing at another time, will perhaps be easier to answer if we ask it first concerning human bodies—say, one young in 1900, and one old in 1950.

One sense, which the assertion that they are "the same" human body can have is that the relation of the first to the second is the relation *"having become."* If this relation does obtain between the 1900 body and the 1950 body, then they are "the same" body even if no likeness, other than that each is a human body, is discoverable between them—not even, let us suppose, likeness of pattern of finger prints because the old man anyway happens to have lost his hands.

If, on the other hand, it is not true that the body in view in 1900 *has become* the one we view in 1950, then they are not "the same" human body even if the likeness between them is so extensive and evident as to make the first clearly recognizable in the second; for it may be that the once young man who has become the old man we now behold is not the young man we knew in 1900 but, perhaps, is his identical-twin brother.

Thus likeness, no matter how great, does not constitute proof of identity unless the characteristic in respect of which it obtains is, and is known to be, *idiosyncratic,* and hence identificatory. Yet the more nearly idiosyncratic, i.e., *the rarer,* is the characteristic (or the combination of characteristics) in respect of which the likeness obtains, and *the more minute* is the likeness in respect of it, *the more probable* it is empirically that the relation between the human body in view in 1900 and that in view in 1950 is that of "having become," and hence that they are "the same" body.

These remarks concerning the meaning of "the same," and

of "not the same," when one or the other of these two relations is asserted to hold between a body at a given time and a body at a different time, apply also in all essentials where minds instead of bodies are concerned: a mind at a given time is *"the same mind"* as one at an earlier time if and only if the mind in view at the earlier time *has become* the mind in view at the later time.

5. **Conceivable forms of discarnate "life".** Regarding the question, in what sense of "living" could such part of the personality as persisted after death be said to continue living, the following several senses suggest themselves.

(i) The particular set of dispositions one had specified as those in the survival of which one is interested might continue to "live" only in the sense in which a machine—here a psychological robot—continues to exist without losing the capacities for its distinctive functions, during periods when it is not called upon to perform them but lies idle, inactive. Even in the case of the body, it is still alive when in deep sleep or in a faint, but is more alive, or alive in a somewhat different sense or in ways more typically human, when it is awake and responding to visual, auditory, and other stimuli from its environment, and acting upon it.

Similarly, in the case of the psychological part of the personality, it might when discarnate be "alive" only in a minimal sense analogous to that in which the comatose or anaesthetized body is nevertheless alive. At any given time of a person's life, much the larger number of his capabilites exist only in such dormant condition. Probably, at the time the reader was reading the beginning of the present paragraph, the capability he does and did have to remember, say, his own name, was wholly latent. Even the enduring of a personality's dispositions in a dormant state, however, would constitute the basis of the possibility of sporadic brief exercise of some of them if and when direct or indirect contact happened to occur between that otherwise wholly dormant personality and the organism of a medium. Temporary exercise of the dispositions constituting the automatic, mechanical constituents of a mind—to wit, associations of ideas, memories, etc.—is the most which the majority of mediumistic communications appear to testify to.

(ii) A second possibility is that some of the "internal" mental dispositions of the person concerned, i.e., some of his psychico-psychical dispositions, should not only persist but actually be exercised, though without critical control. This would mean mental "life" in the sense in which dreaming or idle reverie is a species of mental life.

(iii) Or, thirdly, mental life of a more active kind might consist in a reviewing of the incidents of one's *ante mortem* life, with an attempt as one does so to discern causal connections between one's experiences, one's reactions to them, and one's later experiences or activities. Especially if, as psychoanalysis and some experiments with hypnosis appear to testify, memories one is not ordinarily able to revive are nevertheless preserved; and they were accessible in one's discarnate state; then much wisdom that was latent in them, but which one had at the time been too passionately engrossed to harvest, might in that discarnate state be distilled out of them by reflection.

(iv) Or again, one's capacity for intelligent control and purposive direction of creative thought might be exercised. "Life" would then mean, for example, such creative purely mental activity as a mathematician, or a musical composer, or a poet, or a philosopher, etc., can, even in the present life, be absorbed in at times of bodily idleness and of abstraction from sense stimuli.

(v) Or, fifthly, "life" could mean also response—then telepathic or clairvoyant—to stimuli from a then non-physical environment; and voluntary, "psychokinetic," reaction upon the excarnate personalities, or the possibly impersonal constituents, of that non-physical environment.

This would be discarnate post mortem "life" in the fullest sense. It is the "life" to the reality of which, as we shall see, the so-called Cross-correspondences appear to testify more strongly than do any of the other kinds of *prima facie* evidence of survival. As C. D. Broad has rightly remarked, "if the dispositional basis of a man's personality should persist after his death, there is no reason why it should have the same fate in all cases. In some cases one, and in others another of the various alternatives . . . . might be realized. It seems reasonable to think that the state of development of the personality at the time of death, and the circumstances under which death takes place, might be relevant factors in determining which alternative would be realized."[2]

6. H. H. Price's depiction of a post mortem life in a world of images. One of the objections most commonly advanced by educated and critical persons against the survival hypothesis is that it is *unintelligible*—that no conception of discarnate life that is not patently preposterous is imaginable. Our discussion of the meaning of the hypothesis that the human personality survives after the death of its body may therefore turn next to the description Professor Price has given of a clearly imaginable and plausible "Next World" and of what the content of life in it would be—thus effectively disposing of that objection. His description is contained in a lecture entitled "Survival and the Idea of 'Another World'."[3]

The "Next World" he depicts would be of the same kind as the world we experience during our dreams. When we dream, we perceive things, persons, and events more or less similar to those which we perceive normally as a result of stimulations of our sense organs by the physical world. In dreams, however, this is not the cause of our perceptions of objects, for no physical objects such as perceived are then stimulating our senses. Yet what we perceive engages at the time our thoughts and emotions. The behavior of the dream objects, of course, is often very different from that of the physical objects they resemble, but the anomaly is not realized until we wake up. So long as the dream lasts, we are not aware that it is a dream but take it to be reality, just as we do the objects and events we perceive while awake.

The "Next World," then would, like our nightly dream world, be a world of mental images. It would, as Price puts it, be an *"imagy"* world, not one which, like Utopia or Erewhon, is *imaginary* in the sense of imaged but not believed to exist.

---

[2]*Personal Identity and Survival*, The Thirteenth F. W. H. Myers Lecture, 1958. London, *Soc. for Psychical Research*, p. 31. This lecture provides an admirably systematic, analytical discussion of the various aspects of its topic. The reader is also referred to Ch. 21, "Some Theoretically Possible Forms of Survival" of the present author's *Nature, Mind, and Death*, Open Court Pub. Co. La Salle, Ill. 1951, pp. 484-502.

[3]*Proc. Soc. for Psychical Research*, Vol. LX:1-25, January 1953.

In the experience of a discarnate human personality in that world, *imaging* would replace the *perceiving* normally caused by stimulation of the sense organs. It would replace it "in the sense that imaging would perform much the same function as sense-perception performs now, by providing us with objects about which we could have thoughts, emotions and wishes. There is no reason why we should not be 'as much alive,' or at any rate *feel* as much alive, in an image-world as we do now in this present material world, which we perceive by means of our sense-organs and nervous system. And so the use of the word 'survival' ('life after death') would be perfectly justifiable" (p. 6).

Moreover that image-world would for us be just as real as the physical world is for us now, or as the objects seen in our dreams are real so long as we do not wake up. What one *can* say of the dream objects is that, although they resemble physical objects, they are *not really physical;* but one cannot say that they are *not real* in the sense of not existing. The laws of their behavior are different from those of the behavior of the physical objects they resemble, and this is what makes the dream world an "other" world. But its being other does not make it delusive unless one believes it to be the same world—i.e., unless one believes that the laws of behavior of *its* objects are those of the behavior of physical objects. And such belief is not a necessary nor a usual part of the dream state.

Moreover, if telepathy should be part of the equipment of the discarnate personality, then that personality's image-world would not be entirely subjective. It would, to some extent, "be the joint product of a group of telepathically interacting minds and public to all of them" (p. 16). Yet each mind would, to a considerable extent, build his own dream world—his memories providing the "material" for it; and his desires, whether conscious or unconscious, determining the "forms" the memory material would be given (p. 17). Thus there would be not just one Next World, but many—some, overlapping to some extent, and others "impenetrable to one another, corresponding to the *different* desires which different groups of personalities have" (p. 19).

This description of a Next World as a wish-fulfilment world may seem wishfully rosy; but Price makes very clear that it would be so only to the extent that one's wishes happened to be themselves beautiful ones rather than, some of them, disgraceful. And most of us have some of each kind even if we repress and hide the latter from other persons and largely from ourselves too.

7. **The architect of a person's heaven or hell.** But the words "desires," "wishes," and "aversions," which Price uses to designate the psychological generators of our dream images, are perhaps not the best after all by which to describe the subjective architect of a person's *post mortem* image world. For the architect we can observe at work in ourselves even now, building up every day for us imaginal and conceptual contents of belief, is rather attitude, emotion and disposition. Suspiciousness, for example, paints as devious the persons it meets. Jealousy paints its object as unfaithful; hatred, as hostile; contempt, as despicable. Trustfulness, on the other hand, sees others as honest; magnanimity, as worthy; love, as lovable; friendliness, as well-disposed; considerateness, as respectable; and so on.

It is not so much the "wish," then, that is "father to the thought," as it is the attitude or disposition one brings to one's contacts with others. It determines what one *imagines* and *believes* them to be, as distinguished from what one strictly *observes* and *finds* them to be. Moreover, what a person imagines and believes another to be affects his own behavior; which in turn tempts the other to play up, or down, to the role thus handed to him! What kind of world each person *now* lives in therefore depends to some extent on what kind of psychological spectacles he wears, through which he looks at the empirical, truly objective facts. To that extent each of us, *here and now*, is living in a hell, purgatory, or heaven he himself constructs. How much more, then, is this fatally bound to be the case when he lives wholly in a dream-world—whether an *ante* or a *post mortem* one; that is, in a world from which the objective, stubborn facts perception supplies are absent, and absent therefore also their sobering effect on one's subjective imaginings!

8. **Life after death conceived as physical reembodiment.** There remains to mention, besides the possible forms of discarnate life considered in Sec. 5 above, also the conception of life

after death according to which such life consists of reembodiment of the "essential" part of the personality in a neonate human or possibly animal body; and whether immediately at death, or after an interval during which consciousness possibly persists in one or another of those discarnate forms. This is the hypothesis of metempsychosis, palingenesis, or reincarnation, which has commended itself to numerous eminent thinkers, Professor Broad among them. Nothing more will be said about it in this chapter, however, since Part V is to be devoted to a detailed discussion of it.

What has been said in the present chapter will have made evident that any answer based on empirical facts—no matter of what kinds these might be—to the question whether the human personality survives the death of its body, will automatically be as ambiguous, or as unambiguous, as the question itself happens to be as asked by a given inquirer. Whether the answer, when unambiguous, turns out to be that survival—in whatever specific sense is then in view—is certainly or probably a fact, or certainly or probably not a fact, will of course depend on what the empirical evidence on which it is based happens to be. But to have purged of ambiguity the expression "survival after death" will at all events entail that, when one asks whether "survival" is a fact, one will then know just what it is that one wants to know.

Chapter XV

SURVIVAL AND PARANORMAL OCCURRENCES

In chapter II, we examined the chief of the arguments alleged to prove the reality of a life after death, and we found that, because of one or another defect, each failed to prove it or even to establish that it is probably a fact. On the other hand, we surveyed in Chapter III both the current empirical and the theoretical arguments that purport to show that survival of consciousness after death is impossible; and, after clarifying in Part II the key concepts employed in those arguments, we found in Part III that the arguments quite fail to prove the alleged impossibility. The positive upshot, then of Parts I, II, and III is that persistence of consciousness in some form after death is both theoretically and empirically possible: *theoretically possible* since analysis of the supposition of such persistence finds no contradition implicit in it; and *empirically possible* since that supposition is not inconsistent with any definitely known empirical facts.

The task before us is now to inquire whether there are any empirical facts at all that would establish the reality of survival or, failing this, would show it to be more probable than not.

1. **Where empirical evidence of survival might be found.** Obviously, neither any commonly known facts nor any of the recondite facts of the natural sciences provide evidence of survival; for otherwise survival would hardly be in doubt. Hence, if any empirical evidence at all is to be found that consciousness continues after death, that evidence must be sought among paradoxical occurrences of the kinds termed "supernatural" by naive persons, but to-day designated simply as "paranormal" by persons too critical to assume tacitly as do the former that Nature can comprise only what is known and understood as of now.

The term "paranormal" has—in addition to its freedom from the religious or superstitious connotations of "supernatural"—the virtue of being free also from the special assumptions that are packed into such terms as "parapsychological," "paraphysical," or "parabiological." For "paranormal" means only that the kinds of occurrences so labelled are contrary to what is "normal," i.e., contrary to what "the common sense of the epoch" regards as possible. As Dr. W. F. G. Swann has pointed out, each theory—whether of the nature of the world or of man—that meets with enough success in accounting for the facts it concerns to gain wide acceptance, "grows around itself an aura of common sense, the common sense of its epoch." But knowledge and understanding increase as a result of man's taking novel or neglected facts into account, and in time new or improved theories supersede the old. "And so the center of gravity of common sense changes with the epoch, and the nonsense of the past becomes the common sense of the future."[1]

Since occurrences ostensibly paranormal thus necessarily constitute the sort of evidence we shall have to examine in our presentation of the case for the reality of survival, we need first to sharpen our concept of paranormality by considering in more detail the nature of the criterion we tacitly employ when we class a given occurrence as paranormal. The most painstaking attempts to formulate it the present writer knows are those of Prof. J. B. Rhine and of Prof. C. D. Broad. Let us examine each in turn.

2. **Critique of Rhine's account of what marks an event as paranormal.** Paranormal occurrences have also been designated "metapsychical," "parapsychological," or simply "psi" phenomena. Prof. Rhine ordinarily employs one or the other of the last two of these terms. According to him, what marks certain phenomena as parapsychological is their *non-physical* character: they "defy physical explanation and require a psychological one. They always happen to people (or animals) or involve some associated or at least suspected personal agency or experience; . . . . they

---

[1]Nature and the Mind of Man, Lecture, delivered at the Stated Meeting of the Franklin Institute, Wednesday February 15, 1956. Pub. in *Jl. of the Franklin Institute*, Vol. 261 No. 6. June, 1956. The passages quoted above are from p. 593.

definitely appear to challenge explanation by physical principles."[2]

The required psychological explanation, however, is not supplied by Rhine, who does not even formally supply criteria of what he means by "physical" or by "psychological." Moreover, the character of being incapable of explanation in physical terms, or more exactly, in terms of the "the physics of today"[3] is not peculiar to parapsychological phenomena for, as made clear in our chapter VIII, this same inexplicability in purely physical terms attaches also to *normal* states of consciousness, i.e., to the contents of introspection: however *dependent on* physical processes in the brain these may be, they *are not identically* those physical processes themselves. Indeed, even the purposiveness which seems to characterize all life processes down to those of unicellular organisms is still to be accounted for adequately in terms purely of physics, notwithstanding the attempts to do so made by Schroedinger and others.[4] And of course, that there is in the personality of man "a world of distinctively mental reality"[5] is no new discovery made for us by parapsychology. For, as C. W. K. Mundle pointedly noted in his review of *New World of the Mind*, "surely one's best evidence for [the existence of a "world of the mind"] is still the introspective awareness one has of what goes on in one's own mind."[6]

That telepathy and clairvoyance are non-physical phenomena is shown, Rhine contends, by the fact that "they defy any application of the inverse square law of decline of effect with distance."

The trouble with this contention, however, is that telepathy and clairvoyance have *not* been shown to be independent of dis-

---

[2]*New World of the Mind.* Wm. Sloane Associates, N. Y. 1953, p. 150.

[3]*Parapsychology, Frontier Science of the Mind,* pub. Charles C Thomas, Springfield, Ill. 1957, p. 7.

[4]E. Schroedinger: *What is Life?* 1946. Concerning the purposive character of biological processes, see for instance E. W. Sinnott: *Cell and Psyche, the Biology of Purpose,* 1950; H. S. Jennings: Some Implications of Emergent Evolution, in *Science* Jan. 14, 1927; E. Rignano: The Concept of Purpose in Biology, *Mind,* Vol. XL, no. 159 July 1931; and *The Nature of Life,* 1930.

[5]Rhine, *New World of the Mind,* p. IX.

[6]*Jl. of the Am. Soc. for Psychical Research,* Vol. XLVIII:165, No. 4, Ocotber. 1954.

tance. What *has* been shown is only that distances of a few hundred or even a few thousand miles do not affect *the excess of correct guesses over chance expectation,* which has characterized the results of telepathy and clairvoyance experiments. For these experiments are not quantitative in the sense this term ordinarily has in science, namely, that the cause and the effect are each measured, and that a certain magnitude of the effect regularly corresponds to a certain magnitude of the cause. The magnitude of the "sender's" telepathic action is not measured, nor is the magnitude of the "receiver's" impression. But it is the magnitude of his impression—not the degree of correctness of the information received—which, if the energy involved is physical, would be expected to decrease according to the inverse square law when the distance increases. That is, the receiver's *impression* would be of a telepathic "shout" when the distance is short, and of a telepathic "whisper" when the distance is long. And the question whether this is or is not actually the case is not decided at all by the fact that the *degree of correctness* of the telepathic information was the same at great as at small distances: this fact is irrelevant because the information conveyed in a whisper can be exactly the same information as that conveyed in a shout.

Nor, again, have the "sending" and the "receiving" been timed with the extreme precision which would be necessary to vindicate the supposition that no more time is taken by telepathy over relatively long distances than over short; for the speed of telepathy might happen to be of the same order of magnitude as the speed of light—which is a purely *physical* phenomenon—and, in order to prove that the speed of light is finite, timings vastly more precise than any ever made of telepathy were necessary.

What the "quantitative" experiments with telepathy and clairvoyance have quantified is merely the *probability that there is a causal connection* between the fact to be guessed and the guess made of it. To have shown that the magnitude of this probability was significantly higher than chance is, of course, an epoch-making achievement; but it does not constitute quantification of the cause or the effect, and hence does not show that telepathy and clairvoyance are independent of distance even over the few thousand miles available on the surface of the earth for experimentation.

The criticisms made in what precedes of Rhine's attempt to state what marks an event as parapsychological do not, of course, in any way reflect on the value or the originality of his experimental work. The importance of that work and of the similar work it has inspired others to do is outstanding, for it has definitely shown, by methods similar to those used in certain of the other fields of scientific research, that telepathy, clairvoyance, and precognition really occur and do not depend on the use of the known sense organs.

Nor, on the other hand, were those criticisms intended as an argument that the processes at work in paranormal phenomena are somehow ultimately physical; for what is important in those phenomena is that their occurrence points to the existence of forces and of facts which, whether or not themselves somehow physical, are anyway novel to contemporary science and therefore compel it to revise its conception of the limits of the really possible.

Those criticisms were intended only to make evident on the one hand that Rhine has not proved that the phenomena in view are non-physical; and on the other that some *positive* criterion of non-physicality would be required if the "parapsychological" character of an occurrence were to be applicably defined as consisting in the "non-physicality" of the occurrence. For it is one thing to say of certain occurrences that *we do not know them to be* physical; and it is quite another thing to say that they *are* non-physical. The burden of proof squarely rests on the person who, as Rhine does, asserts the latter. He does not, however, supply the proof, but leaves us with only the fact that the phenomena in view are ones for which we have at present neither a physical nor a psychological explanation. As we pointed out, however, this is true also of some occurrences not termed paranormal, and therefore does not mark off the former from the latter.

The importance Rhine attaches to the "non-physicality" he claims for paranormal phenomena appears to derive from the philosophical implications as regards freedom of the will, moral responsibility, and the validity of human values, which he believes such non-physicality would have—but which in fact it would not have at all.[7]

3. **Broad's analytical account of the marks of paranormality.** The clearest, most adequate and most useful analysis of the notion of paranormality to be found in the literature of the subject is probably that formulated by C. D. Broad in an essay entitled "The relevance of psychical research to philosophy."[8] He writes that "there are certain limiting principles which we unhesitatingly take for granted as the framework within which all our practical activities and our scientific theories are confined. Some of these seem to be self evident. Others are so overwhelmingly supported by all the empirical facts which fall within the range of ordinary experience and the scientific elaborations of it . . . that it hardly enters our heads to question them. Let us call these *Basic Limiting Principles.*"[9]

A "paranormal" event would then be one whose occurrence violates one or more of those principles and therefore proves that, although they have very wide validity, nevertheless it is not as commonly assumed strictly unlimited.

Broad formulates nine of those principles but makes no claim that the list is exhaustive. They fall into four groups. Those of the first group relate to Causation in general; those of the second, to the action of mind on matter; those of the third to the dependence of mind on brain; and those of the fourth to the ways of acquiring knowledge. The following sketchy account of them will be adequate for our present purpose of making clear the distinction between normality, which they define, and paranormality, which consists of exceptions to one or another of them.

---

[7]See on this point, in *Jl. of Philosophy* Vol. LI, No. 25, December 9, 1954, an article by Rhine on The Science of Nonphysical Nature, especially p. 809; and the present writer's comments upon it entitled The Philosophical Importance of 'Psychic Phenomena', especially pp. 816-17. Rhine's conception of "non-physicality" is devastatingly criticized by the physicist, R. A. McConnell, in his review of Rhine and Pratt's recent book, *Parapsychology, Frontier Science of the Mind*, in *Jl. of the Amer. Soc. for Psychical Research*, Vol. LII:117-20, July, 1958, No. 3.

[8]It originally appeared in the Journal, *Philosophy*, and is reprinted in Prof. Broad's book, *Religion, Philosophy and Psychical Research*, Harcourt, Brace and Co., New York 1953, pp. 7-26.

[9]*Op. cit.* p. 7.

(I) An event cannot have effects before it has itself occurred. (Hence "precognition," which would be causation, by an as yet future event, of a present perception of it, would contravene this principle and would therefore be paranormal.)

Then come two other principles regarding causation, which in substance are that causation at a distance in space or in time is impossible without some intermediary chain of causes and effects.

(II) Next is the principle that it is impossible for an event in a person's mind to cause *directly* any material event other than one in his own brain. (This would preclude psychokinesis or telekinesis, e.g., the influencing of the fall of dice by mere volition; and occurrence of it would therefore be paranormal.)

(III) Then comes the principle that some event in a person's living brain is a necessary condition of any event in his mind. (Continuation of consciousness after the body's death, which this principle would preclude, would therefore be paranormal.)

(IV) Lastly, four principles concerning the acquisition of knowledge: (a) that physical events or things can be perceived only by means of sensations caused by them in a percipient's mind. (Clairvoyance, i.e., extrasensory perception of physical events or things, would be ruled out by this principle; and occurrence of it would therefore be paranormal.)

(b) That it is impossible for a person A to know what experiences another person B is having or has had, except by perceiving and interpreting sensory signs of them made by B then or earlier. (Telepathy, which would be extrasensory cognition of another person's experiences, would conflict with this principle, and would therefore be paranormal.)

(c) That it is impossible for a person to know the future, except by inference from data and rules of inference relevant to them, known to him personally or through testimony; or by noninferential expectations resulting from associations formed in the past and presently stimulated. (Precognition, which would violate this principle, would then be paranormal.)

(d) That a person can know the past only from memory, or from testimony as to memories, or from records of perceptions or of memories, or by inference from present data and relevant rules of sequence. (A violation of this principle would constitute "retrocognition," which would therefore be paranormal.)

4. **The chief kinds of ostensibly paranormal occurrences.** Some kinds of paranormal occurrences have no obvious bearing on the question of survival after death; yet almost any of them can have, indirectly if not directly. Hence brief description of the chief kinds of which cases have at times been reported is appropriate at this point.

In many of them some person, referred to variously as a "psychic," "sensitive," "automatist," or "medium," apparently plays some role. The term "medium" was originally used to mean that the person so described functioned as an *intermediary* through whom communication takes place between the deceased and the living. The term, however, and those other terms too, will here be employed in the broader sense usual to-day, of a person in whose presence paranormal phenomena occur at times, and on whose presence their occurrence is somehow dependent.

Paranormal occurrences are commonly divided into two classes—the *physical* and the *mental;* and within each, two sub-classes may be distinguished. As will appear, however, the four resulting sub-classes are not as sharply separate as could be wished, and the placing of a given paranormal occurrence in one rather than in another of them is sometimes rather arbitrary. Also, some phenomena have both physical and mental features. Nevertheless, the following classification is convenient.

(1) The first of its four classes is that of occurrences that are *physical* and in addition *extrasomatic;* that is, external to the bodies of all the persons present. Examples would be paranormal raps on tables, walls, or other objects; motions of objects without their being touched, or moved by any other normal cause; paranormal sharp decreases of temperature in some part of a room; materialization apparently out of nothing, or dematerialization, of flowers, of hands or other parts of human bodies, or of other objects. Apparitions of the dead or the living would come under this heading if perception of them is due to a somehow physical stimulus. Usually, however, they are more plausibly classed as hallucinations and therefore as mental.

(2) The second category is that of *physical* phenomena that

are *somatic* in the sense of taking place in or occurring to the body of the medium or of some other person present. Examples would be the levitation of the body—that is, the rising of it in the air and floating or moving there unsupported; or again, temporary paranormal immunity of parts of the body to fire; or paranormally sudden healing of wounds or diseases; or extrusion from the body of the entranced medium of a mysterious substance which has been termed ectoplasm, which varies in consistency, and which is capable of taking on various shapes and of exerting or conveying force.

Paranormal occurrences classed as *mental,* on the other hand, consist in a person's acquisition of information somehow otherwise than, as normally, through the employment of his sense organs. Here again, we may distinguish two sub-classes.

(3) One comprises paranormal mental experiences of the kinds termed *extrasensory perceptions,* whether occurring spontaneously or under laboratory conditions. Examples would be *Precognition,* that is, not discursive inference but detailed and correct virtual perception, perhaps in a dream or in a waking hallucination, of events that have not yet occurred; or the guessing, correctly to an extent significantly above chance in a large number of trials, of the order the cards will have in a pack *after* it will have been shuffled. Also, *Retrocognition,* which is quasi perception similarly detailed and correct of past events one has never perceived or perhaps even known anything of. Again *Telepathy,* that is, communication between minds independently of the channels of sense and notwithstanding distance and intervening material obstacles; *Clairvoyance,* that is, virtual perception of objective events or things that are not at the time accessible to the organs of sense. A special case of this would be *Object-reading* (sometimes inappropriately called Psychometry,) namely, correct virtual perception of facts and events in the life of a person with whom a given object has been closely associated, but who, or whose identity, is unknown to the percipient.

Again, hallucinations, whether waking or oneiric, that are veridical in the sense that their content includes, or their occurrence correctly signifies, particular facts not otherwise known to the percipient. Apparitions of the dead or of the living would often be instances of this; also what are termed heautoscopic hallucinations (or "out-of-the-body," or "projection," experiences,) namely, experiences in which a person observes his own body and its surroundings from a point in space external to it, as we all do the bodies of other persons.

(4) Lastly, there are the *communications* that come through the automatic speech or writing of a medium; or according to some agreed code, through paranormal raps or paranormal motions of an object in the presence of a medium; and that convey information that turns out to be veridical but was not obtained by the medium in any of the normal ways. The communications, usually but not always, purport to emanate from the surviving spirits of persons who have died, who claim to be temporarily occupying or indirectly using the body of the medium, or to be causing the raps or motions of objects that answer questions and spell sentences according to a code.

Another classification of ostensibly paranormal occurrences—which cuts across that just presented—divides them into the *spontaneous*, the *experimental*, and the *mediumistic* ones. Evidently, the class of mediumistic occurrences may overlap to some extent the other two of these.

The existing evidence that phenomena occur that are paranormal in the sense defined is much stronger for some of the kinds mentioned than for some of the others. It is strongest and practically conclusive in the case of extrasensory perception—especially of precognition, clairvoyance, and telepathy since, for the testing of these, certain experimental methods, and statistical procedures for the treatment of the results obtained by those methods, have been devised and employed; and in this way demonstration of the reality of these paranormal perceptions has to some extent been made repeatable.

5. **Questions relevant to reports of paranormal occurrences.** If one's interest in reports of ostensibly paranormal occurrences or in observations of them one may personally have made is, as in these pages, the scientific and philosophical rather than the religious or sentimental, then certain questions present themselves which it is important to distinguish and to keep in mind.

They fall into four groups according as they concern (a) the *genuineness* or *spuriousness* of a given ostensibly paranormal occurrence; or (b) the *testimony* available for the occurrence of a putative instance of a paranormal kind of phenomenon; or (c) the *observation* made by the witness of the particular occurrence concerned; or (d) what the occurrence, if genuinely paranormal and if correctly observed and reported, *signifies*.

Let us examine each of these more particularly.

(a) That a given apparently paranormal occurrence is *genuinely* so means that the manner of its production really constitutes an exception to some one of the "basic limiting principles" stated by Broad. On the other hand, that it is *spurious* means that the manner of its production is really normal, or perhaps merely abnormal in the sense of unusual; but is not paranormal, i.e., does not, but only seems to, violate one of those limiting principles.

If it is spurious, it may be so because of *deliberate fraud* on the part of the purported medium or of some other person; or because of *unconscious fraud* by a medium or by someone else present. Unconscious fraud in the case of a physical phenomenon could mean for example, that the medium, in a trance state akin to somnambulism, is using his hands or some other normal means of moving objects without realizing that, for the purposes of the occasion, this is illegitimate though it is quite natural from the standpoint of the dreamed situation that constitutes the content of his consciousness at the moment.

Deliberate fraud in the matter of communications allegedly from spirits would mean that, in so far as the content of the communication corresponds to true facts relating to the deceased and peculiar enough to identify him, those facts had previously been ascertained in some normal manner by the supposed medium.

(b) Concerning now the *reports* that are made of particular supposedly paranormal occurrences, the questions to be answered are those relevant to the validity and the value of *testimony* in general. They are (1) whether the witness is *truthful*, i.e., not deliberately mendacious; (2) whether he is *objective*, i.e., impartial not biased by wishful belief in the occurrence or non-occurrence of phenomena of the kind he testifies he perceived or failed to perceive; (3) whether the report is *precise, detailed,* and *full,* rather than vague, superficial, or inclusive only of the more striking features of what occurred or of the conditions under which it was observed; and (4) whether the report *is, or is based on, a record* made at the time the occurrence was being witnessed; or if not, made then how soon after; or on no record but only on what is remembered at the time the report is written.

(c) As regards the *observer* as such, rather than as reporter, the main question would be whether he has, and used, the possibly special critical powers necessary for competence to perceive correctly what occurred, under the conditions that existed at the time. Such critical powers would include familiarity with the psychology of hypnosis and of hallucinations; also, familiarity with the devices or accessories employed in conjuring tricks; and, more generally, with the psychology of illusions of perception. The latter has to do with the *practical* difficulty under some circumstances of distinguishing, in what one believes oneself to be perceiving, between what is *strictly* being observed and what is automatically and unconsciously being added to it—i.e., supplied by one's past experience of what did occur in various past cases to which the present one is similar in obvious but perhaps unessential respects. The performances of illusionists make one perceive things that are really not occurring; and thus bring acutely home the extent of what, in perception, is *supplied by* interpretation based on habit and on the expectations it generates, as distinguished from what is strictly and literally *observed.* This additive activity, however, occurs not only when one witnesses conjuring tricks, but constantly. But, in most though not in all ordinary instances of it, what it supplies is correct instead erroneous.

It should be mentioned in this general connection that experimenting parapsychologists, and the research officers or research committees of the societies for psychical research, are in general familiar with and fairly expert at guarding against the various sources of possible error that were considered in what precedes. The purported paranormal phenomena brought to their attention are investigated usually with care and competence. Hence although the accounts of them published in the proceedings and journals of those societies are not necessarily beyond question;

nevertheless they cannot as a rule be just shrugged off as probably naive. To do so is what would be naive.

(d) Finally comes the question as to what a given occurrence, if genuinely paranormal and correctly observed and reported, *signifies;* i.e., what the true explanation of it is. For example, in the case of precognition, what does it signify as to the relation between causality and time. Or, in that of "out-of-the-body" experiences, do they signify that man's mind is detachable from and capable of existing and of functioning independently of his body. Again, in the case of telekinesis, of levitation, or of so-called "poltergeist" phenomena, is the occurrence due to paranormal psychokinetic action by excarnate "spirits" whether human or other; or to such action by some dissociated part of the medium's personality. Or, in the case of communications purportedly from spirits of the dead, is what they really signify only that the medium has paranormal capacities of telepathy, clairvoyance, or retrocognition which—rather than communication from the deceased—supply him with the recondite correct information the communications contain. Or, on the other hand, do these really emanate from some part of the personality of the deceased that has survived the death of his body; and if so what specific part, and in just what sense can it be said to be still "living."

Chapter XVI

PARANORMAL OCCURRENCES, SCIENCE, AND SCIENTISTS

In the next two chapters, some well-attested concrete examples of the kinds of paranormal occurrences that appear to constitute empirical evidence of survival will be cited and discussed. But the occurrences the reports describe are so shocking to the scientific commonsense of the present epoch that some remarks are called for at this point concerning the relation of paranormal occurrences to science, and concerning the attitude prevalent among scientists towards reports of them.

1. **Reports of paranormal occurrences commonly dismissed offhand by scientists.** During the last seventy-five years, many facts which there is strong reason to regard as paranormal have been recorded as a result of painstaking investigations made by some highly capable individuals, by the societies for psychical research, and more recently by the parapsychology laboratories. The majority of scientists, however, still do not bother to acquaint themselves with those facts, or at most only superficially; and yet are in general ready to dismiss on *a priori* grounds any reports of them, much as Faraday did reports of levitation when he wrote: "Before we proceed to consider any question involving physical principles, we should set out with *clear ideas* of the naturally possible and impossible." Premising then that creation or destruction of force is impossible, Faraday went on to declare that since levitation of an object "without effort" would constitute creation of force, it therefore "cannot be."[1] As the late Professor James H. Hyslop, founder of the American Society for Psychical Research, wrote some forty years ago, "Science, content, without thorough inquiry, to confine its investigations to the

---

[1] *Experimental Researches in Chemistry and Physics*, London 1859, pp. 478-9.

physical world in which it has achieved so much, will not open its eyes to anomalies in the realm of mind and nature and so degenerates into a dogmatism exactly like that of theology."[2]

The following recent statement by an eminent biologist may be cited as a quaint example of such ingenuous dogmatism: "Bordering all branches of science there is of course a 'lunatic fringe' of wishful thinkers to be found defending some bogus cancer cure, mysterious radiation effect, or species of dualism. Among the latter should be classed postulates of cellular intelligence or memory, vital force, perfecting principle, cosmic purpose, extrasensory perception ("ESP"), telepathy, telekinesis, clairvoyance. . ."[3]

These words, of course, automatically relegate offhand to the "lunatic fringe" of science such naturalists and biologists as Alfred Russel Wallace, Charles Richet, Hans Driesch, H. S. Jennings; such physicists as Sir William Crookes, Lord Rayleigh, Sir Oliver Lodge; the astronomer Camille Flammarion; and philosophers like Henry Sidgwick, William James, and Henri Bergson—to mention only a few of the eminent men who have thought that some of the things listed by Prof. Muller deserve serious consideration. If because of this these men belong to the lunatic fringe of science, then many of us would be proud to find ourselves included in it on the same grounds.[4]

2. **What accounts for the dogmatism of scientists on the subject of paranormal events.** Statements by scientists, such as that of Prof. Muller quoted above, compel us to ask what accounts for the dogmatism they exemplify; for the truly scientific attitude is not dogmatic but open-minded. It is free alike from adverse and from favorable prejudice. It welcomes facts as such, no matter whether they confirm or invalidate the assumptions or theories on which they have bearing. Its first commandment is

[2]*Contact with the other world.* The Century Co. New York, 1919, p. 425.

[3]Science Fiction as an Escape, an article by Hermann J. Muller, Nobel prize in biology, President of the American Humanist Association; in *The Humanist*, Vol. XVII:338, No. 6, Nov.-Dec. 1957.

[4]The remarks in the remainder of this chapter were originally presented by the writer as one of the addresses at the Fiftieth Anniversary Celebration of the American Society for Psychical Research, held on March 2, 1956. The addresses were published in the *Journal* of the Society, Vol. L, No. 4. October, 1956.

to investigate and observe. In short, disinterested curiosity—the passion to know the truth—is the one scientific passion. It is a stern censor, which rules out of scientific judgments factors such as arrogance, dogmatism, hopes or fears, and wishful belief or disbelief—factors which so often vitiate the judgments of ordinary men. Such is the scientific attitude. It is altogether admirable, and the command over the forces of nature, which adherence to it and to the methods it dictates has put into the hands of man, testifies to the fruitfulness of that attitude.

But the fact that, in so far as it has actually been the attitude of scientists, they have accomplished wonders; and that these wonders have given magical prestige to the very words, Science, and Scientist—this fact does not at all guarantee that when a man who is by profession a scientist speaks, what he says always represents one of the fruits of scientific investigation. For scientists are men and usually have their share of the typical human frailties. They do park some of these outside the doors of their laboratories, for inside, of course, they either live up to the demands of the scientific attitude as characterized above, or they achieve little. But outside they are as prone as other men to pride of profession and of position; and the prestige with which the name, Scientist, has come to endow them in the public eye easily provides for many of them an irresistible temptation to pontificate concerning various questions which fall outside their professional competence, but about which naive outsiders nevertheless respectfully ask them to speak because they are known as Scientists, and Scientists, by definition, are persons who know! The oracular role which this flattering deference invites them to play leads them almost fatally to assume on such occasions that their utterances have authority; for the idea a person harbors of himself is largely determined by the picture of him which others hold out to him.

Now, that pleasing though mainly subconscious picture of himself as an oracle is what is affronted when outsiders venture to call to the attention of a scientist certain facts, such as those psychical research investigates, which seem to clash with certain assumptions of the science of his time. It is on such occasions that the admirable scientific attitude described above easily deserts him and that, as the late Dr. W. F. Prince charged, proved, and illustrated by quoting the words of some twenty scientists from Faraday, Tyndall and Huxley to less eminent ones—it is on such occasions that the outraged scientist is prone to become unscientifically emotional, obscurantistic, inaccurate, illogical, evasive, dogmatic, and even personally abusive.[5]

3. **Why the paranormal phenomena are regarded as impossible.** The remarks made up to this point about scientists have concerned only the psychological or more specifically the emotional factors that account for the abandonment of the scientific attitude by so many scientists when their attention is invited to the existing evidence, experimental and other, that paranormal phenomena of various kinds really occur. But something must now be said also as to the source of the quite dispassionate firm conviction of many of them that, in the light of modern scientific knowledge, those phenomena cannot possibly be real and can only be semblances, delusions, or frauds.

Let us note first that, when a scientist declares that something, which belongs to the field of his scientific competence, is *possible,* there is no mystery as to the basis of his assertion. It rests either on the fact that he or some other scientist has actually done or observed the thing concerned; or else that it is anyway not incompatible with anything which science has so far established.

Again, when a scientist declares something to be *impossible by certain means under certain conditions,* then the basis of his assertion is likewise not mysterious. It is that he or some other scientist has actually tried to cause that thing in that manner under those conditions, but that it did not in fact then occur.

On the other hand, when a scientist declares something to be impossible, *period;* that is, impossible without qualification, then it is a mystery indeed how he could possibly know this. In such cases, the ground of his assertion is only that occurrence of the thing concerned would clash with some principle which the science of his time has somehow come to accept and which

---

[5]The Enchanted Boundary, *Boston Soc. for Psychic Research,* 1930; see especially pp. 19-133.

is thus part of "the scientific commonsense of the epoch", but which has not in fact been established by science. Such a "principle"—however plausible and however wide its utility as a working assumption—becomes a sheer dogma if the scientist's faith in it is so boundless that it causes him to deny *a priori* or to ignore facts actually observed, that constitute exceptions to it. Assertion that they are impossible because they would clash with it then is pure dogmatism, even if unawares.

The clash of the facts observed may be either with the over-all metaphysical creed of the science of the time or, more narrowly, with one or another of the specific articles of it. These are certain of the "basic limiting principles" of the then current scientific thought, to which reference was made in Sec. 3 of Chapt. XIV, and which the scientist uncritically assumes to have *unlimited* validity, whereas what scientific experience would really warrant him in concluding would be only that it has *very wide* validity.

4. **Clash of a reported occurrence with the metaphysical creed of the natural sciences.** The reference made above to "the over-all metaphysical creed of the science of the time" calls for some words of explanation; for a scientist is likely to deny emphatically that science has any truck with that vain and vaporous thing called Metaphysics, which he is more than glad to leave to philosophers or other unscientific thinkers.

As Prof. Ch. Perelman has pointedly remarked somewhere, however, a person's repudiation and scorn of metaphysics is no guarantee•that he does not himself harbor unawares some metaphysical creed—in which case he is the more helplessly captive in that mental prison because he does not suspect its existence or perceive its walls.

How this is possible becomes evident as soon as one realizes what constitutes a metaphysical creed. It is something which, if put into words, takes the form: "To be real is to have characteristic C." The word "real," as occurring in it, is essentially *a value term,* which specifically means "supremely or alone existent, important or significant." Hence, to *have* a metaphysical creed is to proceeed in all one's activities and judgments, *and whether consciously or unawares,* under the assumption that only what has characteristic C exists, or at least is worth taking into consideration. This is what "to be real" means in, for example, the metaphysical creed that to be real is to be some *material* event, process, or thing, (whether at the macroscopic, directly perceivable level, or at the atomic or sub-atomic levels explored by theoretical physics.)[6] And just this materialistic metaphysical creed is, in fact, that of most of the practitioners of the natural sciences—physics, chemistry, astronomy, biology, physiological and behavioristic psychology, and the rest.

It is harbored by them, however, without recognition of the fact that it simply consists of their personal inclination and commitment to dedicate their efforts to the investigation of only the material part of the world, and hence to ignore or deny mental events as such, or at least deny them any efficacy.

The material world, of course, is highly important to us, and study of it by scientific methods has yielded a vast amount of valuable knowledge. The scientists who have elected the material world as their field of exploration can justly be proud of what they have achieved; and one can readily understand that their prolonged attention to it should have brought them to the point of being psychologically unable to notice or even conceive of any facts, events, or processes other than material ones; and hence should have made them unable to suppose that any material event should have a cause or an effect other than one itself material.

This psychological incapacity, however, is only an occupational disease, which does not at all guarantee that there are not "really" such things as thoughts, feelings, mental images, volitions, and other psychological states. It only compels the scientists who are captives within the invisible walls of the materialistic metaphysical creed to assign at any cost a purely material meaning to the words which denote those psychological states. For if one proceeds from the start and all along on the arbitrary metaphysical assumption that nothing is real unless it is some process or part of the material world, i.e., of the perceptually

---

[6]For more detailed discussion of what "real" means as employed in the formulation of a metaphysical creed, see the writer's *Nature, Mind, and Death*, chapt. 6, and in particular Sec. 8 thereof.

public world, then necessarily thoughts, feelings, and the other states accessible only to introspection are conceived either as unreal, i.e., as inefficacious mere appearances; or else as themselves somehow material events.

It is, of course, perfectly legitimate and proper to push as far as it is successful the attempt to account in purely material terms for all material events, including all the activities of human bodies. But at the many points in, for example, human willed acts, where no material event can be observed that would account for those acts, there is no rational justification for insisting wilfully that their causes *must*, somehow, anyhow, be material events; so that when, for example, I wrote the present words, my thoughts and my desire to formulate them in writing cannot possibly have been what caused the writing of these words. What accounts for but does not justify that insistence is only the quite arbitrary metaphysical creed, harbored and uncritically cherished by most natural scientists, that only what is material is real and can have efficacy; and therefore that not only the vast majority of material events, but all—absolutely all without exception— must have purely material causes.

Nothing but Prof. Muller's pious adhesion to that particular metaphysical creed dictated his naive relegation of dualism, of extrasensory perception, and of any but material explanations, to the "lunatic fringe" of science. For of course to ascribe some material event to a mental cause *is cheating* at the game in which he like other natural scientists are engaged, to wit, that of seeking *material* explanations for all material events; just as, while playing chess, moving the king two steps at a time would be cheating. Yet the fact that it would be cheating *at chess* is not evidence at all that the king is inherently incapable of being moved more than one step at a time! Similarly, that to ascribe to a mental cause a material event not in fact otherwise explained *is* cheating *at the material-science game,* is no evidence at all that causation of that material event by a mental event is inherently impossible.

The substance of the following remarks may be put both summarily and picturesquely in the apt words used by Professor C. D. Broad in the preface to his Tarner Lectures at Cambridge

University in 1923. What he said there was that the scientists who regard the phenomena investigated by psychical researchers as impossible seem to him to confuse the Author of Nature with the Editor of the scientific periodical, *Nature;* or at any rate seem to suppose that there can be no productions of the former that would not be accepted for publication by the latter!

Chapter XVII

INSTANCES OF OCCURRENCES *PRIMA FACIE* INDICATIVE OF SURVIVAL

1. **Apparitions and hauntings.** Apparitions, some precognitions or retrocognitions, and also the so-called "projections" or "out-of-the-body" experiences, all putatively come under the technical psychological category of hallucinations, that is, of "abnormal misinterpretations of ideational experiences as perceptions . . . . . in hallucination the error of perception goes so far as to suppose facts present to a sense which is actually receiving no relevant stimulation."[1]

More explicitly, a hallucination is essentially a mental image —visual, auditory, tactual, or/and other—that has the vividness of a sensation and that, as usual in the case of sensations, is automatically taken to be perception of a physical object or event, although none such as perceived is actually stimulating the relevant sense organ (s). Ordinary dreams are the most common hallucinations: in them, physical objects seem to be perceived and, until one awakens, are not realized to have been physically non-existent. Hallucinations thus are not inherently pathological but only sometimes so (as, for example, in *delirium tremens.*)

To say that an experience is, or is only, a hallucination is, of course, not at all to account for its content or for its occurrence, but is merely to say, as made clear above, that the experience is *not* due to stimulation of the relevant sense organ (s) at the time by a physical object of the kind seemingly perceived. Nor does an experience's being a hallucination in the least dispose of the question whether the experience is *veridical* in the sense of being a true sign of some fact it appears to signify, e.g., of some crisis being faced by the person whose apparition is perceived; or of some future or past occurrence, as in precogni-

---

[1]H. C. Warren: *Dictionary of Psychology.* Houghton Mifflin Co. Boston, 1934.

tion or retrocognition; or, as in "out-of-the-body" experiences, of actual observation of one's own body and of other things— extrasensorily but accurately—from a point distant in space from the body.

This is important to remember when a particular hallucination is more specifically characterized, perhaps, as oneiric, or as hypnagogic, or hypnopompic; or (as in the case of "out-of-the-body" experiences) as heautoscopic, etc.; for these adjectives are names only of sub-classes of hallucinations, not at all of causes or of processes that would account for the particular content of the hallucination, or dispose of the possibility of its being veridical in the sense stated above.

With these words of caution in mind we may now consider first some concrete instances of the putatively hallucinatory experiences commonly termed apparitions of the dead. I say "putatively" because the possibility must not be ruled out *a priori* that apparitions are material even if only tenuously so as compared with the "materializations" we shall consider later.

In Chapter II we had occasion to cite an exceptionally well attested case of the kind of paranormal occurrence generally regarded by those who witness it as most evidential of survival of the human personality, namely, "ghosts," or "apparitions of the dead."

The case was that of the numerous apparitions at the beginning of the 19th century of the form of the deceased Mrs. Butler in a Maine village, to which the Rev. Abraham Cummings (A. M. Brown University 1776) had proceeded in order to expose what he had assumed must be a hoax. He, however, was then himself met in a field by what he terms "the Spectre." His statement of this meeting reads: "Sometime in July 1806, in the evening I was informed by two persons that they had just seen the Spectre in the field. About ten minutes after, I went out, not to see a miracle, for I believed that they had been mistaken. Looking toward an eminence, twelve rods distance from the house, I saw there, as I supposed, one of the white rocks. This confirmed my opinion of their spectre, and I paid no more attention to it. Three minutes after, I accidentally looked in the same direction, and the white rock was in the air; its form a complete

Globe, white with a tincture of red, like the damask rose, and its diameter about two feet. Fully satisfied that this was nothing ordinary, I went toward it for more accurate examination. While my eye was constantly upon it, I went on four or five steps, when it came to me from the distance of eleven rods, as quick as lightning, and instantly assumed a personal form with a female dress, but did not appear taller than a girl seven years old. While I looked upon her, I said in my mind, 'you are not tall enough for the woman who has so frequently appeared among us!' Immediately she grew up as large and as tall as I considered that woman to be. Now she appeared glorious. On her head was the representation of the sun diffusing the luminous, rectilinear rays every way to the ground. Through the rays I saw the personal form and the woman's dress."[2]

In the pamphlet the Rev. Mr. Cummings reproduces some thirty affidavits which he had obtained at the time from persons who had seen or/and heard the Spectre; for the apparition spoke, and delivered discourses sometimes over an hour long. Some of the witnesses believed the apparition was from Satan, others from God. It presented itself sometimes "to one alone . . . . sometimes she appeared to two or three; then to five or six; then to ten or twelve; again to twenty; and once to more than forty witnesses. She appeared in several apartments of Mr. Blaisdel's house, and several times in the open field . . . There, white as the light, she moved like a cloud above the ground in personal form and magnitude, and in the presence of more than forty people. She tarried with them till after daylight, and vanished" (p. 29). On one occasion, one of the men present, Capt. Butler, "put his hand upon it and it passed down through the apparition as through a body of light, in the view of six or seven witnesses" (p. 30). Several of the witnesses report, as does the Rev. Mr. Cummings, that the apparition begins as a formless small luminous cloud, which then grows and in a moment takes the form of the deceased Mrs. Butler. (This incidentally, was what occurred when; over fifty years ago in New York, the present writer wit-

---

nessed in red light but not under test conditions a purported gradual materialization of a man's body.)

The *prima facie* evidence of survival provided by an apparition is greatest when it supplies information that was unknown to the percipent. Among a number of well attested reports of just this, two, which are so clear-cut that they have become classics in this field, may be cited briefly.

One is of the case of a travelling salesman, whose sister had died in 1867, and who in 1876 was in his hotel room at noon in St. Joseph, Mo. smoking a cigar and writing up the orders he had obtained: "I suddenly became conscious that some one was sitting on my left, with one arm resting on the table. Quick as a flash I turned and distinctly saw the form of my dead sister, and for a brief second or so looked her squarely in the face; and so sure was I that it was she, that I sprang forward in delight calling her by name, and, as I did so, the apparition instantly vanished . . . I was near enough to touch her . . . and noted her features, expression, and details of dress, etc. She appeared as alive."

He was so moved by the experience that he cut his trip short and returned to his home in St. Louis, where he related the occurrence to his parents, mentioning among other details of the apparition that on the right side of the girl's nose he had noticed a bright red scratch about three fourths of an inch long. "When I mentioned this," he states, "my mother rose trembling to her feet and nearly fainted away, and . . . . with tears streaming down her face, she exclaimed that I had indeed seen my sister, as no living mortal but herself was aware of that scratch, which she had accidentally made while doing some little act of kindness after my sister's death. She said she well remembered how pained she was to think she should have, unintentionally, marred the features of her dead daughter, and that unknown to all, she had carefully obliterated all traces of the slight scratch with the aid of powder, etc., and that she had never mentioned it to a human being from that day to this."[3]

---

[3]A full account of the case appears in Vol. VI:17-20, *S.P.R. Proceedings*, 1889-90. It is reproduced in F. W. H. Myer's *Human Personality and its Survival of Bodily Death*, Vol. II:27-30.

The other famous case—the Chaffin will case—concerns not a similarly waking vision, but one occurring as either a vivid dream, or in a state between waking and dreaming. The essential facts are as follows. On November 16, 1905, James L. Chaffin, a North Carolina farmer, made a will attested by two witnesses, in which he left his farm to his son Marshall, the third of his four sons; and nothing to the other three or to his wife. On January 16; 1919, however, he made a new will, not witnessed but legally valid because wholly in his own handwriting. In it, he stated first that it was being made after his reading of the 27th chapter of Genesis; and then that he wanted his property divided equally between his four children, and that they must take care of their mother. He then placed this holograph will at the 27th chapter of Genesis in a Bible that had belonged to his father, folding over the pages to enclose the will.

He died on September 7, 1921, without, so far as ascertainable, ever having mentioned to anybody the existence of the second will. The first will was not contested and was probated on the 24th of the same month by its beneficiary, Marshall Chaffin.

Some four years later, in June, 1925, the second son, James Pinkney Chaffin began to have very vivid dreams that his father appeared to him at his bedside, without speaking. Later that month, however, the father again appeared at the bedside, wearing a familiar black overcoat, and then spoke, saying "you will find my will in my overcoat pocket." In the morning, James looked for the overcoat, but was told by his mother that it had been given to his brother John, who lived twenty miles away. Some days later, James went to his brother's house, found the coat, and examined it. The inside lining of the inside pocket had been stitched together. On cutting the stitches, he found a little roll of paper on which, in his father's handwriting, were written only the words: "Read the 27th chapter of Genesis in my Daddie's old Bible." He then returned to his mother's house, accompanied by his daughter, by a neighbor, and by the neighbor's daughter. They had some trouble finding the old Bible, but when they finally did, and the neighbor opened it at the 27th chapter of Genesis, they found the second will. The testator's wife and James P. Chaffin's wife were also present at the time. The second will was admitted to probate in December of the same year.[4]

Hauntings are apparitions that recur and that seem to be connected with a place rather than intended for a particular witness. A famous, well-attested case is that of the Morton ghost. It is described by Miss R. C. Morton (pseudonym) in Vol. VIII, 1892, of the S.P.R. Proceedings, pp. 311/332, who at that time was a medical student and apparently viewed the occurrences without fear or nervousness but only with scientific curiosity. The case dates back to 1882.

Miss Morton states that, having one evening gone up to her room, she heard someone at the door, opened it, and saw in the passage the figure of a tall lady, dressed in black, whose face was hidden by a handkerchief held in her right hand. She descended the stairs and Miss Morton followed; but the small piece of candle she carried went out, and she returned to her room. The figure was seen again half a dozen times during the next two years by Miss Morton, once by her sister Mrs. K, once by the housemaid, and once by Miss Morton's brother and by a boy. After the first apparition, Miss Morton made it a practice to follow the figure downstairs into the drawing room. She spoke to the apparition but never got any reply; she cornered it several times in order to touch it, but it then simply disappeared. Its footsteps were audible and characteristic, and were heard by Miss Morton's three sisters and by the cook. Miss Morton stretched some threads across the stairs, but the figure passed right through them without detaching them. The figure was seen in the orchard by a neighbor as well as in the house by Miss Morton's sisters E. and M., by the cook, by the charwoman, and by a parlormaid, and by the gardener. But Miss Morton's father could not see it even when he was shown where it stood. The apparition was seen during the day as well as at night. In all about twenty people saw it, some of them many times; and some of them not having previously heard of the apparition or of the sounds. The figure was described in the same way by all. The apparitions con-

---

[4]*Proc. of S.P.R.*, Vol. 36:517-24, 1927.

tinued to occur until 1889. The figure wore widow's cuffs, and corresponded to the description of a former tenant of the house, Mrs. S., whose life there had been unhappy.

The weight of apparitions as evidence of survival is decreased by the fact that there are numerous cases on record of apparitions of the living. Many of them are cited in Gurney, Myers, and Podmore's *Phantasms of the Living*.[5] Like apparitions in general, they are most impressive when more than one of the percipient's senses is affected—for instance, touch and hearing, or touch and sight. Several such cases are described on pp. 446 ff. of the book just cited. One is that of a girl, reading at night in her room, who suddenly "felt" (heard?) some one come into the room but, looking, could see no one. Then, she writes, "I felt a *kiss* on my forehead—a lingering, loving pressure. I looked up without the least sensation of fear, and saw my lover standing behind my chair, stooping as if to kiss me again. His face was very white and inexpressibly sad. As I rose from my chair in great surprise, before I could speak, he had gone, how I do not know; I only know that, one moment I saw him, saw distinctly every feature of his face, saw the tall figure and broad shoulders as clearly as I ever saw them in my life, and the next moment there was no sign of him" (p. 447). A few days later, she heard that her lover had at the time been riding a vicious horse which, in order to unseat him, reared perfectly straight and pressed its back against a wall, with him between, making him lose consciousness — his last thought having been that he was dying and that he wanted to see his fiancee again before he died. It turned out, however, that only his hand had been severely injured, so that, for some days, he could not write to tell her what had occurred.

Such cases of apparitions of the living, veridical in the sense stated earlier, are most plausibly accounted for as telepathically caused hallucinations since they cannot really be apparitions of the dead. If, however, they are considered together with the cases of "out-of-the-body" experience — so-called "projection of the double"—of which instances are cited in Sec. 2 of the present

---

[5] In two vols. 1886. Abridged edition prepared by Mrs. Henry Sidgwick. One vol. 1918, Kegan Paul, Trench, Trubner and Co. London; E. P. Dutton and Co., New York.

chapter, then what suggests itself is that what is seen in cases of apparitions — whether of the living or of the dead — is the "projected," i.e., externalized, "double" assumed to be possessed by man but to be normally collocated with the body. It is conjectured that at death the dislocation of it from the body is complete and permanent, whereas in apparitions of the living, the dislocation is temporary and incomplete in that a connection— the reported "silver thread"—remains between the externalized "double" and the body. If this should actually be the state of affairs, then apparitions would not really be visual hallucinations, but rather *sights,* fleeting but genuine, of something very tenuous though objectively present at the place where it is perceived.

In the way of this supposition, however, stands a fact to which we shall have occasion to return; namely that, since apparitions are seldom if ever naked, then their clothes too would have to be supposed to have an externalizable "double."

But even when telepathy is admitted to be a fact and is invoked, apparitions veridical in the sense stated remain very difficult to explain plausibly. How difficult will be appreciated by readers who may be interested to look up the seemingly far-fetched explanations to which able thinkers have found themselves forced to have recourse when they have insisted on taking scrupulously into consideration *all* the facts on record.[6]

2. **"Out-of-the-body" experiences.** Let us turn next to the "out-of-the-body," experiences alluded to in the latter part of the preceding section, of which many cases have been reported. Those who have undergone the experience generally consider it impressive evidence that the human consciousness is separable in space from the human body and, it would therefore seem, can exist independently of the latter. That experience has variously

---

[6]*Apparitions,* by G. N. M. Tyrrell, with a preface by H. H. Price; Gerald Duckworth and Co. Ltd., revised edition, 1953; A Theory of apparitions, by W. F. Barrett, E. Gurney, and F. Podmore, *Proc. S.P.R.* Vol. II:109-36; 1884. Six theories about apparitions, by Hornell Hart, *Proc. S.P.R.,* 1955-56 pp. 153-239. For additional references on the subject of apparitions, see G. Zorab's Bibliography of Parapsychology, Parapsychology Found'n. Inc. New York 1957, pp. 27-8. Concerning Haunting, see H. H. Price's presidential address to the S.P.R.; *Proc. S.P.R.* Vol. XLV:307-343, 1938-39.

been termed projection of "the double," "ESP projection," projection of the astral body," "out-of-the-body" experience, and "bilocation." In the most striking form of it, the person concerned, having gone to sleep or being under anaesthesia, wakens to see his body inert on the bed and is able to observe it from the same variety of angles as he could the body of another. He is also able to observe the various objects in the room, and in some cases he perceives and is later able to describe persons who came into the room and went out before his body awoke. The thus temporarily excarnate observer may or may not find himself able to travel away from the vicinity of his sleeping body. In some of the cases when he does so and visits a distant place, he is reported to have been seen at that place at the time. These are the cases of "bilocation." A famous one is that of Alfonso de Liguori who in 1774 was at Arezzo, in prison, fasting. On awakening one morning, he stated that he had been at the bedside of the then dying Pope, Clement XIV; where, it turned out, he had been seen by those present.

For the sake of concreteness, a few of the many reports of out-of-the-body experience will now be cited.

Dr. E. Osty, in the May-June issue of the *Revue Métapsychique* for 1930, quotes a letter addressed by a gentleman named L. L. Hymans to Charles Richet, dated June 7, 1928, in which the former relates two such experiences: "The first time it was while in a dentist's chair. Under anaesthesia, I had the sensation of awaking and of finding myself floating in the upper part of the room, from where, with great astonishment, I watched the dentist working on my body, and the anaesthetist at his side. I saw my inanimate body as distinctly as any other object in the room . . . The second time I was in a hotel in London. I awoke in the morning feeling unwell (I have a weak heart) and shortly thereafter I fainted. Greatly to my astonishment, I found myself in the upper part of the room, from where, with fear, I beheld my body inanimate in the bed with its eyes closed. I tried without success to reenter my body and concluded that I had died . . . Certainly I had not lost either memory or self-consciousness. I could see my inanimate body like a separate object: I was able to look at my face. I was, however, unable to leave the room; I felt myself as it were chained, immobilized in the corner where I was. After an hour or two I heard a knock on the locked door several times, without being able to answer. Soon after, the hotel porter appeared on the fire escape. I saw him get into the room, look anxiously at my face, and open the door. The hotel manager and others then entered. A physician came in. I saw him shake his head after listening to my heart, and then insert a spoon between my lips. I then lost consciousness and awoke in the bed." In the same article, Dr. Osty cites the similar experiences of two other persons.

Dr. Ernesto Bozzano cites the case of a friend of his, the engineer Giuseppe Costa who, while asleep, so disturbed the kerosene lamp on his bedside table that it filled the room with dense, choking smoke. Signor Costa writes: "I had the clear and precise sensation of finding myself with only my thinking personality, in the middle of the room, *completely separated from my body,* which continued to lie on the bed . . . I was seized with an inexpressible anguish from which I felt intuitively that I could only free myself by freeing my material body from that oppressive situation. I wanted therefore to pick up the lamp and open the window, but it was a material act that I could not accomplish . . . Then I thought of my mother, who was sleeping in the next room . . . It seemed to me that no effort of any kind was needed to cause her to approach my body. I saw her get hurriedly out of bed, run to her window and open it . . . then leave her room, walk along the corridor, enter my room and approach my body gropingly and with staring eyes." He then awoke. He writes further: "My mother, questioned by me soon after the event, confirmed the fact that she had first opened her window as if she felt herself suffocating, before coming to my aid. Now the fact of my *having seen this act of hers through the wall,* while lying *inanimate on the bed,* entirely excludes the hypothesis of hallucination and nightmare . . . I thus had the most evident proof that *my soul had detached itself from my body during its material existence.* I had, in fact, received proof of the existence of the soul and also of its immortality, since it was true that it had freed itself . . . from the material envelope of the body, acting and thinking outside it."[7] In order to explain this case, however, telepathy plus clairvoyance would be enough.

In some persons, out-of-the-body experience becomes voluntary. The best known account of the process involved is that of the late Sylvan Muldoon,[8] whose description of his own experiences brought him numerous communications from strangers who had themselves had out-of-the-body experiences. Many of these are quoted by him in a later book,[9] including one which, some years before that book appeared, was related to the present writer by the person concerned, Miss Mary Ellen Frallic. Her "projection" experience occurred not during sleep or under anaesthesia, but while walking on the street. She gradually became conscious of rising higher and higher, up to the height of the second floor of the surrounding buildings, and then felt an urge to look back; whereupon she saw her body walking about one block behind. That body was apparently able to see "her" for she noticed the look of bewilderment on its face. Her consciousness of location then shifted a few times from that of the "double" to that of the body, and back, each being able to perceive the other. She then felt afraid, and immediately reentered her body.[10]

Besides Muldoon's account of voluntary "projections," one of the most interesting is by a Frenchman who, under the pseudonym, Yram, wrote in 1926 a book entitled "The Physician of the Soul," which has since been translated under the title *Practical Astral Projection*. In it he describes twelve years of his own experimentation in conscious out-of-the-body experience. Another writer, Oliver Fox, in a book entitled *Astral Projection*, related his own experiences.[11]

---

[7]Quoted in Bozzano's *Discarnate Influence in Human Life*, pp. 112-15, from Giuseppe Costa's *Di la della Vita*, p. 18.

[8]*The Projection of the Astral Body*, David McKay Co. Philadelphia, 1929.

[9]*The Phenomena of Astral Projection*, by Sylvan Muldoon and Hereward Carrington, Rider and Co., London, 1951.

[10]Cf. *op. cit.* pp. 189-90.

[11]Rider and Co. London (no date) A number of interesting cases are quoted in some detail on pp. 220-29 of Dr. Raynor C. Johnson's *The Imprisoned Splendour*, Harper and Bros. New York, 1953. A bibliography of the subject is furnished on pp. 221-22 of Muldoon and Carrington's *The Phenomena of Astral Projection*.

In a number of cases, the projected "double" is reported to remain connected with the sleeping body by a "silver cord" which is extensible in various degrees. Persons who have had the out-of-the-body experience have usually assumed, as did the engineer Giuseppe Costa quoted above, that the spatial separation in it of the observing and thinking consciousness from the body on the bed means that the former is capable of existing and of functioning independently of the latter not only thus temporarily during "projection," but enduringly at death, which is then simply permanent, definitive projection when the "silver cord" snaps.

This conclusion, however, does not necessarily follow, for it tacitly assumes that the conscious "double" is what animates the body—normally in being collocated with it, but also, when dislocated from it, through connection with it by the "silver cord." The fact, however, could equally be that the animation is in the converse direction, i.e., that death of the body entails death of the conscious "double" whether the latter be at the time dislocated from or collocated with the former.

Hence, out-of-the-body experience, however impressive to those who have it, and however it may tempt them to conclude that they then know that consciousness is not dependent on the living material body, does not really warrant this conclusion; but only the more modest one, which, of course, is arresting enough, that correct visual perception of physical events and objects, including perception of one's own body from a point distant in space from it, can occur, exceptionally, at times when the eyes are shut and the body asleep—this fact, of course, not being at all explained by labelling the occurrences of it "heautoscopic hallucinations" since, as pointed out earlier, what is paranormal, instead of merely abnormal, in certain hallucinations is that they are *veridical* in the same sense in which perceptions are so, even if not through the same mechanism.

3. Materializations and other paranormal physical phenomena. Among paranormal phenomena, certain physical ones —especially materializations and the so-called "direct voice"—are easily accepted by persons who witness them as evidence of survival. There are numerous reports, some of them circumstantial and made by careful and experienced observers, of the materialization of portions of human bodies—of hands, for example, which move and grasp and carry things; or of faces or even of entire bodies which act, speak, and breathe like ordinary living human bodies; and after a while dematerialize, suddenly or slowly.

Sir William Crookes, for instance, in an article he published in the Quarterly Journal of Science[12] writes: "A beautifully formed small hand rose up from an opening in a dining table and gave me a flower; it appeared and then disappeared three times at intervals, affording me ample opportunity of satisfying myself that it was as real in appearance as my own. This occurred in the light in my own room, whilst I was holding the medium's hands and feet. On another occasion a small hand and arm, like a baby's, appeared playing about a lady who was sitting next to me. It then passed to me and patted my arm and pulled my coat several times. At another time a finger and thumb were seen to pick the petals from a flower in Mr. Home's button-hole and lay them in front of several persons who were sitting near him . . . I have more than once seen, first an object move, then a luminous cloud appear to form about it, and lastly, the cloud condense into shape and become a perfectly-formed hand . . . At the wrist, or arm, it becomes hazy, and fades off into a luminous cloud. To the touch the hand sometimes appears icy cold and dead, at other times warm and life-like, grasping my own with the firm pressure of an old friend. I have retained one of these hands in my own, firmly resolved not to let it escape. There was no struggle or effort made to get loose, but it gradually seemed to resolve itself into vapour and faded in that manner from my grasp."

Among the materializations of entire bodies that have been reported, those of "Katie King," repeatedly observed by Sir William Crookes under his own conditions as well as by others, and measured, auscultated, tested and photographed by him—

---

[12]Notes of an Enquiry into the Phenomena called Spiritual during the years 1870-73. Reprinted with other articles by Crookes under the title *Researches in the Phenomena of Spiritualism*, Two Worlds Pub'g. Co. 1926. The quotation is from pp. 102-3.

Florence Cook being the medium—are probably the most famous and most carefully described.[13]

The apparent materialization, in whole or in part, of human bodies and of their clothing and accoutrements, is supposed to depend on and to consist at least in part of a mysterious substance that emanates from the medium's body, and to which the name of "ectoplasm" has therefore been given. It seems able to exert or to conduct force. It is said to have various consistencies —sometimes vaporous, sometimes filmy like a veil, sometimes gelatinous, sometimes pasty like thick dough.

The latter was its consistency on the one occasion when in the house of a friend of mine I personally had an opportunity to see in good red light, to touch, and take ten flash light photographs of a substance emanating from the mouth of an entranced non-professional medium; which substance, whether or not it was "ectoplasm," did not behave, feel, or look as any other substance known to me could, I think, have done under the conditions that existed. It was coldish, about like steel. This made it seem moist, but it was dry and slightly rough like dough the surface of which had dried. Its consistency and weight were also dough-like. It was a string, of about pencil thickness, varying in length from some six to twelve feet. On other photographs, not taken by me, of the same medium, it has veil-like and rope-like forms.

Professor Charles Richet, who had many occasions to observe what appeared to be materializations, discusses at one point in his *Thirty Years of Psychical Research*[14] the possibilities of fraud in purported materializations and the precautions necessary to preclude it; and he concludes that, in the case of the best of the available reports of the phenomenon—a number of which he mentions—neither fraud nor illusion is a possible explanation: "When I recall the precautions that all of us have taken, not once, but twenty, a hundred, or even a thousand times, it is inconceivable that we should have been deceived on all these occasions."

Concerning occurrences he personally observed under especially favorable conditions, he writes: "Sometimes these ecto-

[13]*Loc. cit.* pp. 115-28.
[14]Collins and Sons, London, 1923, p. 460. English translation by Stanley De Brath, p. 467.

plasms can be seen in process of organization; I have seen an almost rectilinear prolongation emerge from Eusapia's body, its termination acting like a living hand . . . . I have . . . been able to see the first lineaments of materializations as they were formed. A kind of liquid or pasty jelly emerges from the mouth or the breast of Marthe which organizes itself by degrees, acquiring the shape of a face or a limb. Under very good conditions of visibility, I have seen this paste spread on my knee, and slowly take form so as to show the rudiment of the radius, the cubitus, or metacarpal bone whose increasing pressure I could feel on my knee."[15]

The *prima facie* most impressive evidence there could be of the survival of a deceased friend or relative would be to see and touch his materialized, recognizable bodily form, which then speaks in his or her characteristic manner. This is what appeared to occur in my presence on an occasion three or four years ago when, during some two hours and in very good red light throughout, some eighteen fully material forms—some male, some female, some tall and some short, and sometimes two together—came out of and returned to the curtained cabinet I had inspected beforehand, in which a medium sat, and to which I had found no avenue of surreptitious access.

These material forms were apparently recognized as those of a deceased father, mother, or other relative by one or another of the fourteen or fifteen persons present; and some touching scenes occurred, in which the form of the deceased spoke with and caressed the living.

One of those forms called my name and, when I went up to her and asked who she was, she answered "Mother." She did not, however, speak, act, or in the least resemble my mother. This was no disappointment to me since I had gone there for purposes not of consolation but of observation. I would have felt fully rewarded if the conditions of observation had been such that I could have been quite sure that the material form I saw, that spoke to me and patted me on the head, was genuinely a materialization, no matter of whom or of what. Indeed, mate-

---

[15]*Thirty Years of Psychical Research*, Collins and Sons, London, 1923, p. 469.

rialization of half a human body would, for my purpose, have been even more significant than materialization of an entire one.

I should add, however, that the friend who had taken me to that circle, who is a careful and critical observer, and who had been there a number of times before, told me that on the occasions when a material form that purported to be a materialization of his mother had come out of the cabinet and spoken to him, the form was sometimes recognizably like her, and sometimes not.

Apparitions and genuine materializations (if any) are alike in being visible, and usually in reproducing the appearance of a human body or of parts of one; and, in cases where at least the face is reproduced, sometimes in being recognizably like that of one particular person known to someone present. On the other hand. materializations are tangible whereas apparitions are not so.

The question then arises whether apparitions are incomplete materializations (a mist or haze is visible but not tangible, and yet is material,) or whether materializations are "complete" hallucinations, i.e., hallucinations not only of sight and of sound of voice or of footsteps, but also of the sense of touch and the others. As regards the second alternative, I can say only that if the form I saw which said it was my mother and which patted me on the head, was a hallucination—a hallucination "complete" in the sense just stated—then no difference remains between a complete hallucination on the one hand and, on the other, ordinary veridical perception of a physical object; for every further test of the physicality of the form seen and touched could then be alleged to be itself hallucinatory and the allegation of complete hallucination then automatically becomes completely vacuous.

On the other hand, cases are on record of apparitions of the living but, so far as I know, no good cases have been reported of materializations of the living in the sense that a living person was not merely seen and perhaps heard, but also *tangibly* present at a place distant from that of his body. In such cases of "bilocation" as that of Alphonse of Liguori, who, while in prison at Arezzo, was seen among the persons in attendance at the bedside of the then dying Pope Clement XIV in Rome, the testimony does not, I believe, include any statement that he was *touched,* while there, as well as seen.

But no matter whether we say that apparitions are incomplete materializations, or that materializations are complete hallucinations, a fact remains concerning both, that has bearing on the question whether they constitute evidence of survival after death. It is that both apparitions and materializations wear clothing of some sort; so that, as someone has put the point, "if ghosts have clothes, then clothes have ghosts." That is, if one says that the apparition or materialization *is* the deceased's surviving "spirit," temporarily become perceptible, then does not consistency require one to say that the familiar dress or coat or other accoutrement it wears had a spirit too, that has also survived? On the other hand, if one assumes that the clothing the apparition or materialization wears is materialization only of a memory image of the deceased's clothing, then would not consistency dictate the conclusion that the now temporarily perceptible parts of the deceased's body are materializations likewise only of a memory image of his appearance and behavior?

If one is fortunate enough to witness an apparition, or even better, a materialization where the materialized form duplicates the appearance of a deceased friend or relative, speaks and behaves as the latter did, and mentions facts of an intimate nature which few if any but the deceased and oneself knew, then the temptation may well be psychologically irresistible to believe that the deceased himself is with us again in temporarily materialized form, and therefore that he does indeed survive the death of the body that was his. The remarks made above, however, show that this interpretation of the experience, no matter how hard psychologically it then is to resist, is not the only one of which the experience admits, and is not necessarily the one most probably true.

On this point, some words of Richet—who as we have seen became certain that materializations do really occur—are worth quoting. Comparing the evidence for survival from mediumistic communications with that which materializations are thought to furnish, he writes: "The case of George Pelham [one of Mrs. Piper's best communicators], though there was no materialization, is vastly more evidential for survival than all the materializations yet known . . . materializations, however perfect, cannot prove survival; the evidence that they sometimes seem to give is much less striking than that given by subjective metapsychics," i.e., chiefly, by mediumistic communications (p. 490). It is worth bearing in mind in this connection that in the star case of "Katie King," who claimed to have in life been Annie Owen Morgan, daughter of the buccaneer Sir Henry Owen Morgan, no evidence exists that such a woman did actually live. But unless she actually did, and died, the question whether "her" spirit survived death, and materialized as Katie King, becomes vacuous.

As regards the evidence for survival supposedly constituted by physical paranormal phenomena such as "poltergeist" occurrences, telekinesis, raps, levitation, "direct" voice, etc., H. F. Saltmarsh writes that "in order that events of this kind should have any value as evidence of survival they must possess some characteristic which will connect them with some deceased person. The bare fact that a material object is moved in a way we cannot account for by normal means does not afford any clue to the identity of the agent. All we could say in the most favourable circumstances would be that some unknown agency is involved and that that agency exhibits intelligence; we could not argue that it was, or even had been, human, still less that it was connected with some one particular person. Thus when any special characteristics which might connect them with a deceased person are absent, we can rule out physical phenomena as completely unevidential of survival. Where, however, the phenomena show some special characteristics which connect with some definite deceased person, any evidential value for survival rests entirely on those characteristics."[16]

4. **"Possessions."** Another sort of paranormal occurrence, some cases of which invite interpretation as evidence of survival, is that popularly known as "possession," i.e., *prima facie* possession of a person's body by a personality—whether devilish, divine, or merely human—radically different from his or her own. The most probably correct interpretation of the great majority of such cases

---

[16] "Is Proof of Survival Possible?" *Proc. S.P.R.* Vol. XL:106-7, Jan. 1932.

is that the "possessing" personality is only a dissociated, normally repressed portion or aspect of the total personality of the individual concerned.

The case of the Rev. Ansel Bourne, of Greene, R.I.,[17] the still more famous cases of the alternating personalities of Miss Beauchamp, reported by Dr. Morton Prince, and the Doris Fischer case described by Dr. Walter F. Prince,[18] would be examples of such temporary "possession." The survival interpretation has little or no plausibility as regards most such cases, but is less easy to dismiss in a few others, different from these in that the intruding personality gives more or less clear and abundant evidence of being that of one particular individual who had died some time before.

About as impressive a case of this as any on record is that of the so-called Watseka Wonder. An account of it was first published in 1879 in the *Religio-Philosophical Journal*, and, in 1887, republished as a pamphlet, *The Watseka Wonder*, by the Religio-Philosophical Publishing House, Chicago. The sub-title is "A narrative of startling phenomena occurring in the case of Mary Lurancy Vennum." The author of the narrative was a medical man, Dr. E. Winchester Stevens (1822-1885), who had been consulted at the time in the case.

Two girls were concerned. One, Mary Roff, had died on July 5, 1865 at the age of 18. From an early age, she had had frequent "fits" becoming more violent with the years; she had complained of a "lump of pain in the head" (p. 10), to relieve which she had repeatedly bled herself; and she is stated to have been able, while "heavily blindfolded by critical intelligent, investigating gentlemen" to read readily books even when closed and letters even in envelopes, and to do other tasks normally requiring the use of the eyes (p. 11).

The other girl, Lurancy Vennum, was born on April 16,

---

[17]*Proc., Soc. for Psychical Research*, Vol. VII, 1891-2: A Case of Double Consciousness, by Richard Hodgson, M. D. Pp. 221-57. It is commented upon by William James in Ch. X of his *Principles of Psychology*, 1905, pp. 390-3, who also cites a number of others.

[18]Morton Prince: *The Dissociation of a Personality*, London, Longmans Green, 1906; W. F. Prince: The Doris Case of Multiple Personality, *Proc. A.S.P.R.* Vols. IX and X, 1915, 1916; and in Vol. XI, discussed by J. H. Hyslop.

1864 and was therefore a little over one year old at the time Mary Roff died. At the age of 13 in July 1877, Lurancy, who until then "had never been sick, save a light run of measles" (p. 3), complained of feeling queer, went into a fit including a cataleptic state lasting five hours. On subsequent similar occasions, while in trance, she conversed and described "angels" or "spirits" of persons who had died. She was believed insane and was examined by two local physicians. On January 31, 1878, Mr. Roff, who had heard of Lurancy's case and become interested in it, was allowed by her father to bring Dr. E. W. Stevens to observe her. On that occasion, she became apparently "possessed" by two alien personalities in turn—one a sullen, crabbed old hag, and the second a young man who said he had run away from home, got into trouble, and lost his life (pp. 5,6). Dr. Stevens then "magnetized" her and "was soon in full and free communication with the sane and happy mind of Lurancy Vennum herself" (p. 7). She described the "angels" about her and said that one of them wanted to come to her instead of the evil spirits mentioned above." On being asked if she knew who it was, she said: "Her name is Mary Roff" (p. 7). The next day, "Mr. Vennum called at the office of Mr. Roff and informed him that the girl claimed to be Mary Roff and wanted to go home . . . . 'She seems like a child real homesick, wanting to see her pa and ma and her brothers' " (p. 9).

Some days later, she was allowed to go and live with the Roffs. There, she "seemed perfectly happy and content, knowing every person and everything that Mary knew in her original body, twelve to twenty-five years ago, recognizing and calling by name those who were friends and neighbors of the family from 1852 to 1865, [i.e., during the 12 years preceding Lurancy's birth,] calling attention to scores, yes, hundreds of incidents that transpired during [Mary's] natural life" (p. 14). She recognized a head dress Mary used to wear; pointed to a collar, saying she had tatted it; remembered details of the journey of the family to Texas in 1857 [i.e., 7 years before Lurancy's birth]. On the other hand, she did not recognize any of the Vennum family nor their friends and neighbors, nor knew anything that had until then been known by Lurancy.

Lurancy's new life as Mary Roff lasted 3 months and 10 days. Then Lurancy's own personality returned to her body, and she went back to the Vennums, who reported her well in mind and body from then on. She eventually married and had children. Occasionally then, when Lurancy was visiting the Roffs, the Mary personality would come back for some little time.

What distinguishes this case from the more common ones of alternating personalities is, of course, that the personality that displaced Lurancy's was, by every test that could be applied, not a dissociated part of her own, but the personality and all the memories that had belonged to a particular 18 year old girl who had died at a time when Lurancy was but 14 months old; and that no way, consistent with Dr. Stevens' record of the facts, has been suggested in which Lurancy, during the 13 years of her life before her sojourn with the Roffs, could have obtained the extensive and detailed knowledge Mary had possessed, which Lurancy manifested during the sojourn. For the Vennums were away from Wateska for the first 7 years of Lurancy's life; and when they returned to Watseka, their acquaintance with the Roffs consisted only of one brief call of a few minutes by Mrs. Roff on Mrs. Vennum, and of a formal speaking acquaintance between the two men, until the time when Mr. Roff brought Dr. Stevens to the Vennums on account of Lurancy's insane behavior.

In commenting on various cases of seeming "possession" of a person's organism by a personality altogether different, William James notes that "many persons have found evidence conclusive to their minds that in some cases the control is really the departed spirit whom it pretends to be," but that "the phenomena shade off so gradually into cases where this is obviously absurd, that the presumption (quite apart from a priori 'scientific' prejudice) is great against its being true."[19] He then turns to the Watseka case just described, introducing it by the statement that it is "perhaps as extreme a case of 'possession' of the modern sort as one can find," but he makes no attempt to explain it.

The only way that suggests itself, to avoid the conclusion that the Mary Roff personality which for fourteen weeks "pos-

---

[19]*Principles of Psychology*, New York, Henry Holt and Co., 1905, p. 396.

sessed" Lurancy's organism was "really the departed spirit whom it pretended to be," is to have recourse to the method of orthodoxy, whose maxim is: "When you cannot explain all the facts according to accepted principles, then explain those you can and ignore the rest; or else deny them, distort them, or invent some that would help."

This procrustean method, of course, has a measure of validity, since errors of observation or of reporting do occur. Yet some facts turn out to be too stubborn to be disposed of plausibly by that method; and the present one would appear to be one of them, especially if the conclusion reached in Part III is accepted, that no impossibility either theoretical or empirical attaches to the supposition of survival of a human personality after death.

5. **Memories, seemingly of earlier lives.** Brief mention may be made at this point of another kind of occurrence, of which only a few cases at all impressive have been reported, but which, like those of the other kinds considered in the preceding sections, constitute *prima facie* evidence of survival. I refer to the cases where a person has definite apparent memories relating to a life he lived on earth before his present one, and where the facts and events he believes he remembers turn out to be capable of verification. If these should indeed be memories in the same literal sense as that in which each of us has memories of places he visited years before, of persons he met there, of incidents of his school days, and so on, then this would constitute proof not strictly that he *will* survive the death of his body but that he *has* survived that of the different body he remembers having had in an earlier life.

In Part V, we shall consider in some detail the particular form of possible life after death consisting of rebirth of the individual on earth. A number of the most circumstantial accounts of putative memories of an earlier life will be cited and the alternative interpretations to which they appear open will be examined.

Chapter XVIII

ADDITIONAL OCCURRENCES RELEVANT TO THE QUESTION OF SURVIVAL

Except, perhaps, for a very few cases of "possession" that may be as clear-cut as appeared to be that of the "Watseka Wonder" described in the preceding chapter, the most impressive sort of empirical evidence of survival is that provided by certain of the communications which are received through mediums or automatists, and which purport to emanate from particular deceased persons. Such communications, and the alternative interpretation or interpretations to which they may be open, are what we shall consider in the present chapter.

1. **Communications, purportedly from the deceased, through automatists.** The externally observable facts in the case of communications, purportedly from the surviving spirits of the deceased, are that a person, either in a state of trance or in the waking state, gives out various statements automatically, that is, not consciously and intentionally as in ordinary expression. Such persons are therefore perhaps best referred to as automatists, but actually more often as *mediums*.

The statements may be spelled out letter by letter—a pointer, on which the hand of the automatist rests, moving to the appropriate letters printed on a board (the "ouija" board) without conscious guidance by the automatist, who may the while be looking elsewhere and carrying on a conversation with the persons present. Or the letters may be indicated in some other way, as by paranormal raps or by movements of a table on which the hands rest, when the alphabet is recited and the proper letter reached. Or again, the communications may be written automatically by the hand of the automatist while his or her attention is otherwise engaged; or the statements may be spoken either by the vocal organs of the entranced medium, or at times, in some mysterious way by a voice that seems not to employ the medium's vocal organs and is then termed the "independent voice". But whichever one of these various means is used, the appearances are that the automatist's own intelligence and will do not participate in the framing of the statements made, and that a quite different personality originates them. The hand-writing or the voice, and the locutions, the tricks of speech, and the stock of information manifested, are notably different in the best cases from those of the automatist in her normal state. Indeed, they are often typical of, and usually purport to emanate from, some particular deceased friend or relative of the "sitter," i.e., of the person who is sitting with the medium at the time.

The process of communication sometimes appears to be direct, and sometimes indirect. In the latter case, the intelligence directly in command of the automatist's organs of expression purports to be that of some discarnate person more expert than others at the difficult task of using them. This intelligence, which generally remains the same at many sittings, is known as the medium's "control." Sometimes it utters through the medium's organs statements which it purportedly hears being made by the sitter's deceased friend. On the other hand, when the latter appears to be directly in command of the medium's organs, the "control" appears to function as a helper and supervisor of the communicator's attempt to express himself through those organs; for example, by preventing other discarnate spirits that also desire to use the medium from interfering with the communication going on.

That it is sometimes by no means easy to account for the content, the language, and the mannerisms of the communications otherwise than by the supposition that they really emanate from the surviving spirits of the deceased will now be made evident by citation, even if only in summary form, of communications received by the late Professor J. H. Hyslop, purportedly from his deceased father, through the famous Boston medium, Mrs. Leonore Piper, who was studied by men of science probably for more years, and more systematically and minutely, than any other mental medium.

The first of them to study her was Professor William James. He published a first report about her in 1886. In 1887, Dr. Richard Hodgson, who was secretary of the American Society for Psychical Research and was an experienced and highly critical investigator, undertook and carried on for eighteen years an intensive study of her mediumship. In the course of time, Mrs. Piper made three trips to England, where she was studied by Sir Oliver Lodge, F. W. H. Myers, Henry Sidgwick, and other distinguished investigators.

Professor Hyslop was one of the many persons who had sittings with Mrs. Piper during the years in which Dr. Hodgson was supervising the exercise of her mediumship. In 1901, Hyslop published a long and lucid, circumspect, and detailed report of his sittings with her.[1] For lack of space here, reference will be made only to the communications he received that purported to establish the identity and survival of his father, who, it should be mentioned, had been in no way a public character but had lived a very ordinary and retired life on his farm.

A word must be said first as to the physical manner in which the communications were being delivered by Mrs. Piper at that period of her mediumship. She sat in a chair before a table on which were two pillows. After a few minutes, she would go into a trance and lean forward. Her left hand, palm upward, was then placed on the pillow, her right cheek resting on the palm, so that she was facing left. Her right arm was then placed on another table to the right, on which there was a writing pad. A pencil was then put in her hand, which then began to write.

The communications so received purported to come from several of Professor Hyslop's dead relatives, and in particular from his father. Their content included a statement of Professor Hyslop's name, James; of his father's name, and of the names of three others of his father's children. Also, references to a number of particular conversations the father had had with Professor Hyslop, to many special incidents and facts, and to family matters. Examples would be that the father had trouble with his left eye, that he had a mark near his left ear, that he used to wear a thin coat or dressing gown mornings and that at

---

[1]*Proc. S. P. R.*, Vol. XVI:1-649, 1901.

one time he wore a black skull cap at night; that he used to have one round and one square bottle on his desk and carried a brown-handled penknife with which he used to pare his nails; that he had a horse called Tom; that he used to write with quill pens which he trimmed himself; and so on. A number of these facts were unknown to Professor Hyslop, but were found to be true after inquiry. The communications also contained favorite pieces of advice, which the father had been in the habit of uttering, and these worded in ways characteristic of his modes of speech.

The communications that purported to come from other dead relatives, and indeed those given by Mrs. Piper to scores and scores of other sitters over the years, were similarly of facts or incidents too trivial to have become matters of public knowledge, or indeed to have been ascertainable by a stranger without elaborate inquiries, if at all. Facts of this kind are therefore all the more significant as *prima facie* evidences of identity. It is interesting to note in this connection that if one had a brother in another city, with whom one was able to communicate only through a third party—and this a person in a rather dopy state—and if the brother doubted the identity of the sender of the messages, then trivial and intimate facts such as those cited—some of them preferably known only to one's brother and oneself—would be the very kind one would naturally mention to establish one's identity.

The question now arises, however, whether the imparting of such facts by a medium is explicable on some other hypothesis than that of communication with the deceased. Two other explanations—one normal and the other paranormal—suggest themselves. The first is, of course, that the medium obtained antecedently in some perfectly normal manner the information communicated. One of the reasons why I chose Mrs. Piper's mediumship as example is that in her case this explanation is completely ruled out by the rigorous and elaborate precautions which were taken to exclude that possibility. For one thing, Dr. Hodgson had both Mrs. Piper and her husband watched for weeks by detectives, to find out whether they went about making inquiries concerning the relatives and family history of persons they might

have expected to come for sittings. Nothing in the slightest degree suspicious was ever found. Moreover, sitters were always
introduced by Dr. Hodgson under assumed names. Sometimes,
they did not come into the room until after Mrs. Piper was in
trance, and then remained behind her where she could not have
seen them even if her eyes had been open. On her trips to
England, Mrs. Piper stayed in Myer's house or in that of Sir
Oliver Lodge, and the few letters she received were examined
and most of them read, with her permission, by Myers, Lodge,
or Sidgwick. Many of the facts she gave out could not have been
learned even by a skilled detective; and to learn such others as
could have been so learned would have required a vast expendi-
ture of time and money, which Mrs. Piper did not have. William
James summed up the case against the fraud explanation in the
statement that "not only has there not been one single suspicious
circumstance remarked" during the many years in which she and
her mode of life were under close observation, "but not one suggestion has ever been made from any quarter which might tend
to explain how the medium, living the apparent life she leads,
could possibly collect information about so many sitters by
natural means.[2] Thus, because we do not merely believe but
positively know that the information she gave was not obtained
by her in any of the normal manners, there is in her case no
escape from the fact that it had some paranormal source.

The paranormal explanation alternative to the spiritistic hypothesis is that, in the trance condition, Mrs. Piper, or her dissociated, secondary personalities, possess telepathic powers so extensive as to enable her to obtain the information she gives out
from the minds of living persons who happen to have it; and this
even if at the time it is buried in their subconsciousness, and no
matter whether such persons be at the time with Mrs. Piper or
anywhere else on earth. Or else that, in trance, Mrs. Piper has
powers of retrocognitive clairvoyance so extensive as to enable
her to observe the past life on earth of a deceased person.

---

[2]Cf. the conclusions of Frank Podmore to the same effect on pp. 71-78 of his
"Discussion of the Trance-phenomena of Mrs. Piper," *Proc. Soc. for Psychical Research*, Vol. XIV:50-78, 1898-9, in which he contrasts the rigor of the precautions
against possibility of fraud taken in Mrs. Piper's case with the possibilities of it
that existed in certain famous cases of purported clairvoyance.

But even this supposition is not enough, for besides the recondite true items with which the communications abound, there remains to be explained the dramatic form—the spontaneous give-and-take—of the communications. For this, it is necessary to ascribe to Mrs. Piper's trance personality the extraordinary histrionic ability which would be needed to translate *instantly* the suitable items of telepathically or clairvoyantly acquired information into the form which expression of a memory, or of an association of ideas, or of response to an allusion, etc., would take in animated conversation between two persons who had shared various experiences—many of them trivial in themselves, but because of this all the more evidential of identity. How staggering a task this would be can be appreciated only in extensive perusal of the verbatim records of the conversations between sitter and communicator, and often between two communicators.

Professor Hyslop takes cognizance of the capacity which a hypnotized subject does have for *dramatic imitation* of a person he is made to imagine himself to be and about whom he knows something; and Hyslop stresses the great difference, evident in the concrete, between this and the *dramatic interplay between different personalities*, of which numerous instances occur in the Piper sittings. And he points out also that nothing really parallel to the latter is to be found in the relations to one another of the several dissociated personalities in cases such as that of Morton Prince's Miss Beauchamp.[3] Hyslop had stressed earlier (p. 90) that if normal explanations fail to account for the phenomena he has recorded, then the only alternative to the supposition that he has actually been communicating with the independent intelligence of his father is "that we have a most extraordinary impersonation of him, involving a combination of telepathic powers and secondary personality with its dramatic play that should as much try our scepticism as the belief in spirits."

He concludes: "When I look over the whole field of the phenomena and consider the suppositions that must be made to escape spiritism, which not only one aspect of the case but every incidental feature of it strengthens, such as the dramatic interplay of different personalities, the personal traits of the communicator,

---

[3] *Proc. S.P.R.*, Vol. XVI:269 ff. 1901.

the emotional tone that was natural to the same, the proper appreciation of a situation or a question, and the unity of consciousness displayed throughout, I see no reason except the suspicions of my neighbours for withholding assent" (p. 293).

Another of Mrs. Piper's communicators, who during a period of her mediumship was also her chief "control," was "George Pelham." Early in 1892, a young lawyer, George Pelham, [pseudonym for Pellew] died in New York as a result of an accident. He was an associate of the American Society for Psychical Research and a friend of Dr. Hodgson's, to whom he had said that, if he died first "and found himself 'still existing,' he would 'make things lively' in the effort to reveal the fact of his continued existence."[4]

Some four or five weeks after his death, a communicator purporting to be George Pelham manifested himself at a sitting Mrs. Piper was giving to an old friend of his, John Hart. In the subsequent sittings in which G. P. figured, he was specially requested to identify such friends of his as might be among the sitters; and, out of at least one hundred and fifty persons who then had sittings with Mrs. Piper, G. P. truly recognized thirty former friends; there was no case of false recognition; and he failed in only one case to recognize a person he had known. (This was a young woman whom he had known only when she was a child eight or nine years before.) In each case, "the recognition was clear and full, and accompanied by an appreciation of the relations which subsisted between G. P. living and the sitters." Dr. Hodgson adds: "The continual manifestation of this personality,—so different from Phinuit or other communicators,—with its own reservoir of memories, with its swift appreciation of any reference to friends of G. P., with its 'give-and-take' in little incidental conversations with myself, has helped largely in producing a conviction of the actual presence of the G. P. personality which it would be quite impossible to impart by any mere enumeration of verifiable statements."[5]

In bringing to a close Section 6 of his report, Hodgson states that, although further experiment may lead him to change his

---

view, yet "at the present time I cannot profess to have any doubt but that the chief 'communicators,' to whom I have referred in the foregoing pages, are veritably the personalities that they claim to be, that they have survived the change we call death, and that they have directly communicated with us whom we call living, through Mrs. Piper's entranced organism."[6]

The dramatic spontaneity of some of the communications, and their impressive faithfulness to the manner, thought, and character of the deceased persons from whom they purport to emanate, is testified to similarly in the comments of the Rev. M. A. Bayfield on a communication which purported to come from Dr. A. W. Verrall after his death in 1912. Referring to Verrall's intellectual impatience, Mr. Bayfield writes: "The thing I mean does not readily lend itself to definition, but it was eminently characteristic;" and, after quoting certain passages typical of it in the scripts, he goes on: "All this is Verrall's manner to the life in animated conversation. . . . When I first read the words quoted above I received a series of little shocks, for the turns of speech are Verrall's, the high-pitched emphasis is his, and I could hear the very tones in which he would have spoken each sentence." In commenting on the question whether "these life-like touches of character" are inserted perhaps " by an ingenious forger (the unprincipled subliminal of some living person) *with a purpose,* in order to lend convincing *vraisemblance* to a fictitious impersonation," Mr. Bayfield writes that "nowhere is there any slip which would justify the suspicion that in reality we have to do with a cunningly masquerading 'sub.' Neither the impatience, nor the emphatic utterance, nor the playfulness has anywhere the appearance of being 'put on,'—of being *separable from the matter* of the scripts . . . to me at least it is incredible that even the cleverest could achieve such an unexampled triumph in deceptive impersonation as this would be if the actor is not Verrall himself."[7]

2. **Communications through automatists from fictitious and from still living persons.** Whatever may be the correct explanation of such correct and dramatically verisimilar mediumistic

---

[6]Op. cit. p. 406.
[7]*Proc. S.P.R.* Vol. XXVII:246-49, 1914-15.

communications as those we have just described, the explanation must in one way or another leave room for the fact that in some instances "communications" have been received from characters out of fiction, such as Adam Bede; that, on one occasion, Prof. G. Stanley Hall had, through Mrs. Piper, communications from a girl, Bessie Beals, who was a purely fictitious niece of his invented by him for the purpose of the experiment; that, in 1853, Victor Hugo in exile in Jersey received "communications" from "The Lion of Androcles" and "The Ass of Balaam;" that Dr. S. G. Soal received, through Mrs. Blanche Cooper, communications from, on the one hand, a John Ferguson, who turned out to be a wholly fictitious person, and on the other from a Gordon Davis, whom he had known slightly when both were boys at the same school. Soal had since then talked with him only once, for about half an hour about service matters when both were cadets in the army and met by chance on a railroad platform. Soal later believed him to have been killed in the war; but he was in fact living at the time communications of a number of facts about his life history, past and future, were received by Soal through Mrs. Cooper. "Some of these facts," Soal writes, "were given in the form of verbal statements describing incidents which had happened or which were to happen; other facts such as his vocal characteristics were expressed in a purely physical way," for in this case the personality of the (still living) Gordon Davis appeared to "control" or "possess" the medium; was dramatized and spoke in the first person with the fastidious accent and clear articulation peculiar to Gordon Davis; and apparently believed itself to be a deceased person.[8]

Some five earlier cases of communications purporting to emanate from persons who asserted they had died or who were believed to have died, but who were actually living, are cited by Prof. Th. Flournoy in the third chapter of his *Spiritism and Psychology*.[9] The words " 'Deceiving Spirits,' " which, in quotation marks, he uses as title of that chapter, refer to the fact that Spiritualists are wont to ascribe such spurious communications to

---

[8]*Proc. S.P.R.* Vol. XXXV:471-594, 1926. A Report of Some Communications Received through Mrs. Blanche Cooper.

[9]Transl. by H. Carrington, pub. Harper & Bros. New York, 1911, pp. 72-90.

mischievous, deceitful spirits. But obviously this explanation
would be legitimate only if it had first been independently
established that any discarnate spirits at all exist.

3. **Mrs. Sidgwick's interpretation of the Piper communications.** In an article entitled "Discussion of the Trance Phenomena of Mrs. Piper,"[10] Mrs. Sidgwick, who was one of the
keenest minded women of her time in England, takes into consideration what is known both of the pathological dissociations
of personality, and of the capacity of subjects in deep hypnotic
trance to impersonate anyone whom they have been induced to
believe themselves to be. In the light of all this she argues, not
specifically against the contention that Mrs. Piper's communications provide some evidence of survival after death, but against
the "possession" interpretation of her trance communications;
that is, against the supposition that on those occasions the discarnate spirits of George Pelham, of Prof. Hyslop's father, etc.,
"turn out Mrs. Piper's spirit and themselves take its place in
her organism," (p. 35) i.e., possess it for the time being and employ her organs of expression in the same direct manner as that
in which each of us normally employs his own vocal organs in
oral expression or his own hand in writing.

Mrs. Sidgwick contends that the interpretation most plausible in the light of all the peculiarities of the communications is
that the communicating mind is in all cases Mrs. Piper's own
(entranced) mind; that in the trance condition, her mind has
"an unusually developed telepathic faculty" (p. 34); that the
recondite information her trance mind gives out is obtained by
it telepathically from the minds of living persons having it, or
possibly from the dead; and that the dramatic form which the
presentation of it takes in conversations with the sitter is accounted for most economically, but adequately, if one supposes
that the entranced, dreaming Mrs. Piper believes herself at the
time to be the deceased person whose memories and personality
traits then occupy her mind.

As tending to support this hypothesis against that of direct
possession of Mrs. Piper's organism by the discarnate spirit of

---

[10]*Proc. Soc. for Psych. Res'ch.* Vol. XV:16-38, 1900-01.

G. P. or of some other deceased person, Mrs. Sidgwick points out that some sitters are uniformly more successful than others in getting communications whose content is attributable only to some paranormal source—whether this be telepathy from the sitter, or from other living persons, or from the deceased.

This, Mrs. Sidgwick argues, would indicate that the sitter's state of mind, or his particular type of mind, is somehow a factor in the "communication" process; for if the process depended only on the medium and on temporary possession of her entranced organism by a discarnate spirit, there would be no reason why the communications from a given spirit—say, G. P.'s—should, as in fact is the case, be steadily less evidential of some paranormal origin when made to one particular sitter than when made to a particular other.

This conclusion, however, hardly seems to follow; for the supposition that the sitter contributes something—congeniality, readiness to believe, interest in paranormal phenomena, perhaps; or the opposites—is quite compatible with the communicator's being really who he claims to be. It is a matter of common experience that different persons with whom one converses affect one differently and bring out of him different things—one, trivialities; another, exercise perhaps of such unusual powers, or manifestation of such special interests, as he may have.

Anyway, the question we are at present centrally concerned with is whether proof of survival, or at least evidence definitely establishing it as probable, is provided by the paranormal occurrences cited, and more particularly at this point by mediumistic communications, such as Mrs. Piper's, that contain remote details of some particular person's past life and reproduce with high verisimilitude his tone, mannerisms, and distinctive associations of ideas. Hence, if these do prove or establish a positive probability of survival, then the question whether a surviving deceased person communicates with us directly, by taking possession of the entranced Mrs. Piper's organism, or only indirectly by telepathy in the manner suggested by Mrs. Sidgwick, is of but secondary interest, as having to do merely with the technique of the process of communication.

But the facts cited in Section 2 would by themselves be

enough to show that the content and form of mediumistic communications, even when as impressive as some of those of Mrs. Piper or of Mrs. Blanche Cooper, do not necessarily proceed from discarnate spirits. The question thus forces itself upon us whether some other explanation is available, that would account at once for the communications from fictitious persons; for the correct and dramatically verisimilar communications purportedly from deceased persons who, however, are in fact still living; and also for the similarly impressive communications that likewise purport to emanate from deceased persons, but where those persons had in fact died.

About the only hypothesis in sight that might do all this and that would be other than that of communications from excarnate spirits deceitful or truthful, is the hypothesis of telepathy from the subconscious minds of living persons who have or have had the information manifested in the communications; or/and the hypothesis of clairvoyance by the medium, giving her access to existing facts or records containing the information. For of course the correctness, or not, of the information communicated can be testified to, if at all, only by some still living person's memory or by some still existing facts or documents.

Before inquiring into the adequacy of this hypothesis, however, we shall have to consider the cases of so-called "Cross-correspondences;" for they are the ones most difficult to account for in terms of only that hypothesis. At the same time, they are the ones that provide the strongest evidence of "true" survival.

4. Cross-correspondences. It is unfortunately not possible to give an intelligible concrete presentation of any of the cases of cross-correspondence in the space available here, nor without presupposing special knowledge of Greek and Latin classics by the reader; for the scripts of the automatists involved in the cross-correspondences, and the analyses of them, run to hundreds of pages; their significance turns on references or allusions to recondite points in those classics; and their evidential force can be fully appreciated only after long and careful study of the scripts and of the circumstances under which each individually was produced.

The best that can be done here is therefore only to state in general terms what is meant by the term "cross-correspondences," how the experiment they constitute originated, and who were respectively the automatists, the investigators, and the purported communicators concerned in it.

Cross-correspondences are correspondences between the scripts of different automatists isolated from one another at least to the extent of being kept in ignorance of the contents of one another's scripts. Sometimes, one of the automatists is ignorant of the other's existence. For example, Mrs. Verrall, on Oct. 25, 1901, was asked by Mr. Piddington to try to obtain in her scripts a word to be reproduced in the script of another automatist, Mrs. Archdale, of whom Mrs. Verrall had never heard before. She was told that the supposed "control" of Mrs. Archdale was the latter's deceased son, Stewart. Then Mrs. Verrall remembered that, in a script of hers of Sept. 18, 1901, i.e., over a month before she had come to know of Mrs. Archdale's existence, the name Stewart, had occurred together with two other names. These turned out to be ones closely connected with the deceased boy. Similarly definite correspondences were found between some of Mrs. Verrall's scripts in England in the summer of 1905 and those of another automatist, at the time in India, Mrs. Holland, of whose name Mrs. Verrall was then ignorant, and whose acquaintance she did not make until November 1905.[11] Other automatists besides Mrs. Verrall (lecturer in Classics at Newnham College and wife of Dr. A. W. Verall, Cambridge University classicist) and Mrs. Holland (pseudonym of a sister of Rudyard Kipling,) were Miss Helen Verrall, Mrs. Thompson, Mrs. Forbes (pseudonym), Mrs. Willett (pseudonym), and Mrs. Piper.

The investigators in the series of cross-correspondences were Mr. J. G. Piddington, the Hon. Gerald Wm. Balfour (who later became Lord Balfour), Sir Oliver Lodge, Mr. Frank Podmore, Mrs. Sidgwick, and Miss Alice Johnson, Secretary of the Society for Psychical Research. Dr. Richard Hodgson, in charge of Mrs. Piper's sittings in Boston up to the time of his death in 1905, also participated. And, to some extent, Mrs. Verrall functioned not only as automatist but also as investigator.

---

[11]*Proc. S. P. R.* Vol. XX:205-6, 1906.

The deceased persons from whom purported to come the communications characterized by cross-correspondences were chiefly F. W. H. Myers, author of the classic *Human Personality and Its Survival of Bodily Death,* who had died in 1901; Edmund Gurney (d. 1888), author, with Myers and Podmore's collaboration, of *Phantasms of the Living;* Henry Sidgwick (d. 1900), the distinguished Cambridge philosopher and first president of the S. P. R.; and Dr. Richard Hodgson (d. 1905), Secretary of the A. S. P. R. After Dr. Verrall's death in 1912, communications typical of him and of Prof. Butcher were also received.

The correspondences between the scripts had to do in most cases with rather recondite details of the Greek and Latin classics. To identify them or to understand the allusions to them made in the scripts therefore required considerable knowledge of the classics by the investigators. One of these, Mr. J. G. Piddington, who had the requisite scholarly equipment and ingenuity, and who was much interested in the scripts, found that certain of them, besides having a topic in common, complemented one another in a manner analogous to that in which the individually insignificant pieces of a jigsaw puzzle—or to use his own comparison, the cubes of a mosaic—make a meaningful whole when correctly combined. This complementariness is the distinctive feature of the most evidential of the cross-correspondences.

An additional point of the greatest interest is that the scripts contain numerous statements more or less explicitly to the effect that the discarnate Myers, Gurney, and Sidgwick were the devisers of the scheme of giving out, through automatists isolated from one another, communications that would be separately unintelligible but that made sense when put together or, in some of the cases, when a clue to the sense was supplied in the script of yet another automatist. In this way, the possibility of explaining simply as due to telepathy or clairvoyance the similarities of topic between the scripts of two automatists would be ruled out or greatly strained; and in addition proof would automatically be supplied that the communicators, in their discarnate state, were not mere automata and sets of memories, but retained intellectual initiative and ingenuity; that is, that they were still fully living.

An excellent summary of some of the most evidential cases

of cross-correspondence, with some extracts from the scripts, is presented in a fair and discerning manner by H. F. Saltmarsh in his little book, *Evidence of Personal Survival from Cross Correspondences*.[12] Briefer accounts of the subject—though more ample than the present one—may be found in G. N. M. Tyrrell's *The Personality of Man*, chs. 17 and 18, and in his *Science and Psychical Phenomena*, ch. XVII.[13] It is worth mentioning that Lord Balfour, in his fine "Study of the Psychological Aspects of Mrs. Willett's Mediumship and of the Statements of the Communicators Concerning Process"[14] states that "the bulk of Mrs. Willett's automatic output is too private for publication;" hence that, in his paper, "there must still remain withheld from publicity a good many passages which [he] would willingly have quoted by way of illustration;" and that "it would be impossible to do justice to the argument in favour of spirit communication on the basis of the Willett phenomena without violating confidences which [he is] bound to respect" (pp. 43, 45).

In 1932, Mrs. Sidgwick wrote an account of the history and work of the Society for Psychical Research during its first fifty years of existence. She being at the time President of Honor of the Society, her paper was presented by her brother, Lord Balfour, at the Jubilee meeting of the Society, July 1, 1932. After he had done so, he added that some of the persons present "may have felt that the note of caution and reserve has possibly been over-emphasized in Mrs. Sidgwick's paper." Then he went on: "Conclusive proof of survival is notoriously difficult to obtain. But the evidence may be such as to produce *belief*, even though it fall short of conclusive *proof*." Lord Balfour then concluded with the words: "I have Mrs. Sidgwick's assurance—an assurance which I am permitted to convey to the meeting—that, upon the evidence before her, she herself is a firm believer both in survival

---

[12]G. Bell & Sons, London 1938, pp. viii and 159. At the end is a full list of the discussions of the scripts in the Proceedings of the S. P. R.

[13]Respectively, Penguin Books, New York, 1946, No. A165; and Harper & Bros., New York and London, 1938.

[14]*Proc. S. P. R.* Vol. XLIII:41-318, 1935.

and in the reality of communication between the living and the dead."[15] This belief, he had himself come to share.

Certainly, few persons have been both as thoroughly acquainted with the evidence from cross-correspondences for survival and for communication with the deceased, and at the same time as objective and keenly critical, as were Mrs. Sidgwick and Lord Balfour.

---

[15]*Proc. S. P. R.* Vol. XLI:16, 1932-3.

Chapter XIX

HOW STANDS THE CASE FOR THE REALITY OF SURVIVAL

In Chaps. XVII and XVIII, we considered and to some extent commented upon the chief kinds of paranormal occurrences that appear to constitute empirical evidence of survival. The point has now been reached where we must attempt to say, in the light of the evidence and of the criticisms to which it may be open, how stands today the question whether the human personality survives the death of its body.

1. **What, if not survival, the facts might signify.** Only two hypotheses have yet been advanced that seem at all capable of accounting for the *prima facie* evidences of personal survival reviewed. One is that the identifying items do indeed proceed from the surviving spirits of the deceased persons concerned. The other is that the medium obtains by extrasensory perception the facts she communicates; that is, more specifically, obtains them: (a) telepathically from the minds of living persons who know them or have known them; or (b) by retrocognitive clairvoyant observation of the past facts themselves; or (c) by clairvoyant observation of existing records, or of existing circumstantial evidence, of the past facts.

To the second of these two hypotheses would have to be added in some cases the hypothesis that the medium's subconscious mind has and exercises a remarkable capacity for verisimilar impersonation of a deceased individual whom the medium has never known but concerning whom she is getting information at the time in the telepathic or/and clairvoyant manner just referred to.

In cases where the information is communicated by paranormal raps or by other paranormal physical phenomena, the hypothesis that the capacity to produce such physical phenomena is being exercised by the medium's unconscious but still incarnate mind would be more economical than ascription of that capacity to discarnate minds; for these—unlike the medium and her mind —are not independently known to exist.

It must be emphasized that no responsible person who is fully acquainted with the evidence for the occurrences to be explained and with their circumstances has yet offered any explanatory hypothesis distinct from the two stated above. As of today, the choice therefore lies between them. The hypothesis of fraud, which would by-pass them, is wholly untenable in at least some of the cases; notably, for the reasons mentioned earlier, in the case of the communications received through Mrs. Piper. And, in the case of the cross-correspondences, the hypothesis that the whole series was but an elaborate hoax collusively perpetrated out of sheer mischief for over ten years by the more than half-dozen automatists concerned—and this without its ever being detected by the alert investigators who were in constant contact with the automatists—is preposterous even if the high personal character of the ladies through whom the scripts came is left out of account.

Still more so, of course, would be the suggestion that the investigators too participated in the hoax. In this connection the following words of Prof. Sidgwick are worth remembering. They occur in his presidential address at the first general meeting of the Society for Psychical Research in London, July 17, 1882:

"The highest degree of demonstrative force that we can obtain out of any single record of investigation is, of course, limited by the trustworthiness of the investigator. We have done all that we can when the critic has nothing left to allege except that the investigator is in the trick. But when he has nothing else left to allege he will allege that . . . . . We must drive the objector into the position of being forced either to admit the phenomena as inexplicable, at least by him, or to accuse the investigators either of lying or cheating or of a blindness or forgetfulness incompatible with any intellectual condition except absolute idiocy."[1]

---

[1]*Proc. S.P.R.* Vol. I:12, 1882-3. Cf. in this connection an article, Science and the

2. **The allegation that survival is antecedently improbable.**
The attempt to decide rationally between the two hypotheses
mentioned above must in any case take into consideration at the
very start the allegation that survival is antecedently known to be
improbable or even impossible; or on the contrary is known to be
necessary. In a paper to which we shall be referring in the next
two sections,[2] Prof. E. R. Dodds first considers the grounds that
have been advanced from various quarters for such improbability,
impossibility, or necessity. In view, however, of our own more
extensive discussion of those grounds in Parts I and III of the
present work, we need say nothing here concerning Prof. Dodds'
brief remarks on the subject. Nothing in them seems to call for
any revision of the conclusion to which we came that there is not
really any antecedent improbability of survival (nor any antecedent probability of it.) For when the denotation of the terms
"material" and "mental" is made fully explicit instead of, as
commonly, assumed to be known well enough; and when the
nature of the existents or occurrents respectively termed "material" and "mental" is correctly analyzed; then no internal inconsistency, nor any inconsistency with any definitely known empirical fact, is found in the supposition that a mind, such as it
had become up to the time of death, continues to exist after
death and to exercise some of its capacities. Nor is there any
antecedent reason to assume that, if a mind does so continue to
exist, manifestations of this fact to persons still living would be
common rather than, as actually seems to be the case, exceptional.

3. **What telepathy or clairvoyance would suffice to account
for.** Prof. Dodds considers and attempts to dispose of ten objections which have been advanced against the adequacy of the
telepathy-clairvoyance explanation of the facts. The objections
in the case of which his attempt seems definitely successful are
the following.

(a) The first is that telepathy does not account for the claim

---

Supernatural, by G. R. Price, Research Associate in the Dept. of Medicine, Univ. of
Minnesota. *Science,* Vol. 122, No. 3165, Aug. 26, 1955 and the comments on it by
S. G. Soal, J. B. Rhine, P. E. Meehl, M. Scriven, P. W. Bridgman Vol. 123, No.
3184 Jan. 6/56.
[2]Why I do not believe in Survival, *Proc. S.P.R.* Vol. XLII:147-72, 1934.

made in the mediumistic communications, that they emanate
from the spirits of deceased persons.

Prof. Dodds replies that some of the communications have in
fact claimed a different origin; and that anyway the claim is
explicable as due to the fact that communication with the deceased is usually what is desired from mediums, and that the medium's own desire to satisfy the sitter's desire for such communications operates on the medium's subconscious—from which they
directly proceed—as desire commonly operates in the production
of dreams and in the determination of their content.

(b) A second objection is that no independent evidence
exists that mediums belong to the very small group of persons
who have detectable telepathic powers.

In reply, Prof. Dodds points to the fact that Dr. Soal had
in his own mind formed a number of hypotheses about the life
and circumstances of the—as it eventually turned out—wholly
fictitious John Ferguson (mentioned in Sec. 2 of Chapt. XVIII,)
and that in the communications those very hypotheses then
cropped up as assertions of fact. Prof. Dodds mentions various
other instances where things actually false, but believed true by
the sitter, have similarly been asserted in the medium's communications and thus have provided additional evidence that
she possessed and was exercising telepathic powers.

To this we may add that there is some evidence that the
trance condition—at least the hypnotic trance—is favorable to
the exercise of ordinarily latent capacities for extrasensory perception.[3]

(c) Another objection is that telepathy does not account for
"object reading" where the object is a relic of a person unknown
both to the sitter and to the medium, but where the medium
nevertheless gives correct detailed information about the object's
former or present owner.

Prof. Dodd's reply is in substance that these occurrences are
no less puzzling on the spiritistic than on the telepathic hypothesis. Since much of the information obtained in such cases con-

---

[3]See for instance ESP card tests of college students with and without hypnosis,
by J. Fahler and R. J. Cadoret, Jl. of Parapsychology, Vol. 22:125-36, No. 2, June
1958.

cerns occurrences in which the object itself had no part, the object can hardly be itself a record of it; rather, it must be a means of establishing telepathic rapport between the mind of the sensitive and that of the person who has the information.

And of course the correctness of the information could not be verified unless some person has it, or unless the facts testified to are objective and thus accessible to clairvoyant observation by the sensitive.

(d) To the objection that no correlation is found between the success or failure of a sitting and the conditions respectively favorable or unfavorable to telepathy, Prof. Dodds replies that, actually, we know almost nothing as to what these are.

(e) Another objection which has been advanced against the telepathy explanation of the communications is that the quantity and quality of the communications varies with changes of purported communicator, but not of sitter as one would expect if telepathy were what provides the information communicated.

The reply here is, for one thing, that, as we have seen in Sec. 3 of Ch. XVIII, the allegation is not invariably true; but that anyway changes of purported communicator imply corresponding changes as to the minds that are possible telepathic sources of the information communicated.

(f) Again, it is often asserted that the telepathy explanation of the facts is very complicated, whereas the spiritistic explanation is simple. Prof. Dodds' reply here is that the sense in which greater simplicity entails greater probability is that in which being "simpler" means "making fewer and narrower unsupported assumptions;" and that the telepathy hypothesis, not the spiritistic, is the one simpler in this alone evidentially relevant sense. For the spiritistic hypothesis postulates telepathy and clairvoyance anyway, but ascribes these to "spirits", which are not independently known to exist; whereas the telepathy hypothesis ascribes them to the medium, who is known to exist and for whose occasional exercise of telepathy or clairvoyance some independent evidence exists.

4. **The facts which strain the telepathy-clairvoyance explanation.** In the case of the other objections to the telepathy explanation commented upon by Prof. Dodds, his replies are

much less convincing than those we have just presented. Indeed, they bring to mind a remark made shortly before by W. H. Salter concerning certain features of the cross-correspondences communications: "It is possible to frame a theory which will explain each of them, more or less, by telepathy, but is it not necessary in doing so to invent *ad hoc* a species of telepathy for which there is otherwise practically no evidence?"[4]

The essence of these more stubborn objections is the *virtually unlimited range* of the telepathy with which the automatist's or medium's subconscious mind has to be gifted. It must be such as to have access to the minds of any persons who possess the recondite items of information communicated, no matter where those persons happen to be at the time. Furthermore, the telepathy postulated must be assumed somehow capable of *selecting,* out of all the minds to which its immense range gives it access, the particular one or ones that contain the specific bits of information brought into the communications. But this is not all. The immediate understanding of, and apposite response to, allusive remarks in the course of the communicator's conversation with the sitter (or sometimes with another communicator) requires that the above selecting of the person or persons having the information, and the establishing and relinquishing of telepathic rapport with the mind of the appropriate one, be virtually *instantaneous.* And then, of course, the information thus telepathically obtained must, *instantly* again, be put into the form of a dramatic, highly verisimilar impersonation of the deceased purported communicator as he would have acted in animated conversational give-and-take. This particular feature of some of the communications, as we saw, was that on which—as the most convincing—both Hyslop and Hodgson laid great stress, as do Mr. Drayton Thomas and also Mr. Salter.

Let us now see how Prof. Dodds proposes to meet these difficulties, which strain the telepathy hypothesis, but of which the spiritistic hypothesis would be free.

For one thing, he points to some of Dr. Osty's cases, where "sensitives who do not profess to be assisted by 'spirits'" never-

---

[4]*Journal,* S.P.R. Vol. 27:331, 1932. The remark occurs towards the end of a review of C. S. Bechofer Roberts' The Truth about Spiritualism.

theless give out information about absent persons as detailed as that given by the supposed spirits.

Obviously, however, there is no more reason to accept as authoritative what a sensitive "professes" or believes as to the paranormal source of her information when she denies that it is spirits than when she asserts it. Mrs. Eileen Garrett, who in addition to being one of the best known contemporary mediums, is scientifically interested in her own mediumship, freely acknowledges that she does not know, any more than do other persons, whether her controls, Abdul Latif and Uvani, are discarnate spirits, dissociated parts of her own personality, or something else.

Again, Prof. Dodds argues that recognition of the personality of a deceased friend by the sitter has but slight evidential value, since there is no way of checking how far the will-to-believe may be responsible for it; but that even if the reproduction is perfect, it is anyway no evidence that the personality concerned has survived after death; for Gordon Davis was still living and yet Mrs. Blanche Cooper, who did not know him, did reproduce the tone of his voice and his peculiar articulation well enough for Dr. Soal to recognize them.

Prof. Dodd's reply is predicated on the assumption that, although Dr. Soal was neither expecting nor longing for communication with Gordon Davis, nevertheless the recognition was positive and definite. This should therefore be similarly granted in cases where the person who recognizes the voice or manner of a deceased friend is, similarly, an investigator moved by scientific interest, not a grieving person moved to believe by his longing for reunion with his loved one.

Aside from this, however, the Gordon Davis case shows only that, since he was still living, the process by which the tone of his voice and his peculiar articulation were reproduced by Mrs. Cooper was not "possession" of her organism by his discarnate spirit. Telepathy from Dr. Soal, who believed Davis had died, is enough to account for the vocal peculiarities of the communication, for the memories of boyhood and of the later meeting on the railroad platform, and for the purported communicator's assumption that he had died. But this mere reproduction of voice peculiarities and of two memories, in the single brief conversation of Dr. Soal directly with the purported Gordon Davis, is a radically different thing from the lively conversational intercourse Hyslop and Hodgson refer to, with its immediate and apposite adaptation of mental or emotional attitude to changes in that of the interlocutor, and the making and understanding of apt allusions to intimate matters, back and forth between communicator and sitter. The Gordon Davis communication is not a case of this at all; and of course the precognitive features of the communication by Nada (Mrs. Blanche Cooper's control) at the second sitting, which referred to the house Gordon Davis eventually occupied, are irrelevant equally to the telepathy and to the spiritualist hypotheses.

Prof. Dodds would account for the appositeness of the facts the medium selects, which the particular deceased person concerned would remember and which identify him, by saying that, once the medium's subconscious mind is *en rapport* with that of the telepathic agent, the *selection* of items of information appropriate at a given moment to the demands of the conversation with the sitter can be supposed to take place in the same automatic manner as that in which such selection occurs in a person when the conversation requires it.

The adequacy of this reply is decreased, however, by the assumption it makes that the information given out by the medium is derived from *one* telepathic source, or at least one at a time; whereas in the case of Hyslop's communications purportedly from his father, the items of information supplied were apparently not all contained in any one person's memory, but scattered among several. Hence, if the medium's subconscious mind was *en rapport* at the the same time with those of different persons, the task of selecting instantly which one of them to draw from would remain, and would be very different from the normal automatic selection within *one* mind, of items relevant at a given moment in a conversation.

But anyway the degree of telepathic rapport which Prof. Dodds' reply postulates vastly exceeds any that is independently known to occur; for it would involve the medium's having for the time being all the memories and associations of ideas of the person who is the telepathic source; and this would amount to

the medium's virtually borrowing that person's mind for the duration of the conversation; and notwithstanding this, responding in
the conversation not as that person himself would respond, but
as the ostensible communicator—constructed by the medium out
of that person's memories of him—would respond.

Concerning the cross-correspondences, Prof. Dodds admits
that they manifest pattern, but he is not satisfied that they are the
result of design. Even if they were designed, however, he agrees
with the suggestion others had made that Mrs. Verrall's subconscious mind, which had all the knowledge of the Greek and
Latin classics required, could well be supposed to have designed
the scheme, rather than the deceased Myers and his associates;
for, he asserts, "more difficult intellectual feats than the construction of these puzzles have before now been performed subconsciously" (p. 169). H. F. Saltmarsh, however, suggests "that it
may be unreasonable to attribute to the same level of consciousness intellectual powers of a very high order and a rather stupid
spirit of trickery and deception."[5]

But in any case, more than the construction of the puzzles
would be involved; namely, in addition, *telepathic virtual dicta-
tion* of the appropriate script to the other automatist—whose very
existence was, in the case of Mrs. Holland in India, quite unknown at the time to Mrs. Verrall in England. To ascribe the
script to "telepathic leakage" will hardly do, for, as Lord Balfour
remarked concerning such a proposal made by Miss F. M. Stawell
in the Ear of Dionysius case, "it is not at all clear how 'telepathic
leakage' could be so thoughtful as to arrange all the topics in such
an ingenious way. It seems a little like 'explaining' the working
of a motor car by saying that it goes because petrol leaks out of a
tank into its front end!"[6]

5. **What would prove, or make positively probable, that
survival is a fact.** The difficult task of deciding where the various
kinds of facts now before us, the rival interpretations of them,
and the criticisms of the interpretations, finally leave the case for
the reality of survival requires that we first attempt to specify

---

[5]*Op. cit.* p. 138.
[6]*Proc. S.P.R.* Vol. XXIX:270.

what evidence, if we should have it, we would accept as definitely proving survival or, short of this, as definitely establishing a positive probability that survival is a fact.

To this end, let us suppose that a friend of ours, John Doe, was a passenger on the transatlantic plane which some months ago the newspapers reported crashed shortly after leaving Shannon without having radioed that it was in trouble. Since no survivors were reported to have been found, we would naturally assume that John Doe had died with the rest.

Let us now, however, consider in turn each of three further suppositions.

(I) The first is that some time later we meet on the street a man we recognize as John Doe, who recognizes us too, and who has John Doe's voice and mannerisms. Also, that allusions to personal matters that were familiar to both of us, made now in our conversation with him, are readily understood and suitably responded to by each. Then, even before he tells us how he chanced to survive the crash, we would of course *know* that, somehow, he has survived it.

(II) But now let us suppose instead that we do not thus meet him, but that one day our telephone rings, and over the line comes a voice which we clearly recognize as John Doe's; and that we also recognize certain turns of phrase that were peculiar to him. He tells us that he survived the disaster, and we then talk with ready mutual understanding about personal and other matters that had been familiar to the two of us. We wish, of course, that we could see him as well as thus talk with him; yet we would feel practically certain that he had survived the crash of the plane and is now living.

(III) Let us, however, now consider instead a third supposition, namely, that one day, when our telephone rings, a voice not John Doe's tells us that he did survive the accident and that he wants us to know it, but that for some reason he cannot come to the phone. He is, however, in need of money and wants us to deposit some to his account in the bank.

Then of course—especially since the person who transmits the request over the telephone sounds at times a bit incoherent—we would want to make very sure that the person from whom the request ultimately emanates is really John Doe. To this end, we ask him through the intermediary to name some mutual friends; and he names several, giving some particular facts about each. We refer, allusively, to various personal matters he would be familiar with; and it turns out that he understands the allusions and responds to them appropriately. Also, the intermediary quotes him as uttering various statements, in which we recognize peculiarities of his thought and phraseology; and the peculiar nasal tone of his voice is imitated by the intermediary well enough for us to recognize it.

Would all this convince us that the request for money really emanates from John Doe and therefore that he did survive the accident and is still living? If we should react rationally rather than impulsively, our getting convinced or remaining unconvinced would depend on the following considerations.

First, *is it possible at all* that our friend somehow did survive the crash? If, for example, his dead body had been subsequently found and identified beyond question, then obviously the person whose request for money is being transmitted to us *could not possibly be* John Doe not yet deceased; and hence the identifying evidence conveyed to us over the phone would necessarily be worthless, no matter how strongly it would otherwise testify to his being still alive.

But if we have no such antecedent conclusive proof that he did perish, then the degree of our confidence that the telephoned request ultimately does emanate from him, and hence that he is still living, will depend for us on the following three factors.

(a) One will be the *abundance,* or *scantiness,* of such evidence of his identity as comes to us over the phone.

(b) A second factor will be the *quality* of the evidence. That is, does it correspond *minutely* and in *peculiar* details to what we know of the facts or incidents to which it refers; or on the contrary does it correspond to them merely in that it gives, correctly indeed, the *broad features* of the events concerned, but *does not include much detail?*

(c) The third factor will be that of *diversity of the kinds of evidence* the telephone messages supply. Does all the evidence, for example, consist *only of correct memories* of personal matters and of matters typical of John Doe's range of information? Or does the evidence include also *dramatic faithfulness* of the communications to the manner, the attitudes, the tacit assumptions, and the idiosyncracies of John Doe as we remember him? And again, do the communications manifest in addition something which H. F. Saltmarsh has held to be "as clear an indication of psychical individuality as finger prints are of physical,"[7] namely *associations of ideas that were peculiar to John Doe* as of the age he had reached at the time of the crash?

If these same associations are still manifest, then persistence of them will signify one thing if the communication in which they appear is made not too long after the accident, but a different thing if instead it is made, say, twenty-five years after. For a person's associations of ideas alter more or less as a result of new experiences, of changes of environment, of acquisition of new ranges of information, and of development of new interests. Hence, if the associations of ideas are the same a few months or a year or two after the crash as they were before, this *would* testify to John Doe's identity. But if they are the same a quarter of a century later, then this would testify rather that although some of the capacities he had have apparently persisted, yet he has in the meantime *not continued really to live;* for to live in the full sense of the word entails becoming gradually different— indeed, markedly different in many ways over such a long term of years.

Now, the point of our introducing the hypothetical case of John Doe, and of the three suppositions we made in succession as to occurrences that convinced us, of that inclined us in various degrees to believe, that he had not after all died in the plane accident is that the second and especially the third of those suppositions duplicate in all essentials the evidences of survival of the human mind which the best of the mediumistic communications supply. For the medium or automatist is the analogue of the telephone and, in cases of apparent possession of the medium's organism by the purported communicator, the latter is the analogue of John Doe when himself telephoning. The me-

---

[7]*Evidence of Personal Survival from Cross Correspondences,* G. Bell & Sons, London 1938, p. 34.

dium's "control," on the other hand, is the analogue of the intermediary who at other times transmits John Doe's statements over the telephone. And the fact recalled in Sec. 2 of this chapter —that survival has not been proved to be either empirically or logically impossible—is the analogue of the supposition that John Doe's body was never found and hence that his having survived the crash is not known to be impossible.

This parallelism between the two situations entails that if reason rather than either religious or materialistic faith is to decide, then our answer to the question whether the evidence we have does or does not establish survival (or at least a positive probability of it) must, in the matter of survival after death, be based on the very same considerations as in the matter of survival after the crash of the plane. That is, our answer will have to be based similarly on the *quantity* of evidence we get over the mediumistic "telephone;" on the *quality* of that evidence; and on the *diversity* of kinds of it we get.

6. **The conclusion about survival which at present appears warranted.** To what conclusion, then, do these three considerations point when brought to bear on the evidence referred to in Chapters XVII and XVIII?

The conclusion they dictate is, I believe, the same as that which at the end of Chapter XVIII we cited as finally reached by Mrs. Sidgwick and by Lord Balfour—a conclusion which also was reached in time by Sir Oliver Lodge, by Prof. Hyslop, by Dr. Hodgson, and by a number of other persons who like them were thoroughly familiar with the evidence on record; who were gifted with keenly critical minds; who had originally been skeptical of the reality or even possibility of survival; and who were also fully acquainted with the evidence for the reality of telepathy and of clairvoyance, and with the claims that had been made for the telepathy-clairvoyance interpretation of the evidence, as against the survival interpretation of it.

Their conclusion was essentially that the balance of the evidence so far obtained is on the side of the reality of survival and, in the best cases, of survival not merely of memories of the life on earth, but of survival also of the most significant capacities of the human mind, and of continuing exercise of these.

PART V

Life After Death Conceived As Reincarnation

Chapter XX

THE DOCTRINE OF REINCARNATION IN THE HISTORY OF THOUGHT

In Sections 5 to 8 of Chapter XIV, various forms were described which a discarnate life after death, if there is such, might conceivably take. Another possible form of survival, namely life, incarnate again, of the "essential" part of a personality through rebirth in a new human or possibly animal body, was also mentioned but was not discussed there since Part IV was concerned only with the question of discarnate life after death. In the present and the subsequent chapters of Part V, we return to that very interesting conception of survival, and examine it in some detail.

The content of the belief that the individual "soul" lives in a body on earth not once only but several times has been designated by various names. Metempsychosis, Transmigration, Reincarnation, and Rebirth are the most familiar, but Reembodiment, Metensomatosis, and Palingenesis have also been used. The doctrine has taken a variety of specific forms, some of which will be considered farther on; but there is little warrant either in etymology or in any firmly established usage for regarding one or another of those names as denoting only some particular form of the doctrine that the individual "soul" lives on earth not once only but several times.[1]

The conception of survival as metempsychosis seems fantastic and unplausible to the great majority of people today in Europe and America, notwithstanding that the believers in survival

---

[1]"Rebirth," "Reembodiment," "Reincarnation," and "Transmigration," are self-explanatory. "Metempsychosis" is from the Greek *meta* = after, successive, + *empsychoō* = to animate, from *en* = in + *psyche* = spirit, soul; "Palingenesis," from *palin* = again, anew, + *genesis* = birth, *gignomai* = to be born; "Metensomatosis," from *meta* = after, successive, + *en* = in, + *soma* = body..

among them conceive life after death in terms either more fantastic or merely nebulous. And implausibility — distinguished from grounded improbability—means little else than that the doctrine a person characterizes as implausible is one he has not been accustomed to see treated seriously.

The idea of metempsychosis has appealed to vast numbers of persons in Asia and, even in the West, has commended itself to a number of its most distinguished thinkers from ancient times to the present. In this chapter, we shall cite briefly what some of them have said on the subject. It has in most cases been phrased by them in terms of the words "soul" or "spirit," which we shall retain in presenting their views, instead of using "mind" or "personality" as in our preceding chapters.

Then, in subsequent chapters, we shall examine the objections to which the hypothesis of reincarnation appears open, and the ways, if any, in which they might be met. Finally, we shall consider the facts, such as they are, which have been alleged to constitute evidence of the reality of survival conceived as reincarnation.

1. **W. R. Alger, on the importance of the doctrine of metempsychosis.** The importance of the doctrine of Metempsychosis in the history of mankind may be gathered from the statement with which the Rev. W. R. Alger, a learned Unitarian clergyman of the last century, opens the discussion of the subject in his monumental work, *A Critical History of the Doctrine of a Future Life.* "No other doctrine," he declares, "has exerted so extensive, controlling, and permanent an influence upon mankind as that of the metempsychosis,—the notion that when the soul leaves the body it is born anew in another body, its rank, character, circumstances and experience in each successive existence depending on its qualities, deeds, and attainments in its preceding lives."[2]

Alger cites authority for the fact that at the time of his writing, the adherents of the transmigration doctrine in one or another of the more specific forms under which it has been conceived numbered some six hundred and fifty million; and, in order to account for what he terms "the extent and the tenacious

---

[2] *Op. Cit.,* p. 475, Tenth Edition, Boston 1880; preface dated 1878.

grasp of this antique and stupendous belief" (p. 475), he mentions, among other less potent reasons, the fact that "the theory of the transmigration of souls is marvellously adapted to explain the seeming chaos of moral inequality, injustice, and manifold evil presented in the world of human life . . . . Once admit the theory to be true, and all difficulties in regard to moral justice vanish" (p. 481). Moreover, he writes, "the motive furnished by the doctrine to self-denial and toil has a peerless sublimity" (p. 487).

Alger's book was published in 1860 and ran through ten editions in the course of the succeeding twenty years. In the early editions, notwithstanding the high merits he granted to the reincarnation theory, he apparently rejected it, on the ground that, "destitute of any substantial evidence, it is unable to face the severity of science" (p. 484). But in the fifth of six new chapters which in 1878 he adds in the tenth edition, he considers again the merits of the theory and offers it—though, he emphasizes, in no dogmatic spirit (p. 739)—as probably "the true meaning of the dogma of the resurrection" (p. 735); "the true meaning of the doctrine of the general resurrection and judgment and eternal life, as a natural evolution of history from within" (Preface, p. iv); pointing out (p. 735) that "resurrection and transmigration agree in the central point of a restoration of the disembodied soul to a new bodily existence, only the former represents this as a single collective miracle wrought by an arbitrary stroke of God at the close of the earthly drama, (whereas) the latter depicts it as constantly taking place in the regular fulfillment of the divine plan in the creation." The difference, he goes on, "is certainly, to a scientific and philosophical thinker . . . . . strongly in favor of the Oriental theory" (p. 735). For, he somewhat rhapsodically declares, "the thoughts embodied in it are so wonderful, the method of it so rational, the region of contemplation into which it lifts the mind is so grand, the prospects it opens are of such universal reach and import, that the study of it brings us into full sympathy with the sublime scope of the idea of immortality and of a cosmopolitan vindication of providence uncovered to everyone" (p. 739).

One virtue of the reincarnation hypothesis which Alger does

not actually mention concerns the "origin" of the individual human soul if the latter is conceived, as generally by the religious, in spiritual not materialistic terms. For reincarnation provides an alternative to the shocking supposition common among Christians that, at the mating of any human pair, be it in wedlock or in wanton debauch, an all-wise, almighty, and infinitely loving God creates outright from nothing, or extracts from his own eternal being, an immortal human soul endowed arbitrarily with a particular one out of many possible sets of latent capacities and incapacities. In contrast with this the reincarnation theory says nothing about absolute origins, for it finds no more difficulty in thinking of the "soul" as unoriginated than in thinking of it as unending; that is, in conceiving it as evolving from more primitive to more advanced stages, and as extending thus from an infinite past into an infinite future. For if it is conceivable that anything at all should have no absolute beginning, then it is conceivable of a human spirit as easily as of a divine one.

2. **Metempsychosis in Brahmanism and Buddhism.** The transmigration theory, then, presents to us the idea of a long succession of lives on earth for the individual, each of them as it were a day in the school of experience, teaching him new lessons through which he develops the capacities latent in human nature, grows in wisdom, and eventually reaches spiritual maturity.

This idea has for many centuries been widely accepted in Asia. In Brahmanism, the belief is held that the individual ego or spirit, the Atma, has lived in a body on earth many times before the birth of its present body, and will do so again and again after the death of that body; the bodies in which it incarnates being human, or animal, or even vegetable ones according to its *Karma*, that is, according to the destiny it generates for itself by its acts, its thoughts, and its attitudes and aspirations; this evolutionary process continuing until the individual *Atma*, at last fully developed, attains direct insight into its identity with *Brahman*, the World Spirit, and thereby wins salvation from the necessity of further rebirth.

In Buddhism, which, like Protestantism in Christianity, was a reform movement, the belief in reincarnation and *Karma* carried over but with a difference which at first seems paradoxical. For one of the chief teachings of the Buddha is the *Anatta* doctrine—the doctrine namely, that man has no permanent *Atma* or ego, but that the constituents of his nature are always in process of change, more or less rapidly; and that his present being is related to the past beings he calls his, only in being continuous with them as effect is continuous with cause. In Buddhism, the culmination of the long chain of lives, each generating the next, is therefore not described as realization of the identity of *Atma* and *Brahma*, but as extinction of the three "fires"—that is, of craving, ill-will, and ignorance—which, as long as they persist, bring about re-birth. *Their* extinction is the extinction which the word *Nirvana* signifies.

3. **Pythagoras and Empedocles.** But the idea of preexistence, and of repeated incarnations through which the individual progresses has commended itself not only to the minds of men in Asia, but also to numerous eminent thinkers in the West, both ancient and modern.

One of the earliest was Pythagoras, who flourished about 455 B.C. and is believed to have travelled extensively in the East, perhaps as far as India. Little is known with certainty concerning his views, but Ueberweg, in the first volume of his *History of Philosophy*, states that "all that can be traced with certainty to Pythagoras himself is the doctrine of metempsychosis and the institution of certain religious and ethical regulations." The exact nature of his conception of metempsychosis is not known, but an anecdote reported by Diogenes Laertius—according to which Pythagoras allegedly recognized the soul of a deceased friend of his in the body of a dog that was being beaten—suggests that Pythagoras believed that the human soul was reborn at least sometimes in the bodies of animals. Another Greek philosopher of about the same period, namely, Empedocles, also held to some form of the doctrine of the transmigration of souls.[3]

4. **Plato.** But the greatest of the Greek philosophers who taught the doctrine of periodical reincarnation of souls is of

[3]Ueberweg, op. cit. English Trans. 1, pp. 42-63. Scribner's, N.Y., 1898.

course Plato. In the *Phaedrus*, he writes that the human soul, according to the degree of vision of truth to which it has attained, is reborn in a correspondingly suitable body: "The soul which has seen most of truth shall come to the birth as a philosopher or artist, or musician or lover; that which has seen truth in the second degree shall be a righteous king or warrior or lord; the soul which is of the third class shall be a politician or economist or trader; the fourth shall be a lover of gymnastic toils or a physician . . . ." and so on, down to the ninth degree, to which birth as a tyrant is appropriate—Plato adding that "all these are states of probation, in which he who lives righteously improves, and he who lives unrighteously deteriorates his lot." In another passage Plato says that the soul of a man "may pass into the life of a beast, or from the beast again into the man," but that a soul which has never beheld true being will not pass into the human form, since that vision "was the condition of her passing into the human form."[4] In the tenth book of another of the dialogues, *The Republic*, Plato, sets forth similar ideas. He tells of a mythical warrior, called Er, who had been left for dead on the field of battle but who returned to life ten days afterwards and related that he had seen the souls of men awaiting rebirth, beholding a great variety of available lives open to them, and drawing lots as to who would choose first, who next, and so on. Some chose, according to such folly or wisdom as they had, one or another sort of human life; but here too Plato holds to the possibility of rebirth of a man in animal form, saying that Er saw the soul of Orpheus choose the life of a swan, that of Ajax the life of a lion, that of Agamemnon that of an eagle, and so on.[5]

5. **Plotinus.** The next of the great thinkers whose views on reincarnation may be mentioned is the Neo-Platonist, Plotinus, (204-269 A.D.) who was educated in Alexandria under Ammonius Saccas and taught at Rome for some twenty-five years during the middle of the third century, A.D.; and whose philosophical ideas influenced many of the early shapers of Christian theology. In his treatise on *The Descent of the Soul*, he sets forth a view

---

[4]*Phaedrus*, Jowett's translation, pp. 248-249, Scribner's, N.Y., 1908.
[5]*The Republic*, Jowett's translation, pp. 614, 617-20.

of the education of the soul through repeated births in a material body. The soul, he writes, "confers something of itself on a sensible nature, from which likewise it receives something in return . . . ." By a "sensible" nature, Plotinus means here a nature perceptible to the senses, that is, a body. He goes on to say that the soul, ". . . . through an abundance of sensible desire . . . . becomes profoundly merged into matter and no longer totally abides in the universal soul. Yet our souls are able alternately to rise from hence carrying back with them an experience of what they have known and suffered in their fallen state; from whence they will learn how blessed it is to abide in the intelligible world," that is, in the world of abstract forms, which cannot be perceived by the senses but only apprehended by the intellect, and which are the objects of what Plato called the vision of truth, or of true being. Plotinus goes on to say that the soul, "by a comparison, as it were of contraries, will more plainly perceive the excellence of a superior state. For the experience of evil produces a clearer knowledge of good, especially where the power of judgment is so imbecil, that it cannot without such experience obtain the science of that which is best."[6]

6. **Origen.** Among Christian thinkers of approximately the same period as Plotinus, who like him believed in repeated earth lives for the soul, was Origen (c. 185-c. 254, A.D.) one of the Fathers of the Church most influential in the early developments of Christian theology. He held not only, like some of the other theologians of that period, that the human soul preexisted and in some sense lived prior to its entrance into the body, but also that after death it eventually reentered a new body, and this repeatedly until, fully purified, it was fit to enter heaven. This doctrine was later condemned by the second Council of Constantinople, but the following passage, from the Latin translation by Rufinus of Origen's Greek text, of which only a fragment of the original passage remains, leaves no doubt that Origen professed it: "Everyone, therefore, of those who descend to the earth is, according to his deserts or to the position that he had there, ordained to be born in this world either in a different place, or

---

[6] *Five Books of Plotinus*, translated by Thos. Taylor, London, 1794, pp. 279-80.

in a different nation, or in a different occupation, or with different infirmities, or to be descended from religious or at least less pious parents; so as sometimes to bring about that an Israelite descends among the Scythians, and a poor Egyptian is brought down to Judaea."[7]

7. **The Jews, Egyptians, Celts, and Teutons.** Having alluded in what precedes to the influence of Neo-Platonism and in particular of Plotinus on the early Christian theologians, it may not be amiss to mention briefly two or three statements in the new Testament, which have often been cited as indicating that belief in preexistence and rebirth was not uncommon among the persons to whom Jesus spoke, and indeed as suggesting that perhaps he himself accepted it or at least regarded it as plausible.

In the ninth chapter of the Gospel according to St. John, we have the story of the man born blind, whom Jesus saw as he passed by. "His disciples asked him, 'Rabbi, who sinned, this man or his parents, that he was born blind?" Jesus answered, "It was not that this man sinned, or his parents, but that the works of God might be made manifest in him." The point is that the answer of Jesus does not deny that the man could have sinned before birth, but denies only that this actually was the cause of his blindness. More explicit and positive is the assertion by Jesus, twice reported in the Gospel according to St. Matthew, that John the Baptist was Elijah: "And if you are willing to accept it, he is Elijah who is to come. He who has ears to hear, let him hear." And farther on: "But I tell you that Elijah has already come, and they did not know him, but did to him whatever they pleased

---

[7]Origen: *De Principiis* IV Cap. 3, 10, 26, 23. The Latin of Rufinus' translation is given as follows on p. 338 of Vol. 5 of *Die Griechischen Christlichen Schriftsteller der Ersten Drei Jahrhunderte:* Unusquisque ergo descendentium in terram pro meritis vel loco suo, quem ibi habuerat, dispensatur in hoc mundo in diversis vel locis vel gentibus vel conversationibus vel infirmitatibus nasci vel a religiosis aut certe minus piis parentibus generari, ita ut inveniat aliquando Israheliten in Scythas descendere et Aegyptium pauperem deduci ad Iudaeam.

The fragment, which is all we have of Origen's own Greek of the passage, reads: *kai para toisde ē toisde tois patrasin ōs dynasthai pote Israēlitēn pasein eis Schythas kai Aigypton eis tēn Ioudaian katelthein*

. . . . . . Then the disciples understood that he was speaking to them of John the Baptist" (XVII, 12, 13.).

At all events, the doctrine of the transmigration of souls was a part of the Jewish esoteric mystical philosophy known as the Kabbala, the origin of which is very ancient, apparently antedating even the Christian era. The doctrine is mentioned in the later Zoharistic works, but "is never found systematically developed" there; rather, wherever it occurs, it is tacitly assumed as well known, and no explanation is given in detail.[8] The following passage is quoted from the Zohar (ii, 99b) by C. D. Ginsburg: "All souls are subject to transmigration, and men do not know the ways of the Holy One, blessed be he; they do not know that they are brought before the tribunal, both before they enter into this world and after they quit it, they are ignorant of the many transmigrations and secret probations which they have to undergo . . . . . But the time is at hand when these mysteries will be disclosed."[9] The same author, in a footnote (p. 125) writes: "According to Josephus, the doctrine of the transmigration of souls into other bodies . . . . . was also held by the Pharisees . . . . . . restricting, however, the metempsychosis to the righteous. And though the Midrashin and the Talmud are silent about it, yet from Saadia's vituperation against it . . . . . there is no doubt that this doctrine was held among some Jews in the ninth century of the present era. At all events it is perfectly certain that the Karaite Jews firmly believed in it ever since the seventh century . . . . . St. Jerome assures us that it was also propounded among the early Christians as an esoteric and traditional doctrine which was entrusted to the select few; . . . . and Origen was convinced that it was only by means of this doctrine that certain Scriptural narratives, such as the struggle of Jacob with Esau before their birth, the reference to Jeremiah when still in his mother's womb, and many others, can possibly be explained."

---

[8]M. Gaster: *Hastings Encyclopedia of Religion and Ethics*, Art. Transmigration, p. 439. Cf. G. Scholem: *Major Trends in Jewish Mysticism*. Schoken Pub. House, Jerusalem, 1947 pp. 281 ff.

[9]*The Essenes, The Kabbalah*, Routledge and Kegan Paul, London, 1955, pp. 124-5.

In the ancient world, the belief in reincarnation was anyway widespread. Herodotus, Plato, and other Greek writers report it of the Egyptians of their time; Herodotus, for example, writing (Bk. II, Sec. 123): ". . . the Egyptians were the first to teach that the human soul is immortal, and at the death of the body enters into some other living thing then coming to birth; and after passing through all creatures, of land, sea, and air (which cycle it completes in three thousand years) it enters once more into a human body at birth. Some of the Greeks, early and late, have used this doctrine as if it were their own . . ."[10]

Both Caesar and Valerius Maximus definitely state that the Druids of ancient Gaul held the belief in reincarnation; and there is evidence also that it was present among the early Teutonic peoples.

8. **Hume.** Let us, however, now turn to more recent times and see what some eminent modern philosophers have had to say concerning metempsychosis. The first I shall mention is one of the greatest in the history of modern thought—the skeptical philosopher, David Hume. In one of his essays, he emphasizes on the one hand the weakness of the metaphysical and of the moral arguments for the immortality of the soul, and on the other, the strength of the physical arguments for its mortality; and he then concludes the passage with the statement that "the *Metempsychosis* is therefore the only system of this kind [that is, the only conception of immortality] that philosophy can hearken to."[11]

9. **Kant.** Another and no less famous philosopher, who also gave some thought to the idea of preexistence and of rebirth, was Immanuel Kant. In a passage of his celebrated *Critique of Pure Reason,* he notes that "generation in the human race . . . . . depends on . . . . many accidents, on occasion, ... on the views and whims of government, nay, even on vice;" and he remarks that "it is difficult to believe in the eternal existence of a being whose life has first begun under circumstances so trivial, and so entirely dependent on our own choice." Kant then points out that the

---

[10]Bk. III. Sec. 123. Tr. by. A. D. Godley, Putnam's N. Y. 1921.
[11]*Essays and Treatises on Various Subjects,* Boston, 1881. Second of the two, *Essays on Suicide,* p. 228.

strangeness, which attaches to the supposition that so important
an effect arises from such insignificant causes, would disappear
if we should accept the hypothesis that the life of the human
spirit is "not subject to the changes of time . . . neither beginning
in birth, nor ending in death," and that the life of the body,
which so begins and so ends, "is phenomenal only;" that is to
say, if we should accept the hypothesis that "if we could see ourselves and other objects *as they really are,* we should see ourselves in a world of spiritual natures, our community with which
did neither begin at our birth nor will end with the death of
the body."[12] Indeed, a more recent philosopher, James Ward,
who in his Gifford Lectures calls attention to this passage, states
in a note that Kant, in his lectures on metaphysics shortly before
the publication of the *Critique,* dogmatically taught both the preexistence and the immortality of the soul.[13]

10. **Fichte.** Another German philosopher, Fichte, contrasts
the spiritual part of himself, which he conceives as the will to
obey the laws of reason, with the sensuous other part, and conjec-
tures that the latter may have the form of a succession of incarnate lives. He writes: "These two orders,—the purely spiritual
and the sensuous, the latter consisting possibly of an innumerable
series of particular lives,—have existed in me from the first moment of the development of my active reason . . . . My sensuous
existence may, in future, assume other forms, but these are just
as little the true life, as its present form."[14]

11. **Schopenhauer.** Another German philosopher, Schopenhauer, had some acquaintance with the thought of India, and a
good deal of sympathy with certain of its features—in particular
with its doctrine of repeated births. In the third volume of his
great work, *The World as Will and Idea,* he has a chapter on
"Death and its relation to the indestructibility of our true nature." This true nature he conceives to be not the intellect,
which is mortal, but "the character, i.e., the will" which is "the

---

[12]*Critique of Pure Reason,* M. Mueller's Transl. MacMillan's 2nd ed. pp. 625-6.
[13]James Ward, *The Realm of Ends,* p. 404.
[14]*The Vocation of Man,* Bk. III, Transl. by Wm. Smith, Pub. London 1848,
p. 162.

eternal part" of us and comes again and again to new births. This doctrine, he goes on, is "more correctly denoted by the word palingenesis [that is, new births] than by metempsychosis" since the latter term suggests that what is reborn is the whole *psyche*, whereas not the intellectual part of it, but only the will, is born again.[15]

12. **Renouvier.** One of the most distinguished French philosophers of recent times, Charles Renouvier, also endorses the doctrine of reincarnation. In the course of the exposition of his elaborate theory of monads, of indestructible germs, and of the origin and destiny of personality, he writes: "But it is not once only that each person must live again on earth owing to the actualization of one of those seminal potencies; it is a certain number of times, we do not know how many . . . ." And again, speaking of the several individuals which are the several lives of one person, he writes: "These individuals, whom memory does not tie together, and who have to one another no earthly genealogical relationships, also have no memory of the person whom each of them comes to continue on earth. Such forgetting is a condition of any theory of preexistence . . . . the person, reintegrated in the world of ends, recovers there the memory of its state in the world of origins, and of the diverse lives which it has gone through, in the course of which it has received the lessons and undergone the trials of the life of pain."[16]

13. **McTaggart.** To be mentioned next in our partial list of recent and contemporary eminent thinkers who have regarded with favor the theory of metempsychosis are three distinguished British philosophers. The first is John McTaggart, who in 1906 published a book entitled *Some Dogmas of Religion*. The whole of its fourth chapter is devoted to a discussion of the idea of human preexistence. He states that this "renders the doctrine of a plurality of lives more probable." This doctrine "would, indeed, be in any case the most probable form of the doctrine of immortality" (p xiii). Farther on, McTaggart points out that

---

[15]Vol. III:300, Haldane and Kemp's translation. Kegan Paul, Trench, Trubner Co. London, 1906.

[16]*Le Personnalisme*, pp. 125-126. Felix Alcan, Paris 1903.

if both preexistence and immortality are true, then "each man
would have at least three lives, his present life, one before it,
and one after it. It seems more probable, however, that this
would not be all, and that his existence before and after his
present life would in each case be divided into many lives, each
bounded by birth and death." And he adds that there is much
to be said for the view that [such] a plurality of lives would be
the most probable alternative, even on a theory of immortality
which did not include preexistence (p. 116).[17]

14. **Ward.** James Ward, cited above as having called attention to what Kant had to say on the subject of the human spirit's
existence before the birth and after the death of its body, himself
considers various theories of a future life in the 18th of his
Gifford lectures. One of these theories is that of metempsychosis.
He examines some of the chief objections to it which have been
advanced, and he suggests more or less plausible ways in which
they may be met. He concludes that "we must at least insist . . . .
that if such life [to wit, a future life] is to have any worth or
meaning, a certain personal continuity of development is essential. From this point of view, death becomes indeed a longer
sleep dividing life from life as sleep divides day from day; and
as there is progress from day to day so too there may be from life
to life."[18]

15. **Broad.** Lastly, the distinguished Cambridge philosopher, C. D. Broad, at the end of his discussion of the empirical
arguments which may be advanced in support of the idea of survival after death, points out that the hypothesis as to what specifically may survive, which he has himself offered, "has certain
advantages for those who favor the theory of metempsychosis, as
Dr. McTaggart does."[19] And, in a later work where at one point
he discusses what McTaggart says on the subject, Broad states
that, to himself, the theory of preexistence and plurality of lives
seems to be one "which ought to be taken very seriously, both on

---

[17]Op. Cit. London, Edw. Arnold, 1906.
[18]*The Realm of Ends*, Cambridge Univ. Press N.Y. 1911, p. 407.
[19]*The Mind and its Place in Nature*. Harcourt Brace & Co. New York, 1929,
p. 551.

philosophical grounds and as furnishing a reasonable motive for right action . . . . We shall behave all the better if we act on the assumption that we may survive; that actions which tend to strengthen and enrich our characters in this life will probably have a favorable influence on the dispositions with which we begin our next lives; and that actions which tend to disintegrate our characters in this life will probably cause us to enter on our next life "halt and maimed." If we suppose that our future lives will be of the same general nature as our present lives, this postulate, which is in itself intelligible and not unreasonable, gains enormously in concreteness and therefore in practical effect on our conduct.[20]

The preceding citations from authors who have expressed opinions favorable in various degrees to the idea of reincarnation have been limited to philosophers, and even so have not included all those who could be listed. But numerous poets also have viewed the doctrine sympathetically. Persons interested to know what these have had to say, or in citations from various other quarters of opinions commendatory of the doctrine of rebirth, will find quotations in several fairly accessible books, among which may be mentioned E. D. Walker's *Reincarnation, A Study of Forgotten Truth,* G. de Purucker's *The Esoteric Tradition,* and Paul Siwek's *La Réincarnation des Esprits.*[21]

16. **Various forms of the doctrine of reincarnation.** Some of the statements which have been quoted in what precedes will have indicated that believers in reincarnation do not all conceive the doctrine in exactly the same manner. Many of them, for example, believe that a man may be reborn as an animal, and hence that some of the animals are animated by souls which have been and probably again will some time be lodged in human bodies. Others believe that once a soul has reached the human level, it will not thereafter be reborn as an animal. Again, differences of opinion exist as to the interval of time between in-

---

[20]*Examination of McTaggart's Philosophy.* Cambridge, University Press 1938, p. 639

[21]Respectively, Houghton Mifflin, Boston, 1888; Theosophical University Press, Point Loma, Calif., 1935, Vol. II, Chs. XIX, XX, pp. 620-47; Desclée de Brouwer, Rio de Janeiro, 1942, Introduction and Part I.

carnations. For example, L. A. Waddell, who accompanied the
expedition of Sir Francis Younghusband to Tibet at the beginning of the present century, and who has written extensively on
the religion of the Tibetan Lamas, mentions that when the
Dalai Lama dies, the selection of his successor is based on the
belief that his spirit is immediately reincarnated as a new born
infant.[22] Search is then made for a child born at that time, to
whom certain additional tests are then applied.

Other believers in reincarnation hold that a long interval
normally elapses between two incarnations—centuries, or indeed
sometimes a thousand years or more—and offer accounts of the
manner in which they think the discarnate soul employs these
lengthy periods.

Another interesting form of the belief in reincarnation is
that held, according to Delafosse, by one of the West African
tribes, the Mandingos. They do not think of reincarnation as
universal. They believe that the spirit of a dead man, which they
call his *niama* "can reside where it likes—in the corpse, in the
hut, in a sacred object, or in the body of a living being whose
niama it absorbs." The spirit of a man for whom the due rites
have not been performed may reincarnate itself in a solitary animal, or in a human being, who goes mad."[23] This particular
version of the idea of reincarnation is interesting as being virtually identical with the familiar ideas of "obsession" or "possession"; although, in these as traditionally conceived, what incarnates temporarily in the "possessed" person, is not, as in the
Mandingo belief, a discarnate human spirit, but a devil. Some
West African tribes more easterly than the Mandingos apparently
do not conceive reincarnation in this manner, but in its ordinary
sense, according to which the body the discarnate human spirit
enters is that of a child about to be born, not an adult body with
a spirit of its own that has to be displaced or is made insane by
the invasion of another spirit. A conception of reincarnation
similar to that of the Mandingos appears in some of the communications of automatists emanating purportedly from discar-

[22]*Lhasa and its Mysteries*, Dutton and Co., N. Y. 1905, p. 28.
[23]Delafosse, Haut-Sénégal-Niger, III, 165 quoted in *Hastings' Encyclopedia of
.Religion and Ethics*, Art. Transmigration.

nate spirits. For example, in Ch. XV of a book entitled *Thirty Years Among the Dead*,[24] the author, Dr. C. A. Wickland, transcribes communications, uttered by his wife while entranced, from purported spirits who said that during life they had had some acquaintance with the teachings of modern Theosophy and [apparently misconceiving these] that they endeavored to reincarnate by invading the bodies of several of Dr. Wickland's patients. These, as in the Mandingos' belief, had gone mad, i.e., seemingly obsessed or possessed by some personality other than their own.

---

[24]Spiritualist Press, London, no date.

Chapter XXI

DIFFICULTIES IN THE REINCARNATION HYPOTHESIS

The mere fact that the reincarnation hypothesis, in one form or another, has been treated with respect by some thinkers of high eminence, and even has been accepted by some of them, does not prove that reincarnation is a fact. Moreover, critics of the doctrine have advanced various objections to it, purporting to show that it can not possibly be true. We must now consider them and decide whether they do or do not establish the impossibility. And, if we find that they do not really do so, we shall then have to ask whether any empirical evidence at all exists that shows or tends to show that reincarnation occurs.

1. **The materialistic objection to any form of life after death.** The first objection likely to suggest itself to the contemporary Western educated mind would be that a mind cannot exist without a living body, nor therefore pass from a dying body to a living one born later. This objection, if sound, would rule out not only metempsychosis, but also the possibility of any form of survival. But it need not detain us here since, as we saw in Part III, the basis of it consists not of established facts, but only of one or another of the materialistic interpretations of the facts. And, as we took pains to make clear, these interpretations are in no way authoritative but amount only to this: that in them, a legitimate program—that of searching for *material* causes—is illegitimately erected unawares into the metaphysical dogma that none but material causes can exist at all. Moreover in Part IV, various facts were cited which lend some empirical support to the hypothesis that the mind survives the body's death.

The question before us in the present chapter is therefore only whether, if survival is indeed a fact, any good reasons exist for believing that it cannot take the form which the reincarnation hypothesis describes; namely, in its most plausible version, that, following the body's death, there is first a period of discarnate existence whether short or long; and then rebirth, in an infant body, of such of the capacities of the mind of the deceased person as had constituted the basis for acquisition by it of the other capacities it did acquire—and indeed also for acquisition of various others which it did not in fact acquire because external circumstances presented no need for them, or no opoprtunity to acquire them.

2. **The objection that we have no memory of having lived before.** A *prima facie* plausible objection to the reincarnation hypothesis is that we have no memory whatever of having lived before our birth. But if this objection has any force at all, then it has far too much; for, since we have also no memory of the first few years of our present life, it would then follow equally that we did not then exist. Indeed, the case is really worse than this, for we have also no memories at all of the great majority of the days of our life. My own belief, for example that I was alive and conscious on say, the third of December, 1930 is not based on my memory of that day, for I recall nothing whatever in connection with it; and probably nobody else recalls having observed me on that particular day. That belief of mine is in fact only an inference, based on the vacuous premise that human consciousness is continuous—except for periods of unconsciousness in dreamless sleep, in anesthesia, in coma, or otherwise!

It may be said, of course, that although we have no conscious memories of our days of early childhood, or of most of our days since then, yet memories of them persist subconsciously and can be made manifest by automatic writing as induced in her patients by, for example, the late Dr. Anita Mühl, or by the techniques of psychoanalysis; or by suggestions of age-regression, given under hypnosis. But then we naturally find ourselves led to ask how far back such revival of memories can be made to go. Memories of the intra-uterine experiences of the foetus have apparently been obtained; and in some cases, purported memories pertaining to past incarnations. If the latter are dismissed as mere in-

ventions of the mythopoeic faculty, induced by the suggestions
of age-regression, then, on the very same ground, it will be necessary to dismiss also alleged memories of intra-uterine experiences;
and indeed, also abnormally obtained memories of the years of
infancy and even of subsequent years, except where the reality
of the events purportedly remembered happens to be in some way
independently verifiable. But then, what shall we say about the
few reported cases where it is claimed that verification was made
also of facts purportedly remembered from an earlier incarnation? We shall return to this claim farther on, when we come
to ask whether any positive empirical evidence exists in support
of the reincarnation hypothesis. At -this point, however, we are
concerned only with the allegations that absence of memory of
earlier lives is empirical evidence that we had no such lives; and
the outcome of the preceding remarks is that absence of memory
of an event, and especially of a long past event, never proves that
one did not experience the event. Positive memories *can* be evidence concerning one's past, but absence of memories of it proves
nothing at all about it.

3. **The objection that memory is indispensable to identity
of person.** Another objection to the transmigration hypothesis is
that personal identity is wholly dependent on memory; and hence
that, without memories of earlier lives, there is no difference at
all between rebirth of "one" person, and death of one person followed by birth of a *different* person.[1] This objection, however,
would be easily disposed of by the supposition that, although
memory of earlier lives is absent during any one life, such memory
is periodically regained at some point during the interval between consecutive lives; or, possibly, is regained at the end of
the series of earthly incarnations if the series does have an end.
The supposition that, at *some* time, memory of earlier lives is
recovered suffices to make rebirth of *one* person mean something
different from death of one person followed by birth of *another*
person. Absence now of such memory entails only that we cannot tell *now* which of those two possibilities is the fact.

---

[1]Leibniz; *Philosophische Schriften*, ed. Gerhardt, IV. 300.

4. **The objection that, without memory of one's acts, nothing is learned from their consequences.** An objection which has been made to the transmigration hypothesis—or at least to the assumption usually coupled with it that wisdom is gained and moral lessons learned gradually from the consequences brought about by right and wrong acts—is that, without memory of the act, or thought or feeling or attitude, which brought about a given consequence, the relation of cause and effect between them is not perceived; and hence that no moral lesson is learned or any wisdom gained from such features of our lot in the present life as are consequences of right or wrong conduct in preceding lives.

A sufficient answer to this objection is that perception of the consequences of our conduct is one way, but not the only way, in which growth in wisdom, virtue, or ability, can be brought about by those consequences. An act of which we retain no memory may nevertheless have the remote effect of placing us eventually in a situation conducive to the acquiring of the wisdom, virtue, or ability, lack of which made us act as we did in the forgotten past. If, as the *Karma* doctrine of the Hindus asserts, our conduct in one incarnation automatically tends to have this very sort of consequence in one or another of our later lives, then lack of memory of those past lives does not prevent our growing morally and spiritually, in this indirect manner, owing to the nature of our conduct in unremembered earlier lives. Moreover if, as already suggested may be the case, memory of preceding lives is regained in the discarnate interval between incarnations, this would make growth in wisdom possible not only in the manner just described, but also by discernment of some of the consequences of certain of one's acts in earlier lives.

5. **The objection that wisdom, virtue, knowledge, and skills are not innate, but are gradually acquired after birth.** It may be objected, however, that whatever such growth we achieve in a given incarnation, whether in the indirect manner described, or directly out of perception of the consequences of acts done in the present or in a previous incarnation, that growth anyway does not carry over from past lives to the present one. For children are not born with knowledge that fire burns, but have to learn

it again in this life no matter how many times in past lives they may have touched fire and got burnt. Similarly, children have to be taught not to lie and not to take the property of others; they are not born with ready-made mathematical or musical or other skills, any more than with a ready-made moral conscience, but acquire all these by processes open to observation. No matter what they may have learned in past lives, their education—moral, intellectual, aesthetic, and of other sorts—certainly seems to have to start from scratch in the present life.

Reflection, however, makes evident that what has just been said is not quite the whole story. Skills, habits, knowledge, and other varieties of what psychologists call "conditionings" indeed have to be painstakingly acquired during the years of life. But what we come equipped with at birth is not these things; it is only certain instincts and certain aptitudes—an aptitude being a capacity to acquire, when subjected to the relevant stimuli, certain more determinate capacities of the kinds mentioned above. In these native aptitudes, human beings differ considerably one from another. One person will learn quickly and easily what another, even with great effort, is able to learn but slowly and imperfectly.

In this connection, it is useful to dwell on the fact that if any one of us, had been taken away in early childhood from the family where in fact he grew up, and had been placed instead among the Pygmies of Africa, or among the Eskimos, or among the Chinese; or indeed, in his native country, in a family markedly different in economic, cultural and social respects from that in which he was born; then he would, on the basis of his very same stock of native aptitudes, certainly have developed a personality vastly different from his present one. Reflection on this indubitable fact is likely to make the personality he now calls his Self appear to him analogous rather to some particular one of the various roles which a given actor is capable of playing. And this reflection is then likely to lead a person to identify his true Self with his native set of basic aptitudes, rather than with the accidental particular personality—i.e., the particular memories, skills, habits, and so on—generated through the interaction between those aptitudes and the particular environment in which his body happens to have lived.

It is true that, when discussing reincarnation, Professor James H. Hyslop writes: "It is personality that we want, if survival is to be in any way interesting to us, and not only personality, but we want a personal consciousness of this personal identity."[2] But in the light of the remarks just made this demand, though natural enough, appears rather naively wilful.

The supposition just considered, that if reincarnation is a fact then what a man brings to a new birth is not a developed mind or personality but only certain aptitudes, has commended itself also to some other writers who, however, have worded it somewhat differently. Professor Broad, for example, suggests that what transmigrates, if anything does, might not be a mind but only something which he calls a "psychogenic factor," the nature of which, however, he does not describe beyond saying that, from combination of it with a brain, a mind emerges—somewhat as common salt emerges out of the combination of sodium and chlorine, neither of which by itself has the properties of salt.[3] Again, Professor Francis Bowen, in an article in the Princeton Review for May, 1881, quoted at considerable length by E. D. Walker,[4] offered a similar hypothesis, wording it, however, in terms of Kant's distinction between man's Intelligible Character, which is noumenal, and his Empirical Character, which is phenomenal—a distinction only alluded to in the particular passage of Kant's Critique we cited earlier, but which Kant formulates explicitly elsewhere in a different connection.

But if transmigration is to be conceived as a process of growth, it is necessary to assume that the activities and experiences of each incarnation result not only in the acquisition of particular skills, tastes, habits, knowledge, etc., on the basis of the aptitudes (or "psychogenic factor," or "Intelligible Character") brought from past lives; but in addition result in some alteration

---

[2]*Borderland of Psychial Research*, Turner & Co. Boston, 1906, p. 368.

[3]*The Mind and its Place in Nature*, Harcourt Brace & Co. New York, 1929, p. 535.

[4]*Reincarnation, A Study of Forgotten Truth*, Houghton Mifflin, Boston, 1888, pp. 102 ff.

of that stock of aptitudes itself—enhancement of some of them, deterioration of others, perhaps acquisition of new ones, and possibly loss altogether of certain others. And Broad indeed postulates for the psychogenic factor capacity to be modified to some extent by the experiences and activities of the mind which has resulted from the combination of the psychogenic and the bodily factors.

6. **Native aptitudes, heredity, and growth of the self.** It may be contended, however, that a person's native aptitudes or anyway some of them are a matter of heredity; and that if they are derived thus from his ancestors then they are not derived from strivings or experiences of his own past lives. But McTaggart, whose favorable opinion of the transmigration hypothesis was cited earlier, argues that the facts of heredity are at least not incompatible with transmigration. "There is no impossibility," he writes, "in supposing that the characteristics in which we resemble the ancestors of our bodies may be to some degree characteristics due to our previous lives." He points out that "hats in general fit their wearers with far greater accuracy than they would if each man's hat were assigned to him by lot. And yet there is very seldom any causal connection between the shape of the head and the shape of the hat. A man's head is never made to fit his hat, and, in the great majority of cases, his hat is not made to fit his head. The adaptation comes about by each man selecting, from hats made without any special reference to his particular head, the hat which will suit his particular head best." And McTaggart goes on to say: "This may help us to see that it would be possible to hold that a man whose nature had certain characteristics when he was about to be reborn, would be reborn in a body descended from ancestors of a similar character. His character when reborn would, in this case, be decided, as far as the points in question went, by his character in his previous life, and not by the character of the ancestors of his new body. But . . . . . the character of the ancestors of the new body, and its similarity to his character," would be what "determined the fact that he was reborn in that body rather than another."[5] And in

---

[5] *Some Dogmas of Religion*, Edward Arnold, London, 1906, p. 125.

answer to the question as to how each person finds the body most appropriate to him, McTaggart refers to the analogy of chemical affinities.

McTaggart, it must be emphasized, is not contending that some of the characteristics—or let us say more specifically, aptiitudes—which a person possesses *were* gained in an earlier life and brought over to the present one at birth. He is contending only that this supposition is not incompatible with the inheritance of aptitudes from one's ancestors.

But the compatibility of the two, or not, turns on whether heredity accounts for *every* aptitude a person is born with. If it does, then the supposition that any aptitudes at all are brought from a past incarnation becomes wholly idle. Indeed, no room at all is left for it, since if something *did* have a certain origin, then it did not have a different one!

The assumption, however, that heredity does account for *all* of a person's native aptitudes is a good deal more sweeping than present-day knowledge of heredity warrants. Hence, if a given aptitude a man has does not happen to be traceable to his parents or known ancestors, his having brought it over from an earlier life remains conceivable.

But just what, in McTaggart's simile, the "hat" and the "head" may respectively consist in literally, can become clear only in the light of analysis of the notions of an "aptitude" and of the corresponding "skill."

An aptitude, it will be recalled, is the capacity to acquire a specific capacity under given circumstances; and the specific capacity concerned is a skill in so far as it is voluntary. Moreover, that a given person did possess aptitude for acquisition of a given skill is shown by his having in fact acquired it. But the factors on which his having acquired it depended are several.

One was possession by him of such *bodily* organs of sensation or of action as may be necessary for exercise of the skill concerned. For example, no matter how musically gifted otherwise a man may be, he cannot acquire high skill as a violinist if his fingers are short, thick, and stiff.

A second factor consists in possession of *psychological* aptitude for acquisition of the skill concerned, in addition to such bodily aptitude as the skill may require.

The third factor consists of the *external opportunities or/and stimuli* which the person in view has had for acquisition of that skill. A man's capacity to acquire ability to swim, for instance, would have no opportunity to realize itself if he were to spend his whole life in the desert.

And a fourth factor is *interest* in acquisition of the skill concerned. Aptitude and opportunity for acquisition of the skill might exist, yet interest in acquiring it might be lacking. Or the interest might exist but remain latent in the absence of external circumstances that would arouse it. Or the interest might exist and be patent, but the person might have no aptitude for acquisition of the particular skill. The interest is therefore a factor additional to the other three.

Which of the four factors, we may now ask, would constitute the "hat" in McTaggart's simile, and which of them the "head"?

The first factor—bodily aptitude—is plausibly a matter of biological heredity and would therefore be part of the "hat." Whether or how far the second factor—psychological aptitude—is also purely a matter of biological heredity is dubious. So when, as often is the case, a given aptitude is not traceable to the parents or the known ancestors, the supposition that it has been brought over from an earlier life remains possible. The aptitude concerned would then be part of the "head."

The third factor — the external circumstances which permitted acquisition of the skill for which aptitude existed—would evidently be another part of the "hat." And the fourth factor—existence of latent interest in acquisition of the skill concerned—can, like the aptitude for that skill, be supposed to be a carryover from an earlier life and thus to be part of the "head." Indeed, that interest, which amounts to a craving to acquire that skill, can be supposed to operate as the quasi "chemical affinity" McTaggart invokes, by which the aptitude to acquire that skill is brought to incarnation in a family that provides not only the appropriate bodily heredity, but also eventually the kind of external circumstances necessary for development of the particular skill concerned.

Chapter XXII

INCOMPETENT KINDS OF EVIDENCE
FOR AND AGAINST REINCARNATION

In Chapter XXI, we examined a number of difficulties in the way of the reincarnation hypothesis, and found them far from sufficient to show that it cannot be true, or even that it is more probably false than true. We now come to the question whether any empirical evidence is available that would tend to support the hypothesis. In the present chapter, certain facts will be considered which have sometimes been offered as evidence of reincarnation but which, as we shall see, admit of some different and more plausible explanation. And since, in Part IV, we came to the conclusion that some positive evidence exists for survival— survival discarnate for the time being anyway—of some components of the personality of deceased persons, the facts on which we shall comment in the present chapter will include the testimony on the subject of reincarnation contained in certain communications which purported to emanate from surviving spirits of the deceased.

1. **"Déjá vu" experiences.** An experience sometimes thought by the persons who have it to be evidence that they have lived before their present life is the experience psychologists have labelled "déjá vu," i.e., "already seen," "seen before." It is what occurs when a person "recognizes" some situation which in fact he never experienced before—for example some street or house in a town he is now visiting for the first time, and of which he has never seen a picture or description. In such cases, the person concerned sometimes interprets the fact that what he is seeing for the first time in his life nevertheless feels familiar to him, as being evidence that he must have seen it in an earlier life.

The true explanation, however, is usually that the new situation is similar in prominent respects to some situation he has experienced before in his present life but which he does not at the moment recall; and that, although the two situations also have dissimilarities, nevertheless the points of likeness between them are sufficient to generate the feeling of familiarity which, normally, is a *sign* that the object or situation arousing it was experienced before. A striking example of such spurious recognition occurs when we "recognize" a person whom we have in fact never met before, but who happens to be the twin of an acquaintance we then mistakenly believe ourselves to be facing at the moment.

Another explanation, however, perhaps fits better some instances of "déjá vu"—those where the person concerned feels that he so remembers the conversation he is now hearing, or the house he is now entering for the first time, that he can tell what the person who speaks next is going to say, or what a given door in the house leads into.

In such cases, what he now feels he already knows may be something which he is now paranormally precognizing. Or it may be something which he paranormally precognized a short time before, but only subconsciously, or perhaps the night before in a dream he does not remember—the later parts of the past precognition being now brought to consciousness by the present perceptual fulfillment of the earlier parts.

Whether or not this explanation happens to be the correct one in a given case, the fact that precognition has been experimentally proved to occur sometimes[1] means that explanation of a "déjá vu" experience in terms of paranormal precognition must not be ruled out *a priori,* and that the normal type of explanation must not be made a Procrustean bed, which every fact of this kind, no matter how recalcitrant, shall be stretched or trimmed to fit into.

2. **Illusions of Memory.** Mnemonic illusions are another type of experience capable of causing a person to believe that he has lived other lives than his present one. The late Prof. J. H.

---

[1]See for instance "Experiments in Precognitive Telepathy" by S. G. Soal and K. M. Goldney, *Proc. S.P.R.* Vol. 47:21-150; 1943; and summary in *Modern Experiments in Telepathy,* by S. G. Soal and F. Bateman, Yale Univ. Press 1954, pp. 123-31.

Hyslop mentions an example of such an illusion, which, although the experient did not interpret it as memory of an earlier life, nevertheless strikingly illustrates the possibility of mnemonic illusion.[2] The person concerned was a friend of Dr. Hyslop's, and, in conversation with another, mentioned that he remembered the Harrison presidential campaign and described in considerable detail many of the incidents in it. He, however, had been born in 1847, whereas the Harrison campaign had taken place in 1840. The explanation of his "memories" of the campaign turned out to be that what he really remembered were the vivid images of the campaign which he had formed in childhood as a result of the elaborate descriptions of it which uncles of his who had taken part in it and with whom he went to live at the age of eight, delighted to rehearse, in his hearing, for their friends and neighbors. He had remembered the images, but not how his mind had come to be furnished with them.

3. **Paranormal retrocognitions.** But a person's belief that he had an earlier life may be a conclusion he bases on a dream or vision which subsequent historical research shows to have corresponded in recondite details to some historical event antedating his birth—which details he certainly never learned in a normal manner. A tempting interpretation of such an experience is that he actually witnessed the event in an earlier life, and that the vision or dream is a memory image of it, carried over from that earlier life to the present one.

An example of a vision which would lend itself to such an interpretation, although in fact it was not so interpreted by the two ladies who had the vision, is that of Miss Moberly and Miss Jourdain at Versailles, related in their much discussed book entitled *An Adventure*.[3] A more plausible interpretation of the facts as reported—which is the interpretation they themselves adopted—is that their vision was a case of retrocognitive clairvoyance.

4. **Testimony, purportedly from discarnate spirits.** Another

---

[2]*Borderland of Psychical Research*, Turner & Co., Boston, 1906, pp. 371-2.

[3]London, Faber & Faber, 1911. By 1947 the book had had four editions and many printings.

kind of empirical evidence alleged by some to substantiate, or
to invalidate, the belief in reincarnation consists of the declara-
tions on the subject contained in the mediumistic communications from purported discarnate spirits.

In 1856, Hypolite Denizard Rivail, better known by his pen
name of Allan Kardec, published *Le Livre des Esprits,* consisting
mainly of communications, dictated through unnamed "diverse
mediums" by various purported discarnate spirits in answer to
questions asked by Kardec—these questions and answers being
then published by him in the book at the behest of those spirits.
One of the central doctrines proclaimed by them is that of reincarnation. The following, which is a translation of Sec. 166 of
the 1947 amplified edition, is a typical passage (from Chapter
IV pp. 147/8):*

Q. How can the soul, which has not reached perfection during corporeal life, complete its purification?

A. By undergoing the trials of a new life.

Q. How does the soul accomplish this new life? Is it by its
transformation into Spirit?

A. The soul, by purification, undoubtedly undergoes a transformation, but for this it needs the trials of a new life.

Q. The soul then has several corporeal lives?

A. Yes, we all have several lives. Those who assert the contrary wish to keep you in the ignorance in which they
themselves are; it is their desire.

Q. It seems to follow from this principle that the soul, after
having left one body, takes on another; in other words,
that it reincarnates in a new body. Is this what we are to
understand?

A. Evidently.

Interesting additional information concerning *Le Livre des
Esprits* is provided by Alexander Aksakof, one of the early investigators of psychic phenomena, in an article entitled "Researches on the Historical Origin of the Reincarnation Specula-

*Ed. Griffon d'Or, Paris, 1947.

tions of French Spiritualists."[4] He states that, in 1873 in Paris, he heard that a somnambulist, Celina Japhet (real name, Bequet) had contributed largely to the work. He called on her, and she told him among other things, that she was "a natural somnambulist from her earliest years;" that, in 1845 she went to Paris, made the acquaintance of a magnetizer, M. Roustan, and became a professional somnambulist under his control, giving "medical advice under the spiritual direction of her grandfather, who had been a doctor;" and that "in this manner in 1846 the doctrine of Reincarnation was given to her by the spirits of her grandfather, of St. Theresa, and others." Aksakof states at this point that "as the somnambulic powers of Madame Japhet were developed under the mesmeric influence of M. Roustan, it may be well to remark in this place that M. Roustan himself believed in the plurality of terrestrial existences." Aksakof's account of what Madame Japhet told him goes on to relate that from 1849 until 1870, she was a member of a spirit circle in Paris which met once or twice a week, and of which Victorien Sardou was a member; that, after a while, she became a writing medium and that the greater part of her communications were obtained in this manner; and that "in 1856 she met M. Denizard Rivail, introduced by M. Victorien Sardou. He [Rivail] correlated the materials by a number of questions; himself arranged the whole in systematic order, and published *The Spirits' Book* without ever mentioning the name of Madame C. Japhet, although three quarters of this book had been given through her mediumship. The rest was obtained from communications through Madame Bodin, who belonged to another spirit circle. . . . . After the publication of *The Book of Spirits* . . . . . he quitted the circle [Mme. Japhet's] and arranged another in his own house, M. Roze being the medium." Aksakof's article ends with the words: "All that I have herein stated does not affect the question of Reincarnation, considered upon its own merits, but only concerns the causes of its origin and of its propagation as Spiritism."

Another Frenchman, Alphonse Cahagnet, published in 1848 a book, *Arcanes de la Vie Future Dévoilés,* translated under the

[4]*The Spiritualist,* Aug. 13, 1875, pp. 74-5.

title of *The Celestial Telegraph,* and containing, like Kardec's, communications purporting to emanate from discarnate human spirits, who on the contrary deny that reincarnation occurs. For example:

Q. You are convinced that we never more appear on earth, to be again materialized?

A. We are born, and die but once; when we are in heaven, it is for eternity.[5]

In England, the famous medium, D. D. Home, denied and ridiculed the doctrine; and communications through mediums in English speaking countries, when touching at all on reincarnation, have in most cases denied it. For example, Dr. C. A. Wickland, in his book, *Thirty Years Among the Dead,* already mentioned, reports many communications received through his own wife as medium, including some purporting to come from deceased persons who while on earth had accepted and taught reincarnation, but who in those communications repudiate the doctrine. Prominent among these are the purported spirits of Ella Wheeler Wilcox (pp. 411-5) and of Mme. Blavatsky (pp. 420-7).

Their testimony, however, is hardly more impressive than that of Allan Kardec's spirits on the opposite side of the question. For instance, what the supposed spirit of Ella Wheeler Wilcox says is that she "would not care to come back. . . . .would not like to come back to this earth plane again to be a little baby;" that she does "not see why" she should come back! But obviously, if our likes and dislikes as regards our own future fate, settled the question of what it actually will be, then few of us would die, or become bald or wrinkled, or ever catch cold; for few persons indeed like these prospects.

The utterances of the purported Blavatsky spirit are much more categorical: "Reincarnation is not true," the spirit says, "I have tried and tried to come back to be somebody else, but I could not. We cannot reincarnate. We progress, we do not come back."[6] But although more downright, these statements are no

[5]Sec. 83, p. 111 of the 1851 First American Edition.
[6]*Op. cit.* Chapt. XV, p. 421.

more impressive than those of the Wilcox spirit; for it would be strange indeed that, as those statements would have it, not only the other alleged spirits of former Theosophists quoted in the same chapter, but the spirit of the very foundress of the modern Theosophical movement, should *expect and try to reincarnate just a few years after death,* notwithstanding her own explicit teaching that the interval between incarnations averages from 1000 to 1500 years; notwithstanding her own definite condemnation of the belief of "the Allan Kardec school . . . . . in an arbitrary and immediate reincarnation;"[7] and notwithstanding her own teaching that reincarnation takes place not by trying for it, but automatically at the end of many centuries spent in the blissful "devachan" dream world. And it would be equally strange that reincarnation should now be denied—on the ground of the gratuitous assumption that "progressing" and "coming back" are mutually exclusive—by the very same Mme. Blavatsky who had affirmed reincarnation on the ground that we progress *by coming back,* as does the schoolboy progress by coming back to the same school after vacations and learning each time new lessons, which the school well can teach him but which he cannot all learn in a single term.

Thus, if the utterances of the purported Blavatsky spirit should be considered evidence at all for anything, it would then rather be for truth of the Blavatsky teaching that the purported spirits who speak or write through a medium are instead only what is left of a personality when, some time after death, what she calls "the second death" has taken place; that is, when the higher active, thinking and judging mind has withdrawn from and left behind the lower, passive part, consisting of the habits, passions, memory images, and desires. This unthinking shell of the personality, she taught, borrows from the medium's living mind and is in this way temporarily able to act the part of a true spirit.

It would seem, then, that the misconceptions of Mme. Blavatsky's teachings evident in the statements of her alleged spirit through Mrs. Wickland, and uniformly also in the statements

---

[7] *The Key to Theosophy,* 3rd. ed. 1893, pp. 90, 98, 129.

of the alleged spirits of former disciples of hers, are in fact simply the misconceptions of those teachings present in Mrs. Wickland's own mind.

As regards the modes of thought and the style of the communications attributed in Dr. Wickland's book to the spirit of Ella Wheeler Wilcox, the present writer is not in position to judge whether they are typical of the thought and style of the prototype. But in the case of those attributed to Mme. Blavatsky's spirit, the intellectual content of most of the utterances in the eight pages of its communications is of the feeble quality which is rather usual in "spirit" messages; and which, if the messages really emanated from the particular spirits claimed to be their authors, would cause one to weep for the then degeneration patently undergone after death by the minds of such of them as, like Mme. Blavatsky's, were anyway vigorous.

In this connection, it is interesting to note that the purported Blavatsky spirit says at one point: "Some may say this is not Madam Blavatsky. . . .They may say, she would not say so and so, she would not talk so and so,—but it is Madam Blavatsky" (p. 424.). This would indicate that the would-be-Blavatsky "spirit" was conscious of the incongruity of its own utterances to the mind and personality of its claimed prototype.

Anyway, assuming for the purposes of the argument that the communications by mediums do come from discarnate human spirits, and even that these spirits are the particular ones they say they are, the really important point with regard to their denials of the reincarnation doctrine is that *their* lack of memory of lives earlier than their recent one on earth proves exactly nothing; just as the fact pointed out earlier that *we* now have no memory of the first few years after our birth or of the vast majority of our days since then, is no proof at all that we were not alive and conscious at those times. And the spirits' denial, or equally their assertion, that they will eventually reincarnate, is not based by them on any claim of paranormal capacity to precognize their own far remote future; nor is there any evidence that they have such capacity. Indeed, A. Campbell Holms, a writer who does not himself believe in reincarnation, but who is familiar with the records of spirit communications and apparently accepts them at their face value, writes: "Spirits long passed over, who appear to discuss matters with moderation and caution, if asked about reincarnation, will usually say that, although it may be true, they have no knowledge of it."[8]

Such "spirits" thus evince greater intellectual responsibility than do either those Spiritualists or Spiritists who naively assume that the mere fact of a person's having died constitutes an answer to the question *how* his surviving spirit knows, or *whether* it knows, that reincarnation is not, or is, a fact. All that a surviving discarnate spirit could competently testify to would be (a) that it has survived its body's death; (b) that, *as yet*, it has not reincarnated; and (c) that it does not, or as the case may be does, "remember" anterior lives on earth.

---

[8]*The Facts of Psychic Science and Philosophy*, London, Kegan Paul, 1925, p. 36.

Chapter XXIII

VERIFICATIONS OF OSTENSIBLE MEMORIES OF EARLIER LIVES

The best evidenced and most evidential case of "reincarnation" known to the present writer is that described in Chapter XVII, Section 4, which was reported by Dr. E. W. Stevens under the title of "The Watseka Wonder." But what it would illustrate is reincarnation only as conceived by the African Mandingos and by Dr. Wickland; that is, as invasion by a discarnate spirit of the body of a grown person whose own personality is thereby more or less completely displaced. Cases of this kind, when they are not explicable as simply dissociations of the personality whose body is concerned, would ordinarily be described as cases of "possession" or "obsession," rather than of reincarnation. For the term "reincarnation" is commonly intended to mean rebirth, in a neonate baby body, of a "spirit" or "soul" which has had earlier lives on earth.

Such claim as can be made that the cases which will now be cited constitute empirical evidence of reincarnation as conceived in the latter way rests not simply on the purported memories of the earlier life or lives, but on the allegation that some of the facts seemingly remembered have been subsequently verified but could not possibly have been learned in a normal manner by the person who has "memories" of them.

1. **The rebirth of Katsugoro.** This case is cited by Lafcadio Hearn in Chapter X of his *Gleanings in Buddha Fields*.[1] He states at the outset that what he is presenting "is only the translation of an old Japanese document—or rather series of docu-

---

[1]Houghton Mifflin, Boston, 1897.

ments—very much signed and sealed, and dating back to the early part of the present [i.e., the 19th] century." The documents were in the library of Count Sasaki in Tokyo. A copy of them was made for Hearn, who made the translation. Reduced to essentials, the facts related in the documents are as follows:

Katsugoro was a Japanese boy, born on the 10th day of the 10th month of 1815, son of Genzo, a farmer living in the village of Nakano Mura, and his wife Sei. One day, at about the age of seven, Katsugoro, while playing with his elder sister Fusa, asked her where she came from before her present birth. She thought the question foolish and asked him whether *he* could remember things that happened before he was born. He answered that he could; that he used to be the son of a man called Kyubei and his wife Shidzu, who lived in Hodokubo; and that his name was then Tozo. When later questioned by his grandmother, he said that until he was four years old he could remember everything, but had since forgotten a good deal; but he added that when he had been five years old Kyubei had died, and that a man named Hanshiro had then taken Kyubei's place in the household; that he himself had died of smallpox at the age of six, when his body was put in a jar and buried on a hill; that some old man then took him away and after a time brought him to Genzo's house, saying "Now you must be reborn, for it is three years since you died. You are to be reborn in this house." After entering the house, he stayed for three days in the kitchen; and he concluded: "Then I entered mother's honorable womb. . . . .I remember that I was born without any pain at all."

After relating all this, Katsugoro asked to be taken to Hodo-kudo to visit the tomb of his former father, Kyubei. His grandmother Tsuya took him there and when they reached Hodokubo, he hurried ahead and, when he reached a certain dwelling, cried "This is the house" and ran in. His grandmother followed and, on inquiry, was told that the owner of the house was called Hanshiro; his wife, Shidzu; that she had had a son, Tozo, who had died thirteen years before at the age of six, his father having been Kyubei. Katsugoro, who was looking about during the conversation, pointed to a tobacco shop across the road, and to a tree, saying that they used not to be there. This was true, and con-

vinced Hanshiro and his wife that Katsugoro had been Tozo, who
had been born in 1805, and had died in 1810. (The year of birth
of a Japanese child, Hearn states in a footnote, is counted as one
year of his age.)

Evidently, Katsugoro's experience, as testified to in the affidavits translated by Hearn and summarized above, is radically
different from that of Lurancy Vennum in the Watseka Wonder
case. Nothing of the nature of obsession or possession appears
in his case. His Katsugoro personality is at no time displaced or
interfered with by that of Tozo, any more than is the personality
of an adult "possessed" by the very different personality that was
his in childhood, but which he remembers. The account presents
Katsugoro as a normal boy, whose memories simply reached
farther back than the time of his birth. Assuming the objective
facts to have been as related in the affidavits translated by Hearn,
the only explanation of them to suggest itself as alternative to
reincarnation is that of paranormal retrocognition, by Katsugoro,
of the various events and surroundings of the short life Tozo lived
in another village some years before Katsugoro's birth, plus unconscious imaginative self-identification by Katsugoro with the
retrocognized Tozo personality. This kind of explanation would
require us to postulate in Katsugoro a capacity for retrocognitive
clairvoyance far exceeding in scope any for the reality of which
experimental evidence exists. And such postulation, if made at
all, would undermine the empirical evidence not only for reincarnation, but equally of course for discarnate survival of the
personality after death.

2. **The rebirth of Alexandrina Samona.** The next case is
the well-attested one of the rebirth of Alexandrina Samona, which
is peculiar in that, according to the accounts of the affair, it involved not only like that of Katsugoro memories of an earlier
incarnation, but also and prominently the announcement by the
girl's discarnate spirit that she was about to be reborn.

The facts were recorded at the time in the Italian periodical
Filosofia della Scienza, and discussed subsequently there and in
the French *Journal du Magnétisme.* The articles—the Italian
ones, translated into French—and the attestations of the several

persons who had first-hand knowledge of the facts, are reproduced *in extenso* together with photographs of the two girls, and discussed, in Dr. Charles Lancelin's book, *La Vie Posthume*.[2]

Alexandrina, aged five years, died in Palermo, Sicily, on March 15, 1910. She was the daughter of Dr. Carmelo Samona and his wife Adela. He recorded the facts and communicated them to the editor of the Italian Journal mentioned above. Three days after Alexandrina's death, her mother dreamed that the child appeared to her and said: "Mother, do not cry any more. I have not left you; I have only gone a little away. Look: I shall become little, like this"—showing her the likeness of a complete little embryo. Then she added: "You are therefore going to have to begin to suffer again on account of me." Three days later, the same dream occurred again.

A friend suggested to Mme. Samona that this meant Alexandrina would reincarnate in a baby she would have. The mother, however, disbelieved this—the more so because she had had an operation which it was thought would make it impossible for her to have any more children.

Some days later, at a moment when Mme. Samona was expressing bitterest grief to her husband over the loss of Alexandrina, three inexplicable sharp knocks were heard. The two of them then decided to hold family seances in the hope of obtaining typtological communications from discarnate spirits. From the very first seance, two purported such spirits manifested themselves: one, that of Alexandrina, and the other, that of an aunt of hers who had died years before. In this manner, Alexandrina's spirit testified that it was she herself who had appeared to her mother in the dream and who had later caused the three loud knocks; and she added that she would be reborn to her mother before Christmas, and that she would come with a twin sister. In the subsequent seances, she insisted again and again that this prediction be communicated to various relatives and friends of the family.

---

[2]Pub. Henri Durville, Paris, no date (about 1920) pp. 309-363. See also the briefer accounts of the case in Ralph Shirley's *The Problem of Rebirth*, Occult Book Society London, no date. Ch. V; and A. de Rochas' *Les Vies Successives*, Chacornac, Paris 1911, pp. 338-45.

On November 22, 1910, Mme. Samona gave birth to twin daughters. One of them closely resembled Alexandrina, and was so named. The other was of a markedly different physical type and eventually proved to have a very different disposition—alert, active, restless and gregarious—whereas Alexandrina II, like Alexandrina I, was calm, neat, and content to play by herself. She had, like her namesake, hyperaemia of the left eye, seborrhea of the right ear, and noticeable facial asymmetry; and, also like her, was left-handed and enjoyed playing endlessly at folding, tidying, and arranging such clothing or linen as were at hand. She insisted, like Alexandrina I, that her hands should be always clean, and she shared the first Alexandrina's invincible repugnance to cheese.

When, at the age of ten, the twins were told of a projected excursion to Monreale where they had never been, Alexandrina asserted that her mother, in the company of "a lady who had horns," had taken her to Monreale before. She described the large statue on the roof of the church there and said they had met with some little red priests in the town. Then Mme. Samona recalled that, some months before the death of the first Alexandrina, she had gone to Monreale with the child and with a lady who had disfiguring wens ("horns") on her forehead, and that they had seen a group of young Greek priests with blue robes ornamented with red.

Attestations were obtained by Dr. Samona from several of the persons who were personally acquainted with the facts—in particular, from his own sister; from his wife's uncle; from an Evangelical Pastor to whom Dr. Samona had related the prediction of the rebirth before it was fulfilled; and from a lady to whom, in March 1910, Mme. Samona had described the dream, and, in June, the seances announcing twins.

The comments relevant to this case are essentially the same as those made on the preceding one, and therefore need not be repeated.

3. **The case of Shanti Devi.** In 1936, a pamphlet was printed by the Baluja Press in Delhi, India, setting forth the results of an inquiry into the case of Shanti Devi by Lala Desh-

bandhu Gupta (Managing Director of the Daily Tej,) Pandit Neki Ram Sharma (a leader in the Nationalist movement,) and Mr. Tara Chand Mathur (an Advocate.) The chief facts recorded in their statements are as follows.

They concern a girl, Kumari Shanti Devi, born October 12, 1926 in Delhi, daughter of B. Rang Bahadur Mathur. From the age of about four, she began to speak of a former life of hers in Muttra—a town about 100 miles from Delhi—saying that she was then a Choban by caste, that her husband was a cloth merchant, that her house was yellow, etc. Later, she told a grand-uncle of hers, Mr. Bishan Chand, that her husband's name in her previous life had been Pt. Kedar Nath Chaubey. The uncle mentioned this to Mr. Lala Kishan Chand, M.A., a retired Principal, who asked to meet the girl. She then gave him the address of "Kedar Nath," to whom he wrote. To his surprise, it turned out that Kedar Nath Chaubey actually existed; and, in his reply to the letter, he confirmed various of the details Shanti Devi had given and suggested that a relative of his in Delhi, Pt. Kanji Mal, interview the girl. When he came to see her, she recognized him as a cousin of her former husband and gave convincing replies to questions of his concerning intimate details.

Pt. Kedar Nath Chaubey then, on November 13, 1935, came to Delhi with his present wife and his ten year old son by his former wife. Shanti Devi recognized Kedar Nath and was greatly moved, answering convincingly various questions asked by him about private matters of her former life as his wife, and mentioning that she had buried Rs. 150. in a certain room of her house in Muttra. After they left, she kept asking to be taken to Muttra, describing various features of the town. On November 24, 1935, she and her parents, and the three inquirers who author the pamphlet, went to Muttra. On the railway platform an elderly man in the group of people there paused for a moment in front of her, and she recognized him, saying that he was her "Jeth," i.e., the elder brother of her former husband.

The party then took a carriage, whose driver was instructed to follow whatever route the girl told him. She mentioned that the road to the station had not been asphalted when she lived in Muttra, and she pointed out various buildings which had not existed then. She led the party to the lane in which was a house she had formerly occupied. In the lane, she met and recognized an old Brahmin, whom she correctly identified as her father-in-law. She identified the old house, now rented to strangers. Two gentlemen of Muttra, who then joined the party, asked her where the "Jai-Zarur" of the house was—a local expression which the party from Delhi did not understand. She, however, understood it and pointed out the privy which, in Muttra, that term is used to designate.

After leaving the old house, and as she led the way to the newer one still occupied by Chaubey Kedar Nath, she recognized her former brother now twenty-five years old, and her uncle-in-law. At the house, she was asked to point out the well she had mentioned in Delhi. There is now no well in the courtyard there, but she pointed out the place where it had been. Kedar Nath then lifted the stone with which it had since been covered. She then led the way to the room she said she had formerly occupied, where she had buried the money. She pointed to the spot, which was then dug up, and, about a foot down, a receptacle for keeping valuables was found, but no money was in it. Kedar Nath Chaubey later disclosed that he had removed it after the death of his first wife, Lugdi, at the age of 23, on October 4, 1925, following the birth of her son on September 25. Later, Shanti Devi recognized her former father and mother in a crowd of over fifty persons.

The pamphlet reproduces also the confirmatory testimony of Kedar Nath's cousin in Delhi, Choubey Kenji Mal, including a statement of the questions he asked Shanti Devi when he interviewed her, and of her replies.

A number of Indian cases, similar in essentials to those of Shanti Devi and of Katsugoro, are described and the relevant attestations of witnesses quoted, in a booklet, *Reincarnation, Verified Cases of Rebirth after Death*, by Kr. Kekai Nandan Sahay, B.A., LL.B., Vakil High Court, Bareilly, India, no date (about 1927).[3]

---

[3]For a photostatic copy of this now rare booklet, the present writer is indebted to the kindness of Dr. Ian Stevenson, of the University of Virginia Medical School.

4. The "Rosemary" case. Another case, and one worth citing here at some length, is the "Rosemary" case. It is of interest for various reasons, but in this chapter in particular because the incarnation to which the purported memories would refer is not, as in the three described above, one which would have terminated only a few years before the beginning of the present life of the person concerned, but instead would date back some 3300 years. The case is reported by Dr. Frederic H. Wood in several books, the essential facts being as follows.[4]

Shortly after the death of his brother in 1912, Dr. Wood's investigations of psychic phenomena convinced him that survival of the human personality after death is a fact. Eventually, as a result of a common interest in music, he became acquainted with the girl referred to in his books by the pseudonym, "Rosemary." Late in 1927, she spontaneously began to write automatically. She viewed this development with repugnance and distrust and, knowing as she did of Dr. Wood's interest—which she had not shared —in psychic phenomena, she turned to him for light on the matter (ATC 19, 20).

Her automatic scripts purported to emanate from the surviving spirit of a Quaker girl of Liverpool, who gave her name as Muriel. At a sitting in Oct. 1928, Muriel brought a new "spirit guide" to take her place, whom she introduced as "the Lady Nona" and described as "an Egyptian lady of long ago." Nona, in the course of the many sittings which followed, stated that she had been a Babylonian princess who had come to Egypt as consort of the Pharaoh Amenhotep III (ca. 1410-1375BC.); that is, some 3300 years ago.

Dr. Wood mentions that, on June 28, 1930, he had, remaining incognito, a seance with a London medium, Mrs. Mason, whose spirit guide, Maisie, described to him both Rosemary and Nona, saying that the latter gave the name of "Ona, Mona, or Nona." The description of her which Maisie gave agreed with that previously given by a "spirit guide" other than Nona, which

_____
[4]*After Thirty Centuries*, Rider & Co. London, 1935; *Ancient Egypt Speaks*, (in collaboration with A. J. Howard Hulme) Rider, London, 1937; *This Egyptian Miracle*, McKay Co. Philadelphia, 1940; 2nd. ed. revised, J. M. Watkins, London, 1955 (Titles abbreviated respectively ATC, AES, TEM.)

occasionally manifested through Rosemary. Maisie also stated that Rosemary had been with Nona in Egypt, and that Nona's name there had been Telika.

On July 3, 1930, Nona confirmed both of these assertions through Rosemary's automatic writing. On December 5, 1931, Nona introduced the word "Ventiu," and later (June 6, 1935) explained that her name had been Telika-Ventiu, which means "The wise woman of an Asiatic race;" "Telika" having been her Babylonian name, and "Ventiu" a name given by the Egyptians to the Asiatic races generally. Dr. Wood surmises that she had first given the pseudonym "Nona" because at that time she wished to be "nameless"; and this because in those early days of her communications she could not be sure that her real name would come through correctly (TEM p. 46).

Dr. Wood mentions that a clay tablet found at Tell el-Amarna in 1887 is generally accepted as evidence that Amenhotep III had married a Babylonian princess.[5] Her name, however, appears nowhere; so that, should a papyrus eventually be found giving it as Telika Ventiu, this would be strongly confirmatory evidence. Nona, when she added the "Ventiu" insisted that it was or would be important as evidence (TEM 49-51, AES 37).

Nona states that she expresses herself by impressing her thoughts on Rosemary's mind, which then spontaneously formulates them in English either orally or in writing. But Nona, in the course of the many years' sittings, has given out orally some 5000 phrases and short sentences in old Egyptian language. In the case of these, Rosemary states that she "hears" the Egyptian words clairaudiently and repeats them aloud—this having first occurred on August 18, 1931 (TEM 171). As she utters them, Dr. Wood records them phonetically as well as he can in terms of the English alphabet. It is unfortunate that he was not then familiar with, and therefore did not use, the more adequate alphabet of the International Phonetic Association; but his recording was anyway good enough to enable an Egyptologist, Mr. Hulme, to identify with but a correction here and there, and to translate the

---

[5]Dr. Wood states in a letter that his authority for this was the late Alan Shorter Assistant Keeper of the Egyptian Antiquities at the British Museum.

first eight hundred of these thousands of Egyptian utterances, which constitute coherent communications manifesting purpose, intelligence, and responsiveness to the conversational situation of the moment. Dr. Wood, in order to qualify himself to meet certain criticisms by Prof. Battiscombe Gunn of Oxford University, then (1937) took up the study of scholastic Egyptian and eventually became able to translate himself the word sounds, which previously he could only record without understanding them.

In the course of the many years of sittings with Dr. Wood, Rosemary has developed ostensible memories, extensive and detailed, of a life of hers in Egypt as "Vola," a Syrian girl brought captive to Egypt, whom Nona befriended (AES Chs. VIII, IX.).

So much being now clear about the ostensible situation and process of communication in the Rosemary case, attention must next be directed to the fact in it which is of central interest in connection with the topic of the present chapter. That fact is Nona's assertion that Rosemary was with her in Egypt, her name then having been Vola; so that *Rosemary would be a reincarnation of Vola.* Nona states further—although this is not essential to the point—that Vola was the daughter of a Syrian king killed in battle with the Egyptians; that she was brought to Egypt as a captive and given to Nona who liked and adopted her, and had her appointed a temple maiden in the temple of Amen Ra; and that the enemies of Amenhotep III, who were plotting to wrest the power from him and were afraid of Nona's influence on him, contrived an accident in which she and Vola drowned together.

In this complex affair the most arresting fact, which has to be somehow explained, is the utterance by Rosemary's lips of those thousands of phrases in a language of which she normally knows nothing, but concerning which Mr. Hulme, an Egyptologist, states that, in the eight hundred of them he had examined, the grammar and the consonants substantially and consistently conformed to what Egyptologists know today of the ancient Egyptian language.

The phrases as uttered supply vowel sounds, which are otherwise still unknown since the hieroglyphs represent only the consonants.[6] There is today no way of either proving or disproving that these vowel sounds are really those of the ancient speech, although a presumption in favor of it arises from the consistency of their use throughout those thousands of phrases, and from the substantial correctness of the xenoglossy as regards grammar and consonants. But in any case, the Rosemary affair remains the most puzzling and yet the best attested instance of xenoglossy on record.

The present chapter, however, is concerned not with xenoglossy as such, but with verifications of ostensible memories of earlier lives. The questions relevant to this in the Rosemary case are therefore two. The first is whether Rosemary's ostensible memories of an earlier life in Egypt as Vola have been verified and are truly memories. And the second is whether the xenoglossy is explicable only, or most plausibly, on the supposition that Rosemary is a reincarnation of a girl, Vola, who supposedly lived in Egypt 3300 years ago.

The first question subdivides into: (a) whether the ostensible memories have been found to correspond to objective facts —as were the ostensible memories of Katsugoro, of Alexandrina, and of Shanti Devi; and if so, (b) whether there are sufficient reasons to believe that Rosemary cannot have come to know or guess those objective facts in some normal manner but have forgotten having done so.

As regards (a), a great deal of the detail supplied is not claimed to have been verified or to be verifiable, and hence, although dramatically impressive, is not evidence at all. This would apply for example, to a large part of the ostensible memory of sights seen on the market place at Thebes (AES 128); for instance, that of "a man with some dear little black and white baby goats to sell." Indeed, another of the putatively remembered sights there—that of camels with tents on their backs in which people travelled—constitutes a difficulty in the way of the memory hypothesis rather than a support of it. For, on the one hand, if scholars are right in maintaining that domesticated camels (as distinguished from camels as food animals) were not used

---

[6]Two exceptions to this are claimed by Dr. Wood; see TEM ist. ed. p. 93. 2nd. p. 95.

in Egypt prior to the Persian conquest in 525 B.C.,[7] then that sight
of domesticated camels in the market place at Thebes during the
reign of Amenhotep III would be anachronistic by some 900
years. And if, on the other hand, another statement by Rosemary,
in rebuttal of the opinion of the scholars on this point, is accepted as correct, then her memory of camels being used as con-
veyances for persons *in Thebes* at that time must be incorrect,
since her rebutting statement is that although there were camels
in Egypt, "the Egyptians. . . .would not use them *in their cities*"
because of their unpleasant habits and smells, but used them in
the desert (TEM 177, italics mine).

Another ostensible memory—recorded on Oct. 7, 1932—con-
tains descriptions of buildings, of steps, of a river in the distance,
of boats, and of a temple with carved figures in front. Dr. Wood
takes this to refer to Karnak, and—relevantly to sub-question (b)
—states that, at the time that memory was recorded, "the normal
Rosemary had taken no special interest either in Thebes or Karnak. She had always refused to discuss or read about them" (AES
129). On an earlier page of AES, however, he described Rosemary as "a well-educated girl" (p. 25); and, as such, it is un-
likely that she had never seen any of the numerous pictures or
photographs of Egypt in history books and magazines.

Relevantly to sub-question (a), Dr. Wood further states that
neither he nor Rosemary have visited Egypt, but intimates that
the content of her memories is consistent with what he subsequently found in guide books and in a certain book of photographs. This, of course, is much less of a verification than was
obtained in the three cases described in the earlier sections of this
chapter. And, concerning the memories relating to Vola as a
maiden serving in the Temple, which have to do with music and
ritual and are of course very interesting in themselves, no objective verifications are offered.

It would seem, then, that much the larger part or perhaps
all of the ostensible memories either lack clear-cut objective veri-

---

[7]Their opinion apparently being based on the fact that camels are not mentioned in the hieroglyphic records until Persian times.

fication, or are susceptible of explanation otherwise than as genuine memories of an earlier life in Egypt.

Let us turn next to the second main question and ask what various explanations of the xenoglossy, of its vast extent, and of its substantial correctness of grammar and consonants, are conceivable; how plausible or the reverse each of them is; and what, if anything, the most plausible imply as to whether Rosemary is a reincarnation of Vola.

(1) What may be called the standard explanation of xenoglossy is that the person manifesting the phenomenon did at one time associate with someone who was in the habit of reciting aloud words and sentences in the foreign tongue concerned; that these sounds, although not understood by the hearer, registered on her subconscious mind as they would on the tape of a recorder; and that later, under the circumstances of the sitting, she reproduces some of them automatically. This explanation, *mutatis mutandis,* would apply to the xenography of the Argentine medium, Sra. Adela Albertelli, as reported by Sr. José Martin to the present writer in correspondence, and through articles in the periodical, *La Conciencia.*

Such an explanation, however, does not apply to the case of Rosemary, both because she never associated with or knew any scholar addicted to such recitations, and because the Egyptian phrases uttered by Rosemary—whether as being Nona's or Vola's—are not random ones but are shaped by the purpose of conveying specific information, and in many cases directly relate to questions or incidents occurring at the moment (TEM Chs. IX, X, XI. Summary, p. 179).

(2) Concerning the hypothesis that all such correct facts about Egypt as Rosemary—whether as Nona or as Vola—relates, are obtained by her through present exercise of retrocognitive clairvoyance, all that need be said is that, even if this should be regarded as plausible so far as knowledge of those facts goes, it would anyway altogether fail to account for the conversational appositeness and responsiveness of the xenoglossy.

(3) A third possible explanation is that which Spiritualists would regard as the obvious one; namely, that Nona is indeed the surviving spirit of Telika, which uses Rosemary as medium.

This, however, would not entail that Rosemary is a reincarnation of Vola, but would leave the matter open. For the mere fact that something is asserted by a discarnate spirit does not automatically guarantee that it is a fact not a mere opinion. That is, the question *how Nona knows* that Rosemary is a reincarnation of a girl whom she knew in Egypt 3300 years ago is just as legitimate but unanswered as would be the question *how I know*, if I were to assert that the eighteen year old daughter of a friend of mine is a reincarnation of a woman I knew in New York 55 years ago, who died shortly thereafter. That Nona is discarnate at the time she makes the assertion, whereas I would be incarnate at the time I made mine, is irrelevant unless one assumes—gratuitously in the absence of independent evidence—that an *ad hoc* cognitive capacity is automatically conferred on a person's spirit by the mere fact of his body's dying.

Anyway, the hypothesis that Nona is the surviving spirit of Telika leaves with us the problem of accounting for such of Rosemary's ostensible memories of herself as Vola as perhaps correspond to objective facts known. That she is a reincarnation of Vola would be a possible explanation of this; but another, which Spiritualists generally would probably regard as more plausible, would be that the alleged memories are dramatic imaginations subconsciously constructed by Rosemary partly out of her years of acquaintance with the contents of her automatic speech and writing, partly out of what any well-educated person knows about Egypt, and partly out of telepathic borrowing from Nona's mind of appropriate items of information or of Egyptian words which the conversational situation at particular times calls for.

(4) Still another possibility would be that Nona is a dissociated part of Rosemary's personality. The fact Dr. Wood stresses (AES 103-5), that the Nona personality is of a type radically different from that of Rosemary, does not invalidate this hypothesis; for such marked difference is almost a normal feature of cases of dissociated personality. In the Beauchamp case reported by Dr. Morton Prince, for example, the contrast was sharp between the "Sally" personality and that of Miss Beauchamp; and so was that between the Eve Black and Eve White personalities in the

recent case of *The Three Faces of Eve,* described by Drs. Thigpen and Cleckley.[8]

But if Nona is a dissociated part of the personality of Rosemary, the xenoglossy remains to be accounted for; and the only supposition in sight which would seem capable of doing so is that of Rosemary's being a reincarnation of some person who lived in Egypt in ancient times, and of whom Nona, or Vola, or both were perhaps even then dissociations.

(5) Finally, of course, there is the possibility that the facts of the case really are just what they purport to be: That Nona is the spirit of Telika surviving discarnate; that Rosemary is a reincarnation of Vola; and that her ostensible Vola memories are —like the ordinary memories of all of us—in the main veridical though occasionally erroneous. This explanation is bound to appear the most likely to Dr. Wood and to Rosemary for the same reason which, when in the theater we watch a well-acted, vividly dramatic presentation of a scene in a play, makes us forget for the time being that it is a play. Dramatic verisimilitude tends to generate belief, and can make fiction more credible than truth. Yet the strange things which this pisteogenic power of dramatic verisimilitude may make credible are not therefore necessarily fiction. Even at the play, the fact may turn out to be that the villain's sword, by a fluke, really does pierce the hero's chest, that the latter is really dying, and that the play is after all not altogether a play!

What now, in the light of the whole preceding discussion, can we conclude as to the evidentiality of the Rosemary case for reincarnation? The answer would seem to be that, granting substantial accuracy to the identification and translation of anyway most of the thousands of Egyptian phrases of the Nona and the Vola personalities, then the fact that those phrases were uttered by Rosemary's vocal organs is explicable at all only on the assumption either that Nona is the surviving spirit of an Egyptian of an ancient period who now uses Rosemary as medium for expression, or that Rosemary is the reincarnation of the spirit of

---

[8]Pub. Secker & Warburg, London, 1957. And, the Beauchamp case, *The Dissociation of a Personality,* New York, Longmans Green, 1906.

such a person, or both. But, in the absence of clear-cut verifications of the ostensible Vola memories by objective facts that Rosemary certainly could not have at some time learned or inferred in a normal manner, the account we have of the case does not provide strong evidence that Rosemary is a reincarnation of Vola, but only suggests and permits the supposition of it. The xenoglossy, however, does provide strong evidence that the capacity once possessed by some person to converse extensively, purposefully, intelligently, and intelligibly in the Egyptian language of three thousand years ago, or anyway in a language closely related to it, has survived by many centuries the death of that person's body.[9]

---

[9] A considerable number of other cases of purported memories of anterior incarnations are cited and critically examined by Dr. Ian Stevenson in a paper which, at the date of the present writing, has not yet been published, but is scheduled to appear in two parts in the April and the June 1960 issues of the *Journal of the American Society for Psychical Research.*

Chapter XXIV

REGRESSIONS TO THE PAST
THROUGH HYPNOSIS

A few of the available cases of spontaneous apparent memory of an earlier life were cited in the preceding chapter. But various attempts also have been made to regress by appropriate commands the consciousness of a hypnotized subject to a time earlier than the birth or conception of his body. We shall now consider some of them.

1. **An experiment in New York in 1906.** In February 1906, in New York, the writer was present at two experiments in regression to the past through hypnosis. The subject was a young woman whose name he does not now remember, and he long ago has lost touch with the young physician, Dr. Morris Stark, who conducted the experiments. But the writer recorded in shorthand at the time the whole of both experiments and still has the typescript of his notes. The girl was familiar with the idea of reincarnation and understood that the experiment was to be an attempt to regress her consciousness to a time anterior to that of the birth or conception of her body. Besides the two sessions the writer recorded, there had been another at which he had not been present, but the seeming success of which had suggested the desirability of a shorthand record. The name, "Zoe," mentioned in the session of Feb. 25, had been obtained at that earlier session. The difference between the tone and the manner of the Zoe personality and those of either the Roman or the Egyptian personality was most impressive.

In the record of the two sessions there are hardly any items that would lend themselves to verification by objective facts and that yet could not plausibly be supposed to have been learned by the subject in a normal manner at some time and subsequently forgotten. Hence such correspondence as may obtain between the statements of the entranced subject and historical facts is hardly evidence of reincarnation or even of paranormal cognition. And the dramatic form and the contents of the subject's statements can most economically be credited to the mythopoeic faculty—stimulated on that occasion by the commands given under hypnosis—which at other times normally gives birth to novels and other works of fiction. The most economical interpretation, of course, is not necessarily the correct one; but, when no item of evidence rules it out, it is methodologically the safest. Accordingly, the record of those two sessions—which antedates not only the recent "Bridey Murphy" experiment but also the publication (in 1911) of De Rochas' *Les Vies Successives* in which he relates his own experiments in regression through hypnosis— is presented here essentially as an interesting concrete sample of the sort of material sometimes obtainable under deep hypnosis when the subject is instructed to go back in time to a life anterior to his present one.

The notes of those two sessions are as follows:

Q. Tell us what you see; where are you now?

A. It is very warm. I am walking out somewhere, the sun is hot, I don't know where I am. It is all growing dark.

Q. The picture will clear up in a minute.

A. The sky is very blue and the sun is very warm, it shines through my sleep. I am walking along the water. The water is very blue and the ships are in the water. I don't know what I am doing here.

Q. What is your name?

A. My name, I don't know. It is very beautiful, not a cloud in the air, there are beautiful trees and plants and a great many people.

Q. How are they dressed?

A. They wear loose, beautiful gowns, not like others I have seen. Their arms are bare, they are talking.

Q. What language? . . . . . .

A. Who are you?

Q. I am a friend of yours.

A. The city is on hills, it hurts my eyes. I live over there. It is getting so warm. Had I not better go home? It is by the water.

Q. What is the name of the water?

A. It is some bay, I don't know the name. The city is in the distance. It might be a river, but I think it is too large for a river. There is a large building here, all open. There are a great many flowers and inside the floors are marble in blocks, some of them are of different colors.

Q. What year?

A. I don't know, I shall have to go and ask some one. There are little statues around. There are wings to the building, people sitting there are looking over the water. Steps lead from the wings to the ground. Back of the building there is some more water. There is a little bridge and you pass over the bridge to go home. It is an arch. I think there must be something very beautiful here; so many of the people have flowers in their hair. It is some feast. They are playing games. One side there is a sandy court. Men are running and jumping over a barrier. The others are looking and cheering. No women out there. I don't find any one I know.

Q. How are you dressed?

A. Just like the others. I have a white robe of some kind, it is clasped on the arm by a gold clasp, a bracelet. My hair is tied up some way. Why did you not speak to me about that before? My hair is all puffed up some way behind. My arms are bare.

Q. What sort of material is your dress made of?

A. It is soft wool of some kind. It looks a little bit coarse, but is very soft. . . . .It is not a feast, just a place where people come for pleasure. The men are doing something else now, jumping and running; they take off their robe when they run.

Q. Who is the emperor, what is his name?

A. I don't believe I know.

Q. Ask some one.

A. I shall see if I can find some one in the building. Is it not curious I don't know?

Q. What is your father's name?

A. He is dead.

Q. What was his name when he lived?

A. It sounds like a silly name, I only know one of his names, Prato, that was the name we called him in the house.

Q. How long has he been dead?

A. About 7 years.

Q. How old are you now?

A. Why, I think I am about 29, I must be because I live in the house over there, and it is my own house.

Q. Are you married?

A. Yes.

Q. What is your husband's name?

A. I will think of it in a minute. They are waiting for me over the bridge. There is a man in the house; he is one of the slaves, I should not speak to him.

Q. What sort of a looking man is he?

A. An ordinary looking man from the mountains, they bring a great many. My husband brings several home every year.

Q. Is he black or white?

A. Oh, white.

Q. What is the name of the country from which he comes?

A. I don't know. It is east somewhere from here. He does not come from the west. Of course he is darker than we are. The east, that is where the war is. My husband is a general, he is away from home.

Q. Do you know your husband's name now?

A. I can't think of his name.

Q. What is the reason you don't remember things?

A. . . . . . You stay with me won't you? Some time you seem to go away from me and then all grows dark.

Q. Who am I.

A. I don't know, just a voice. They are waiting for me, my litter is over the bridge. Don't you think it is beautiful on the bridge? It seems to be a road, a beautiful highway. Oh, I know the reason I could not tell you the emperor's name, we don't have one, we have ten.

Q. What are they called? Consuls?

A. They do not call them by that name. The people are

very dissatisfied. Of course that is a secret, you must not tell that, you are just a voice. They are talking of a war against the Government. There is one of the most wicked ones, his name is Appius, there is a great deal of talk about his crimes, he does as he pleases. He overrides the authority of the generals over the army.

Q. Do you know who Christ was?

A. No, who was he?

Q. What is your religion?

A. We have many Gods.

Q. Have you temples or churches?

A. Each God has a temple, shrines in the houses. We have household Gods. The road is paved up, then we go into the city; there are four slaves. I like black slaves. We go through the streets. You are coming with me are you not? I know all the streets, there are shops and temples and houses. We go through the principal part of the city and come to some beautiful houses. Many of my friends live there. I have one of these houses. Will you come in? The house is very beautiful. You cannot go with me now, because I am going up to my rooms, and you will have to stay here.

Q. Where do you get the black slaves from?

A. From across the sea to the south, we pay more for them than for the others.

Q. How much do you pay?

A. I never buy the slaves. I think my husband said he paid for those who carry my litter 1000.

Q. 1000 what? What is the name of the money?

A. Sesterces. I am tired. I am going to have my hair dressed. My husband is away to the war, I have not thought of his name yet.

Q. What day of the week is this?

A. About the 5th day.

Q. What is the name of that day?

A. I don't know. I can't tell, I have forgotten so many things. That poet is coming in, Marcus, with his silly flowers in his hair. He is coming to bore me now. I want to talk to you. He comes afternoons and reads odes to me. He is harmless. I think he is very lazy. I don't care for his poetry.

Q. Getting suspicious of you, knowing the name of the poet and not that of your husband.

A. He is away so much . . . I am going to have my hair dressed. Wait for me. (She shakes and moves her head) . . . Here I am; I had to wait, I have so much hair; it is blue black, it comes almost to my knees. The girls dress it.

Q. White girls?

A. Yes, I would not have those Nubians dress my hair. My hair dresser is a very pretty girl. My husband bought her for me. I like her very much.

Q. What is her name?

A. I think it is Ena. I have four girls; one has the care of my jewels, another has my robes and Ena dresses my hair. She is the only one that does not pull it. She puts the filets (?) in it. I think four is a nice number. You can get on with four very comfortably. Now that I am dressed, we will go out where the flowers are. We will sit out there, there is a fountain. Everything is very pretty I take so much pleasure sitting here, except when Marcus comes. The sun is very warm, let us sit a little out of the sun. I have never been ill.

Q. How long have you been married?

A. About five years. (A pillow is put behind her.) Why did you not let one of the girls do that? It does not seem as though I was married very much. I have no children. I have a very good time in every way. Life is a very beautiful thing.

Q. Do you remember your husband's name now?

A. I don't seem to be very much interested in my husband. I don't want to ask any one my husband's name.

Q. Ask Marcus whether he has ever written any ode to your husband.

A. He says that he does not write odes to Flavius.

Q. Do you ever hear from him, do you get letters?

A. One of the soldiers comes, from Sextilius; that is my name that is his name too. What do you care about names? . . . Just look at him, look at him, look at his lovelorn face! Who takes Marcus seriously?

Q. What does your diet consist of? What do you have when you arise in the morning?

A. We have fruit, pomegranates and honey and cakes of barley. We eat fish. We have different meats. A great deal of some kinds of fowls.

Q. What is the name of those fowls?

A. I don't believe I know. At the feast we have, oh, so many things. Flavius never gives a feast; he does not like to attend. He only goes because he must go. I love to go; there is music, flowers, wine, fragrant wine, very sweet. They have grapes in this country and the wines are sweet and very good. We have fowls of different kinds. They serve them with all the plumage on. They put them inside the skin after they are cooked. The table looks beautiful. Flavius is much older than I am.

Q. What are these birds served on?

A. Gold and silver dishes of different workmanship . . . One of the ten is Appius Claudius. The Government was not always with these ten, formerly we had one ruler; now there are ten.

Q. How do the ten dress?

A. In purple.

Q. What do they carry?

A. They have a sign of their office, it is a short . . . with a . . . . tip. Appius rides through the streets in his litter. He controls the others. You must not tell any one what I say, my husband would be very angry.

Q. What is the name of your country? Italy?

A. They don't call it that way, the name is something else . . . I had better send Marcus home, he can go and sing odes to some one else. Put the pillows around me. I will go to sleep; you will not mind if I go to sleep? I am so tired. I don't know why. There are clouds; where are you . . . You have taken me somewhere else. You are taking me across the water, we are going south (she laughs) I did not know I could come so quickly. (She looks sideways and laughs.)

Q. What is the matter?

A. I am not dressed well, that is why I laugh. You should not be here.

Q. What is your name?

A. I am Ula.

Q. Ula what?

A. I forget what name . . . Ula Desthenes. You should not be in here. I should not talk to you, where are you?

Q. I am simply a voice.

A. No one is allowed there but we of the temple.

Q. What is the name of the temple?

A. I don't know.

Q. What does it look like?

A. It is not white, it is a different color, red and blue and different colors, and the main color is a sort of a yellowish. It is higher than the other parts of the city. We never go outside. You should not be here.

Q. How old are you?

A. Eighteen.

Q. What is your religion?

A. We worship our mother. She is the mother of everything, everything in the world, the Great Mother. We attend to the temple.

Q. Tell me your duties.

A. We must deck the altars with flowers, we serve at the ceremonies.

Q. Describe the ceremonies.

A. There are priests who officiate at those ceremonies, but we never see them at other times. They wear beautiful robes, incrusted with jewels. On the back is the sun in jewels. We all wear a gold circlet on the head. My robe is white. The priests wear circlets, but not like ours, more like the sun. I don't know everything. The priests come here at the ceremonies and we help them, and we have flowers and something that we burn. It must be some kind of incense. There is chanting and the people are outside, they cannot come where we are. They look on from the distance at the ceremonies. While I have been here a long time, I have not tended the temple long. My father and mother are dead. I have always been here . . . We must never ask questions, we are told.

Q. Who teaches?

A. One of the older ones, an old priestess.

Q. What name is given to you, what are you called?

A. I don't know, the other ones are called priestesses, but we are not, we are just maidens, we serve.

Q. Are you married?

A. Oh no, never. How can you speak of such a thing. I am afraid to speak of such a thing in the temple. They tell us that we would incur the wrath of our Mother, we might die.

Q. What becomes of you when you die?

A. We go to the underworld, and we go through so many places in the underworld! There seem to be dangers; it is not pleasant, but we have to go there, everybody. Then we are told that we go somewhere else after the underworld.

Q. How long do you stay in the underworld?

A. There are two places, we don't stay very long in the first underworld, only so long that we are not afraid any more. There seem to be seven grades of dangers that we must pass; it is more like trials, something you must pass through. You go down to the underworld, and then you are taken by some God who leads you. If you pass through them all with brave courage in your heart . . . You have something to take with you to help you, something you are given, either a word you can repeat, or something, and if you remember that, you can pass. When you reach the seventh gate, according to the way you passed, you are very happy and you dream in happiness, or else you are very miserable, it depends upon the seven gates and how you passed.

Q. What do they give you when you die?

A. I know what it is, something to hang around your neck, some sort of a charm and they make it in the temple, a word or some words in a case, written in a little piece of parchment and hung around the neck of the dead, and no one dies without that, so that they may pass the gates of the underworld. There is a name for the first underworld, it is Amenta.

Q. After you pass through the underworld and the other place, what becomes of you?

A. You may come back. They tell me that one must be very good or one comes back as a very evil person.

Q. Do you come back in the forms of animals?

A. I think they tell me one does if one is wicked.

Q. What animals are there?

A. There are cats. Some are painted in the temple. They do not mean cats, it is some God. There are tall birds with long red bills. They stand motionless all day in the reeds. I am not so tired here.

Q. What do the buildings look like?

A. Flat, with soft colors. There are a great many people in the streets. I can see them all from the windows here. I can see the river.

Q. What is the name of the river? Is it Nile?

A. That sounds like it. It is a sacred river, a beautiful river.

Q. How long ago is this, what year?

A. I don't know how to say what year.

Q. What day of the month?

A. I don't know what you mean.

Q. How do you designate time?

A. Why, there are men who count time from the stars, but I don't understand about it; from the stars and the moon. It is very warm.

Q. Have you change of seasons?

A. Summer all the year round. Are you not afraid they will find you?

Q. They cannot see me. Is it not strange to you to hear a voice?

A. Strange things happen in the temple, the gods speak, we are forbidden to tell. They can make the dead speak.

Q. By what means?

A. They have a good deal of magic. I never see those things, there are some secret ceremonies where the priests are and there is that by which the dead can be made to speak, or they say so, I don't know.

Q. Do you believe it?

A. Yes, I have seen some very wonderful things. They bring the dead to the temple, a dead king or some great person. There is a place, not where our Mother is. This is a great place divided into a separate temple. The temple of our Mother is connected with the other by an underground passage. They bring the dead man there and lay him so that he is very near the gods in the inner shrine. They lay him there by the gods, and in the night they come, the priests, and they walk around in a circle and sing something, a chant that it is forbidden to hear. One of the older priestesses told me this, that is strange, something that no man may hear. They draw a circle with a sacred wand; the temple is very dark, there are no lights in it. They go inside the circle so that those outside may not hurt them, the dead, or something that might hurt them. Then they chant. I am told that upon the dead man comes a flame, a tongue of flame, from the gods, and then they may ask the dead man if he has a burden on his mind to prevent him from passing on. This is only when people die suddenly, when the people are not old but die suddenly in battle before they have had time to say parting words. After this flame comes, the dead man speaks, they say he does, and they remember what he says, and after they have recorded it so that they can give his message, they say "be gone" and he goes. They must remain a long time in the circle, because those outside will hurt them. The next day the dead man may be embalmed. Before that, he cannot go, he would remain chained. That is why they have this ceremony. This is never told outside the temple, those in the street don't know. It is a secret. Something dreadful would happen; I don't know of any secret ceremony, one of the priestesses told me . . . . . There are big flat boats when the kings go out.

Q. What is the name of your King?

A. Why, we call him Ra. They are building his temple in the desert over there, the slaves work there all the time. I am very tired.

Q. How do the people travel?

A. They almost always walk; they wear different colored robes, drapery. They don't wear very much. They have carts in the streets with bullocks. The soldiers ride horses.

Q. Do they have any locomotives?

A. They don't have any locomotives (shakes her head) what are those things? You seem to be always behind me . . . . Ra is the sun. Potas is a God of the underworld.

Q. How are you dressed?

A. I have a white robe, very rich. We have different robes,

jewels on our arms, anklets. We have something on our feet and sometimes walk barefooted.

Q. Is your King's name Rameses?

A. Yes, that is why I said Ra.

Q. Has he any other name?

A. There was a Rameses before this one, he has a great many names, ceremonial names, I cannot remember now.

Q. Do you ever see the Mother?

A. (She motions yes)

Q. What is her name?

A. Isis . . . I am very tired . . . (She awakes)

FEBRUARY 25, 1906.

Q. Zoe, Zoe, how do you do? Good morning, how are you?

A. I can't see, who called me by that name? It is long since any one called me that, it was Zoe. Where do you come from? You speak a dead tongue, . . . something . . . it is confused. Those were happy days in the streets. I have been called nothing for so long.

Q. What country is this?

A. A warm country. Zoe, it is good to hear the name again. The wife of Dedro.

Q. How old are you now?

A. That I forget. I am too old to be alive. Everything is gone, nothing remains but sorrow and hunger; I have had a hard life. Do you remember Metha, years ago, she used to tell me tales. She was a good old crone. Did you know me when I was young? Do you see my wrinkles? Oh, what a change (she shakes her head). I was not bad to look at, was I? My eyes were bright, and I laughed in the street. I was often hungry.

Q. How old were you when you were married?

A. I was very young. Dedro is dead, my children are all gone; I had twelve children, all gone. An old woman sits alone in the sun and thinks, thinks. It is very little profit.

Q. What religion do you follow?

A. Oh, there is a religion, but I know very little about it. The lords govern this realm, the highest one represents the God

. . . . You gave me something, you gave me a gold coin, the only one I ever had.

Q. Was I alone?

A. No, you rode in some sort of a cart, and there were horses, you drove through the streets. I kept it, I never spent it, though many a day I went hungry, and then Dedro came, and he had something, some little saved, he had some business. I had better take Dedro, so they said, so I married Dedro.

Q. Do you remember the marriage ceremony?

A. We have none, what do they care about us? He comes, he takes us and that is all. He often beat me, yes. There is nothing to tell, just a hard, bitter life. . . . It is very warm, the buildings have flat roofs. Mountains way off. You can see the snow in the distance. The plain stretches in sand for miles.

Q. What is the name of the city you live in?

A. It begins with S. I think I can tell you in a few minutes. It is like Saraban, but that is not it. Some great man built the city, I don't know his name.

Q. What is the color of the skin of the people?

A. Pale, no color, rather yellow, but clear. Their eyes are set like mine, slantwise. Our hair is dark. My curls, that was something unusual.

Q. Have you heard of Shinto? What is your god?

A. The god is the sun. We have a temple built up high in the city, the city is built tier after tier. In the temple dwells the Lord, and in the higher temple dwell the priests of the sun. There are many other gods, but the sun is the Lord of all.

Q. What is his name?

A. The Sun God. We know nothing of the temple, they rule the country with a rule of iron, they are oppressors.

Q. What becomes of you when you die?

A. We go to an underworld, we meet our ancestors. If we have revered them, if we have fulfilled our duties, we are passed through happily, if we have not, some fate overtakes us, some punishment. If we fulfill our duties we go to some happy place after the underworld, where we meet them again. I know nothing more.

Q. Do you ever come back to this earth?

A. No, not that I know.

Q. What animals do you use?

A. The camels carry things. There are also little shaggy horses. They don't look like any horses . . . Who are you? Why do you ask me this question?

Q. What is your age, 70, 80?

A. As old as that, 86 I think.

Q. Can you tell the names of some of your children?

A. There were eight girls and four boys. Two boys died. Sina is the youngest, a girl; how hard it is to remember. And Boro, he was my eldest.

Q. Go to sleep; clouds, back, back, back, back. The clouds are going up, what do you see?

A. I don't know where I am. It is dark. The sun is shining now.

Q. What are you, a man or a woman?

(She looks herself over several times.)

A. Why of course, I am a woman.

Q. What do you see?

A. A room I am sitting in, on the floor.

Q. Are there any chairs around? Do you know what chairs are?

A. Whatever they are, there are not any here. I am sitting on a rug. There are cushions.

Q. How are you dressed?

(She looks herself over)

A. Why, I am not very much dressed. (She looks inside her hand, at her arm, etc.) How did I come to be brown? My hand is brown. My arm is bare and covered with bands of some description and a sort of a gauzy shirt and anklets, and that is all.

Q. What is your name?

A. My name is Rella.

Q. Is it a Turkish rug you are sitting on?

A. I don't know what a Turkish rug is. It is very warm. My features are oval, dark eyes, dark brown hair. I dance, there are some others here.

Q. How old are you?

A. I am very young, 16, Rella the dancer.

Q. Are you married?

A. No. I live at a court. There is some monarch, but not a very great monarch, there are others as great as he, and I live here at the Court of Naobas.

Q. Ever heard of Turkey, Persia, China, Japan, Hindustan, Arabia, India?

A. No, India is more like it. We live in the North of our country.

Q. What is your religion?

A. We have a God, the Lord Ganga; he is in the other world.

Q. What becomes of you when you die?

A. We go on to other worlds, there are many . . . . There is a palace and a great pleasure garden, the pleasure garden slopes down to the river.

She awakes.

2. **De Rochas' hypnotic attempts to bring back consciousness of earlier lives.** In a book, *Les Vies Successives,* (Paris, 1911,) Colonel Albert de Rochas (1837-1914) describes experiments, most of them made by himself, with some nineteen persons in whom what he calls "magnetic" sleep was induced, and whose consciousness was then apparently regressed to various ages down to the time of birth, then to intra-uterine life, then purportedly to life as discarnate spirit, and then, still farther back, to one or more earlier lives. Also, *prima facie* progressions of consciousness to ages future to the hypnotized subject's age, and even to future incarnations.

In these experiments, age regressions were induced by means of longitudinal passes, and age progressions by means of transverse passes. But an incident in one of the experiments led De Rochas to remark that, "apparently the mode of magnetization, that is, the direction of the passes, has no great importance" (p. 80, note). He does, however, hold to the idea of a magnetic fluid and of the efficacy upon it of the passes; also to the existence on the subject's body of areas, e. g., the wrists, on which pressure has conjugate hypnogenic and hypnopompic effects; and of a point (the forehead at the root of the nose,) the pressing upon which has mnemonic effects. He seems to overlook or underestimate the fact that such pressings and passes constitute modes of suggestion, and appears to assume that only verbal suggestion is suggestion at all.

In the sixth experiment with the first of the subjects on his list, Laurent, in 1893, De Rochas hit accidentally upon the possibility of regressing the subject's personality to earlier life (p. 57); but it was not until eleven years later (1904) that, having regressed an 18 year old girl, Josephine, to the time of her birth, the idea occurred to him to continue the longitudinal passes (p. 67). This brought forth purported consciousness of the intra-uterine period and of a discarnate period preceding conception. De Rochas says that further deepening of the trance then resulted in manifestation of a personality whose nature at first puzzled him— that of a man who "would not say who he was, nor where he was. He replied in gruff tones, with a man's voice" (p. 68). Eventually, however, this personality declared himself to be Jean-Claude Bourdon, born in 1812 in the village of Champvent, district of Polliat, where he died at 70. He gave various details of his life, but subsequent inquiry turned up no evidence that such a man had lived in Polliat at the time stated.

This experiment was what led De Rochas to subsequent attempts to regress the consciousness of his subjects to earlier lives. Deepening Josephine's trance while the Bourdon personality was manifest brought out the personality of a wicked old woman, who said that she was born Philomene Charpigny in 1702, that she had married a man named Carteron in 1732 at Chevroux; and that her grandfather, Pierre Machon, lived at Ozan. De Rochas states in a footnote that families by the names of Charpigny and Carteron did exist at Ozan and at Chevroux, but that he found no positive trace of Philomene herself (p. 74 n.). Additional deepening of the trance brought out that, in anterior lives, she had been a girl who had died in infancy; before that a bandit who robbed and killed. Then came the shamefaced avowal that, in a life anterior to that bandit incarnation, she had been a big ape!

The attempts to progress Josephine to later ages in her present life brought out various episodes. Those relating to dates near enough to admit of verification—for example, foreseen employment as a salesgirl in the Galeries Modernes at Grenoble—did not come to pass. When progressed to the age of 32, i.e., to 1918, she sees herself back at Manziat where her mother lives. There she is seduced by a young farmer, and has a child who eventually dies. De Rochas then progresses her to the age of nearly seventy when she dies; purportedly then reincarnating first as a girl, Elise, who dies when three years old; and then as Marie, daughter of a man by the name of Edmond Baudin, who runs a shoe store at Saint-Germain-du-Mont-d' Or, and whose wife's name is Rosalie. When progressed to the age of sixteen in that life she says the year is 1970. This means that her birth as Marie would have occurred in 1954.

It would of course be interesting to inquire now at that place whether such a child was in fact born there in or about 1954 to parents of that name and occupation; also, of course whether in her life as Josephine she was indeed seduced in 1918 at Manziat and had a child there. De Rochas gives the seducer's name only as Eugene F., stating in a footnote (p. 78) that he had made inquiries which revealed that a man of that name, born in 1885, son of well-to-do farmers who were neighbors of Josephine's mother, was actually living there in 1911, and that he and Josephine, being of the same age had made their first communion together.

The non-fulfillment of the "Galeries Modernes" episode, however, makes all the more improbable that the later ones of the Josephine life, and of the reincarnation as Marie, have turned out to be veridical. But if hypnotic progression in 1904 to rebirth as Marie Baudin in 1954 should turn out to be corroborated by existence now of such a girl at the place named, this, so far as it went, would lend some weight to the hypothesis that the purported regressions to earlier lives are really this.

De Rochas declares that, by means of passes, one certainly can regress the subject to earlier ages of his present life: "It is not memories that one awakens; what one evokes are the successive stages of the personality" (p. 497). He also declares certain "that in continuing these magnetic operations beyond birth and without need of recourse to suggestions, one makes the subject go through analogous stages corresponding to preceding incarnations and to intervals between them" (p. 497). He adds, however, that "these revelations, when it has been possible to test their veridicality, have not in general corresponded to the facts" (p. 498). In case No. 8, where ten earlier lives are described by the entranced subject, numerous anachronisms occur. And in cases nos. 10, 11, 13, where details susceptible to verification were mentioned, the attempt subsequently made to corroborate them failed to do so. Thus, although the idea of reincarnation evidently appeals to De Rochas—and certain peculiar features of some of his experiments, to which he points, suggest it—he is on the whole far from fully convinced that the regressions under hypnosis which he relates really are regressions to earlier lives of the persons concerned.

In the absence of definite verification of the details they relate, the most plausible explanation of the facts appears to be that they are effects of suggestion and/or of stimulation of the mythopoeic imagination in the trance state. One feature of De Rochas' cases, which also points to this explanation, is that in almost all of them the purported earlier lives of those French subjects are likewise lives as French men or women; which, of course, especially for persons of simple minds, and who had never read much or travelled abroad, would be the psychologically easiest and most natural kinds of earlier lives to imagine.

3. **The "life readings" of Edgar Cayce.** A few words may be added concerning the accounts, purportedly of earlier incarnations of many persons, given by the late Edgar Cayce while in a state of trance. Cayce, who died in 1945, was a farm boy, born in Kentucky in 1877, who had only a grade school education and was a persistent Bible reader. He did not care for farm work and eventually became a photographer's apprentice. It was accidentally discovered that, while in hypnotic trance, he had the capacity to diagnose, and to prescribe often successful treatment for, the illnesses of persons who desired him to do this; and to do it even when the person was far away, provided the latter's name and the place where he was at the moment were given to Cayce. In the course of time Cayce, who had become able to put himself into the state of trance, gave many thousands of such "health" readings. After some years, however, it was found, again acci-

dentally, that while in the trance he could also give what came to be know as "life readings." These purported to report one or more earlier lives on earth of the person concerned, the name he or she had borne then, and the actions or experiences in those past lives which had as remote consequences in the present life certain features of body, mind, or character, and certain special abilities. Although in these readings the persons concerned were generally entire strangers to Cayce and far away at the time, his delineations of their present personality and vocational capacities was often surprisingly accurate. Dr. Gina Cerminara, a psychologist who made a study of the records of these readings, states that obscure historical details mentioned in the accounts of earlier lives of some of the persons who had "life readings"—including "the names of obscure former personalities. . . . . .in the locality"— have been verified by looking up historical records.[1] But, in the absence of citation of specific cases where details of an earlier life were given—as in the cases of Katsugoro, of Alexandrina Samona, and of Shanti Devi—and where careful verification of those details was made and is on record, the mere statement that such verification has been made does not constitute for us empirical evidence that the Cayce "life readings" really describe past incarnations of the persons concerned. And, although correct delineation of the present character and abilities of strangers at a distance would require clairvoyance of a high order, such delineation in itself has no relevance to the matter of rebirth.

Under these circumstances, the chief importance of the Cayce "life readings" in connection with the question as to the reality of reincarnation is the suggestion it affords that the hypnotic trance may be a means of bringing back in certain persons memories of presently verifiable details of earlier lives of their own; and possibly a means of arousing in exceptional individuals retrocognition of the lives of deceased persons, such as Cayce's "life readings" purportedly constituted, but with presently verifiable details.[2]

---

[1] *Many Mansions*, New York, Wm. Sloane Associates, 1950, p. 301.

[2] In 1943, the present writer had a "life reading" of himself done by Cayce. According to it, in his preceding incarnation, his name had been Jean de Larquen, and he had come to America from France as an intelligence officer associated with Lafayette. Such inquiries as he has been able to make have brought no evidence either in the United States or in France that any one ever bore that name.

Chapter XXV

THE CASE OF "THE SEARCH FOR BRIDEY MURPHY"

The widely discussed recent book, *The Search for Bridey Murphy*,[1] sets forth the six attempts made by its author, Mr. Morey Bernstein, between November 29, 1952 and August 29, 1953, to regress the consciousness of a deeply hypnotized subject, "Ruth Mills Simmons" (pseudonym for Virginia Burns Tighe) to a life earlier than her present one; and to obtain from her concerning that life details that would be verifiable but that could not have become known to her in any normal manner.

The experiment appeared to be notably successful, and verification was obtained of a number of the obscure details about Ireland which the entranced subject furnished. This, and the conversational form—reproduced verbatim in the book—in which those intrinsically drab details were supplied by her gave to the idea of reincarnation a concreteness which made it more plausible to many of the readers of the book than had such references to it as they had met with before. And this in turn opened their eyes to the fact that reincarnation, if true, could furnish a rational explanation for the great disparities—otherwise so shocking to the human sense of justice—which obtain from birth between the endowments and the fortunes of different individuals.

In consequence, the book became a best seller almost immediately after publication. The idea of reincarnation, however, runs counter both to the religious beliefs prevalent today in the West, and to certain assumptions which, although really gratuitous, are at present commonly made in Western scientific circles.

---

[1]Doubleday & Co. Garden City, N.Y. January 1956; Pocket Books, Inc. edition, with a new chapter by Wm. J. Barker, New York, June 1956.

Hence the sudden emergence of the reincarnation hypothesis into public attention quickly moved the protagonists both of religious and of scientific orthodoxy to impassioned attacks on the book.

These sociological aspects of the Bridey Murphy case give it exceptional interest even aside from such evidence for reincarnation as it may be thought to provide. They furnish eloquent footnotes to what was said in earlier chapters concerning the psychology of belief and of disbelief both in scientists who approach the "enchanted boundary" of the paranormal, and in custodians of institutionally vested religious dogmas. For these reasons, and because the case is still fresh in the minds of many today, it will be worth while to devote the whole of the present chapter to a review and discussion of the Bridey Murphy affair.

1. **The hypnotist and author, and his subject.** The author of the book, Morey Bernstein, is a Colorado businessman who received his bachelor's degree from the University of Pennsylvania. His studies there apparently did not include a course in abnormal psychology, for it was not until later that—after unexpectedly witnessing a private demonstration of hypnotism—his prior disbelief in the reality of hypnosis gave way. He then proceeded to study the literature of the subject and to experiment with hypnotism. At the time of the first of the "Bridey Murphy" sessions in 1952, he had had some ten years of experience with hypnotism, had hypnotized hundreds of persons and, in many of these experiments had regressed his subjects to various ages of their childhood. Thus, although the later attacks on the book have insistently termed Bernstein an "amateur" hypnotist, he is so in the sense that he has made no charges for services he has rendered as a hypnotist; not in the sense of lacking practical experience or of being but casually acquainted with the standard literature of the field. For as regards these two desiderata, he is doubtless better equipped than were a number of the dentists and physicians in the seminars he attended, who because of their professional degrees, received at the end a certificate of competence to use hypnotism in their practice.

An acquaintance of Bernstein's, familiar with the idea of reincarnation, eventually brought it to his attention; and he then learned that attempts, *prima facie* successful, had been made by some hypnotists to regress their entranced subjects to times earlier than their birth or conception. This led him to undertake a similar experiment on one of his subjects, Virginia Tighe—the "Ruth Simmons" of his eventual book.

Virginia is a young married woman, born April 27, 1923, daughter of Mr. and Mrs. George Burns, who lived in Madison, Wis. Their marriage did not endure and, shortly after Virginia's third birthday, her father's sister, Mrs. Myrtle Grung, took her to Chicago to live with her and her Norwegian husband. There Virginia grew up a normal girl, went through grade and high schools, and eventually attended Northwestern University for a year and a half. At the age of 20, she married a young Army Air Corps man who died in the war a year later. Some time after, in Denver, she married her present husband, businessman Hugh Brian Tighe. They have three children. In Pueblo, Colorado, where they have lived for some years, she and her husband became casually acquainted with Mr. and Mrs. Bernstein.

When Bernstein decided to attempt regressing the consciousness of a hypnotized subject to an earlier life, it occurred to him that the chances of success would be greatest in a subject capable of the state of deep, somnambulistic hypnosis. He then remembered that, some time before he had had any idea that regression to an earlier life might be possible, he had hypnotized Mrs. Tighe twice and that she had readily attained that deep hypnotic state. This, and the fact that she knew nothing of his then recent interest in reincarnation, led him to wish to have her as subject for the regression experiments. Although such leisure as she and her husband had was much occupied with other interests, they eventually consented. The six sessions which are the basis of the book were then held at intervals during the course of the next few months, and were tape-recorded.

2. **Emergence of "Bridey Murphy" during Virginia's trance.** Although neither Virginia nor Bernstein had ever visited Ireland, as soon as she had in deep hypnosis been regressed first to the years of her childhood, and then instructed to go farther back to times anterior to her present life, and to report what scenes she per-

ceived, she began to describe episodes of a life in which she was Bridey (Bridget) Kathleen Murphy, an Irish girl born in Cork in 1798, daughter of a Protestant Cork barrister, Duncan Murphy, and his wife Kathleen. She said she had attended a school run by a Mrs. Strayne and had a brother named Duncan Blaine Murphy, who eventually married Mrs. Strayne's daughter Aimee. She had had another brother who had died while still a baby. At the age of 20, Bridey was married in a Protestant ceremony to a Catholic, Brian Joseph McCarthy, son of a Cork barrister. Brian and Bridey moved to Belfast where he had attended school and where, Bridey said, he eventually taught law at the Queen's University. A second marriage ceremony was performed in Belfast by a Catholic priest, Father John Joseph Gorman, of St. Theresa's church. They had no children. She lived to the age of sixty-six and was— to use her own expression—"ditched", i.e., buried, in Belfast in 1864. Many of her other statements referred to things which it seemed highly improbable that Virginia could have come to know in any normal manner, but which might possibly be verified or disproved. And the "search" for Bridey Murphy is the search that was made for facts or records that would do one or the other.

3. **The chief documents of the Bridey Murphy controversy.** No attempt will be made in what follows to review all the special points on which debate has focused in the Bridey Murphy controversy. But the chief of the documents which together constitute the history of the case, and on which are based the conclusions that will be offered, must be listed. For convenience of reference, a symbol will be assigned to each, made up from initials in the title of the corresponding document.

SSBM. The first published account of the Bridey Murphy regression experiments appeared Sept. 12, 19, and 26, 1954 in *Empire*—the Sunday magazine section of the *Denver Post*—in three articles entitled "The Strange Search for Bridey Murphy" written by Wm. J. Barker, of the *Denver Post* staff.

MAB. This was followed by "More About Bridey," in *Empire* for Dec. 5, 1954.

TSBM. The next document is the book itself, *The Search for Bridey Murphy*, by Bernstein, published in January 1956 by

Doubleday & Co. The last chapter of it gives an account of the results up to that time of the search which the book's editor had instituted through an Irish law firm and various librarians and investigators. Then the *Chicago Daily News*, which was publishing a syndicated version of the book, instructed its London man, Ernie Hill, to go to Ireland for three days and look for additional verifications from Cork to Belfast. In view, however, of the extent of territory to be covered and of the brief time allowed, this assignment could hardly turn out other than, as it actually did, virtually fruitless.

TABM. Next, the editor of the *Denver Post* sent Wm. J. Barker to Ireland for three weeks on a similar assignment. What he found and failed to find was objectively reported in a twelve page supplement to the *Denver Post* for March 11, 1956, entitled "The Truth about Bridey Murphy."

FABI. Then *Life* for March 19, 1956, published an article in two parts, one of which was entitled "Here are facts about Bridey that reporters found in Ireland." This part was stated to have been compiled from the reports of W. J. Barker, Ernie Hill, and *Life's* own correspondent Ruth Lynam.

OSAB. The second part of the *Life* article was entitled "Here are opinions of scientists about Bridey's 'reincarnation.' " It gave an account of views of two psychiatrists, Drs. J. Schneck and L. Wolberg, concerning the case.

SACA. The next document consists of a series of articles published in May and June 1956 by the *Chicago American* and reproduced in other Hearst papers (the *San Francisco Examiner,* the New York *Journal American,*) purporting to show that Virginia's supposed memories of a life as Bridey Murphy in Ireland really were subconsciously preserved memories of her childhood in Madison, Wis. and in Chicago, and of stories about Ireland with which, one of the articles claimed, she had been "regaled" by an aunt of hers who was "Irish as the lakes of Killarney." Another of the *Chicago American* articles had it that the real Bridey Murphy had been found and was a Mrs. Bridie Murphy Corkell, whose house in Chicago was across the street from one of those in which Virginia had lived.

CNCU. Then the *Denver Post,* on June 17, 1956, published

an article by a member of its staff, Robert Byers, captioned "Chicago Newspaper Charges Unproved," and commenting critically on the allegations of the *Chicago American* series of articles.

BSE. Next, on June 25, 1956, *Life* published a short article, "Bridie Search Ends at Last," summarizing the *Chicago American's* contentions and printing a photograph of Mrs. Corkell with her grandchildren.

CFBI. Also in June 1956, Pocket Books, Inc. published the paper back edition of *The Search for Bridey Murphy,* in which a new chapter, "The Case for Bridey in Ireland," by Wm. J. Barker, was added. In it, he gives an effective presentation of the chief conclusions which, notwithstanding various allegations, appear valid in the light of the results of the investigations made by himself and others; and he adds that "Bridey's 'autobiography' stands up fantastically well in the light of such hard-to-obtain facts as I did accumulate" (p. 271).

SRSBM. In the spring of 1956 a book, *A Scientific Report on "The Search for Bridey Murphy,"* edited by Dr. M. V. Kline and containing a chapter each by him and by Drs. Bowers, Marcuse, Raginsky, and Shapiro, and an Introduction by Dr. Rosen, was published in New York by the Julian Press.

HBCL. In October 1956, the *Denver Post* published in six instalments an interview of Virginia in Pueblo by W. J. Barker, entitled "How Bridey Changed my Life," in which she comments on various of the allegations about her that had been published.

In addition to the articles cited above, numerous others concerning the case, by psychiatrists, psychoanalysts, and other members of the professions appeared in a number of periodicals.

TM. For example, the summer 1956 issue of *Tomorrow* magazine contained several.

AW. The case furnished occasion also for a series of articles in the March to December 1956 issues of the monthly theosophical periodical, *Ancient Wisdom*—some dealing with reincarnation itself, and others pointing out the weak spots in the *Chicago American* series.

RIS. In a review of SRSBM in the January 1957 issue of the Journal of the American Society for Psychical Research, Dr. Ian Stevenson, Head of the Department of Neurology and Psychiatry,

University of Virginia School of Medicine, expresses disappointment with the book and states a number of reasons for this.

4. **The Bridey statements that have not so far been verified.** No verification has yet been obtained that a barrister named Duncan Murphy and his wife Kathleen lived in Cork in 1798 and in that year had a daughter, Bridget Kathleen; nor that a Bridget Kathleen Murphy married in Cork a Catholic called Sean Brian McCarthy; nor that she died in 1864 in Belfast; nor that there was in Belfast in her days a St. Theresa's church; nor that it had a priest named John Joseph Gorman who, as Bridey states, performed a second marriage ceremony there.

That no traces of her birth, marriage, or death have been found, however, is not surprising since, aside from some church records, vital statistics in Ireland do not go back beyond 1864. Indeed, that any traces of her or of her people should be found would be the more surprising if an impression is correct, which Bernstein gained early and which the reader may test for himself from the recorded conversations between Bridey and Bernstein—the impression, namely, that her references to her father and to her husband as "barristers" were partly attempts to upgrade her family socially, and partly stemmed from the fact that she had only a vague idea of what their occupations actually were outside the home, or of what a Barrister really was. She states at one place that her father was a "cropper," i.e., a farmer; and she names correctly what crops were raised there at the time. He may well have had also a part-time clerical job, perhaps in a law office. And as regards her husband, Barker, at the end of his chapter in the paper back edition of the book, declares his conviction that Sean (John) Brian M'Carthy was not a barrister but a bookkeeper, who kept books for several of the business houses in Belfast and perhaps also for Queens' College. This would be supported by the fact that, in the 1858-9 Belfast Directory, one John M'Carthy, clerk, is listed; and that, in the 1861-2 Directory, he is listed as a bookkeeper. (*CFBI* p. 287-8)

5. **Examples of the Bridey statements that have been verified.** The statements of the Bridey personality, on the other hand, that have been verified notwithstanding (in the case of some of

them) expert opinion that they could not be correct, are effectively presented with references to the verificatory findings in the chapter Wm. Barker contributed to the paper-back edition of the book. They constitute, as the title of his chapter indicates, The Case for Bridey in Ireland. In order to invalidate it, what would be necessary would be to show that Virginia learned those recondite facts about Ireland of a century ago in a normal manner in the United States. The attempts of the *Chicago American* to show this have patently failed. The most they could be held to have shown would be that *some* of Virginia's statements, *not* those which constitute the case for Bridey in Ireland, are perhaps traceable to experiences of Virginia's childhood in Chicago.

In order to outline all the essential facts, the allegations that they have been explained in an orthodox manner, and the refutations of those allegations, far more space would be required than is available here. But a few samples will make evident the lack of real basis for the belief—now widespread as a result of the wishful attacks of orthodoxy on Bernstein's book—that every puzzling feature of the case for Bridey Murphy in Ireland has now been explained away in a satisfying orthodox manner.

Bridey mentions the names of two Belfast grocers from whom she bought foodstuffs—Farr's and John Carrigan. After considerable search by the Belfast Chief Librarian, John Bebbington, and his staff, these two grocers were found listed in a Belfast city directory for 1865-66 which had been in preparation at the time Bridey died in 1864. Moreover, Barker reports, they were "the *only* individuals of those names engaged in the 'foodstuffs' business," there at the time. Bridey stated also that in her days a big rope company and a tobacco house were in operation in Belfast; and this has been found to be correct. (*CFBI*, 271, 284) She also mentioned a house that sold "ladies things," Cadenns, of which no trace has been found. Directories, however, listed individuals rather than business houses, and the proprietor of Cadenn's house might not have been himself named Cadenn.

Even more impressive than the verification of Farr's and of John Carrigan, however, is the fact that a number of Bridey's statements which according to experts on Ireland were irreconcilable with known facts were shown by further investigation not to be really so. One example would be the following.

The very first of the utterances ascribed to Bridey on the tape of the first session is that (as of age four, i.e., 1802) she had scratched the paint off all her bed, that "it was a metal bed," and that she got an awful spanking. *Life* (in *FABI*) states that "iron bedsteads were not introduced into Ireland until at least 1850." Dr. E. J. Dingwall, however, states that "they were being advertised by the Hive Iron Works in Cork in January 1830 . . . . .Mallett's portable iron bedsteads were often used in Ireland at about that date, although it is somewhat doubtful whether they were at all common about 1802" (*TM*, p. 11). And the *Encyclopedia Britannica* (1950 edition), states that "iron beds appear in the 18th century." So Bridey *could*, in 1802, have had an iron bed in Cork.

But however this may be, attention must now be called to the fact that in the published transcript of the tape recording (*TSBM* p. 112) Bridey does not speak of an *iron* bed at all but of a *metal* bed; and to the recently noticed fact that a careful rehearing of the tape seems to show that the word (which like many others uttered by Virginia in trance is not clearly articulated) was not "metal" but "little," i.e., "little bed."

This is made the more probable by the fact that hardly anybody—least of all a child of four—would ordinarily speak of a *metal* bed, but rather—as all commentators on the episode have indeed done spontaneously—of an *iron* bed; or as the case might be, of a *brass* bed.

One of the *Chicago American's* articles claims that the aunt who brought up Virginia in Chicago remembered such a bed-scratching and spanking incident in Chicago when Virginia was six or seven; and that Virginia remembered it and laughed about it with her aunt when, a dozen years later, she was given a bedroom suite as a birthday present.

Virginia, on the other hand, told Robert Byers *(CNCU)* that she recalls no such incident, and most especially that she never recalled it to a relative when, at the age of eighteen, she was presented with a new bedroom set. Worth bearing in mind in connection with statements alleged to have been made by relatives of hers (unnamed by the newspaper) is Virginia's statement to Barker (*HBCL,* part I) that "both Hugh's and my relatives in Chicago are very much opposed to the whole Bridey phenomenon on religious grounds." This would easily open the door to wishful thinking unawares on their part.

Aside from this, however, it should be noticed that the statement about the bed-scratching and spanking episode is the very first which Virginia, supposedly as Bridey, makes; and that it comes immediately after those which Virginia, as regressed to her own childhood, had made. It is therefore possible that the memory of the incident did belong to her own childhood, rather than to that of the girl who, when asked for her name immediately afterwards, gave it as Bridey.

But in any case, it has *not* been shown that there were no metal beds in Cork in 1802, but at most that they were probably not common there at that time. Hence,—even if Bridey said "metal," not "little"—it has not been shown that she cannot really be remembering a metal bed in Cork in 1802.

Let us turn next to the fact, of which much has been made, that in view of the scarcity of wood in Ireland, Bridey's house in Cork could hardly have been a wooden house.

According to the published transcript of the first session, Bridey, when asked what kind of house she lives in, answers: "it's a nice house. . . . it's a wood house. . . .white. . . . has two floors." But here again, a careful rehearing of the tape appears to show that the word Bridey uttered was not "wood," but "good": ". . . a nice house. . . . a good house. . .;" and this is the more probable because one would not ordinarily speak of a "wood" house, but —as *Life* spontaneously does in its comment—of a *wooden* house or, today, of a frame house.

Again, immediately after quoting the passage quoted above, the *Life* article adds: "and was called 'The Meadows.'" But reference to the passage where "the Meadows" are first mentioned (in the second tape) shows that Bridey did *not* say the house was *called* "The Meadows." The question asked her is "What was the address in Cork?" and her answer is: "That was. . . . .the Meadows. . . . .just the Meadows" (*TSBM* 140; Pocket Books ed. 159). Also, in the third tape, she is asked: "What were the

Meadows in Cork?" and she answers: "There's. . . .where I lived" (*TSBM* 160; Pocket Books ed. 183). Moreover, the *Denver Post* article *(TABM)* reproduces on its p. 9 a section of an 1801 map of Cork showing an area named Mardike Meadows, where some half-dozen houses are indicated.

So Bridey's statements about her house in Cork have not been shown to clash with known facts. On the contrary, her statements turned out to be compatible with what research in Ireland showed the facts in Cork really to have been.

We now pass to Bridey's statement that her husband taught law at the Queen's University in Belfast some time after 1847. *Life* attacks it, not on the ground suggested by Barker that Brian McCarthy was probably not a lawyer after all, but on the ground that there was no law school there at the time, no Queen's *College* until 1849, and no Queen's *University* until 1908.

This, however, is an error; for the facts are that on December 19, 1845, Queen Victoria ordained that "there shall and may be erected. . . . .one College for students in Arts, Law, Physic. . . . which shall be called Queen's College, Belfast" (*CFBI* 278). At the same time, she founded colleges at Cork and Galway. Then, on August 15, 1850, she founded "the Queen's University in Ireland," directing "that the said Queen's Colleges shall be, and . . . .are hereby constituted Colleges of our said University" (*CFBI* 279). So here again Bridey's statement is consistent with the facts, and the allegation that it is not rests on an error concerning the facts.

Again, Bridey spoke of ". . . .tiny little sacks of rice. . ." which were snapped on an elastic band on the leg: "It is a sign of purity" (*TSBM*, 199; Pocket Books ed. 231). *Life's* "Folklore Expert" Richard Hayward is quoted as saying: "Nonsense! Rice has never been a part of the folk tradition in Ireland. Corn, oats or potatoes, yes, for centuries. But rice, never!"

Rice, however, was imported into Ireland about 1750. Doubtless, it took some years for it to become widely known there. And it takes some more years for a "tradition" to develop out of ideas that happen to arise spontaneously in a number of individuals. Rice, being white, would naturally suggest purity to some of its early users. How it eventually came to symbolize fertility is less obvious. But anyway, what is relevant to the question whether Bridey's statement can represent a genuine memory of an earlier life in Ireland is not whether rice has ever been a part of the folk tradition in Ireland; but only whether the *whiteness* of that until then unknown grain is likely to have struck some of its early consumers and to have caused them to think of it as symbolizing purity—as *white* orange blossoms are today used to signify a bride's purity, i.e., virginity. To *this* question, it is highly probable that the answer is Yes. Indeed, rice, as a symbol of purity, may well have been imagined to aid a girl in preserving purity if worn by her in little bags on the leg, as today medals symbolizing holy beings are given children to wear as an aid to them in conducting themselves as their religion expects them to do.

Again, the word Bridey uses to refer to interment of the bodies of the dead is not "burying" but "ditching." *Life* is of course right when it states that "ditch" does not correctly mean "bury." Yet *Life* itself mentions that "ditching" *was* used to designate the mass burials of the many who died during the potato famine of 1845-47. So there can be little doubt that, as Professor Seamus Kavanaugh of University College, Cork, has suggested, a good many persons came to use "ditch" colloquially to mean "bury." Similarly, "croak" does not correctly mean "die;" yet today "to croak" is sometimes slangily used among us to mean "to die."

Again, Bridey said that "tup" meant a rounder; and she used "a linen" to mean a handkerchief. *Life* states that "Scholar Hayward. . . .laughed at *tup, linen*. . . . . .as being any sort of Gaelic." But where Hayward got the idea that Bridey, or Bernstein, claimed that "linen" is a Gaelic word is a complete mystery. Bridey mentions "a linen" at all only when, having sneezed during the fourth session, she said "Could I have a linen?. . . .I need a linen." And Professor Kavanaugh endorsed this use of the word as, in Bridey's days, referring to a handkerchief.

As regards "tup," it is quite true as a matter of linguistics that the word is not Gaelic. It is a Middle English word of unknown origin, which properly means a male sheep but also has slang meanings. Bridey mentions "tup" when asked by Bernstein for some Gaelic words. But Bridey is no linguistician, and reference to p. 156 of *TSBM* makes evident that, for her, "Gaelic" means essentially *the language the peasants use.* Associating as these did with persons who spoke English, some words of this language, such as "tup," doubtless got into the peasants' vocabulary; and Barker states that Professor Kavanaugh indeed found the word in one of his dictionaries in the sense Bridey gave for it *(CFBI,* p. 281).

Again, Bridey used the word "lough" to designate rivers as well as lakes *(TSBM,* pp. 136-7). And *Life*—apparently on Expert Hayward's authority—states that *"Lough* simply does not mean 'river' but 'lake.' " Yet *Murray's English Dictionary*—which presumably is at least as authoritative as Mr. Hayward—gives "low" as an obsolete variant of "lough" and meaning "a lake, loch, river, water" (Vol. VI, p. 271).

Again, Barker states *(CFBI* p. 280) that, notwithstanding Hayward's statement that "no Irishman would refer to another as an *Orange* but always as Orangeman or Orangewoman," he (Barker) "can recall no one in Ireland questioning the slang term *Orange* as a synonym for 'Orangewoman.' "

Of Bridey's mention that she read, or that her mother read to her from, a book on the sorrows of Deirdre, *Life's* would-be invalidation consists of a statement that according to *The English Catalogue*—said to be "a complete list of books published between 1800 and the present"—the first appearance of Deirdre's name in a title is in Synge's play *The Sorrows of Deirdre* published in 1905. But Barker cites to the contrary "a cheap paper-back published in 1808 by Bolton, entitled *The Song of Deirdre and the Death of the Sons of Usnach" (CFBI* p. 278.). So here again Bridey's statement turns out to be consistent with the facts notwithstanding that Virginia Tighe had no normal way of knowing that such a paper-back had existed nor any interest in the question; whereas *Life,* which had such an interest, and whose possible sources of information were surely as ample as Barker's, overlooked that 1808 paper-back.

An additional statement made by Bridey is that in her days one of the coins in use was a tuppence. This is correct; but very few persons know that such a coin was in use in Ireland only between the years 1797 and 1850.

Barker's chapter mentions a number of additional obscure facts testified to in Bridey's tape-recorded statements, which some persons presumably expert in matters of Irish history disputed, but which subsequent investigation turned out likewise to corroborate. Those cited above, however, will suffice to make evident not only that reputed experts are not omniscient, but also that the allegations of critics of disturbing ideas need to be scrutinized with quite as much care as must the assertions of proponents of those ideas. For, as repeatedly has been pointed out in earlier chapters, the temptations to wishful thinking and to emotionally biassed conclusions are even greater on the side of the entrenched religious orthodoxy of the time and place concerned, or on the side of the vested "scientific commonsense of the epoch," than on the side of the protagonists of *prima facie* paradoxical views.

At all events, the items Barker's investigation brought out, about which Bridey was right and the experts were wrong, constitute the central feature of the Bridey Murphy affair so far as concerns the question in view in Parts IV and V of the present work—the question, namely, whether any empirical evidence is available that the human mind survives after death, whether in some discarnate state or in the form of reincarnation. For the evidence, so far as it goes, which the Bridey Murphy case furnishes for survival consists essentially of the fact that those obscure items were correctly supplied by the lips of Virginia in trance, and of the fact that it is hard even to imagine how she could have come to know in a normal manner about the Ireland of over a century ago details so numerous and so uninteresting in themselves—details, moreover, the confirmation of which by researchers in Ireland was so laborious that the wonder is not that some of them have so far eluded verification, but much rather that it has been possible to verify so many of them.

6. **The allegation that the true Bridey statements are traceable to forgotten events of Virginia's childhood.** We may now consider briefly the allegation that the *Chicago American's* articles brought out facts which explain away Virginia's utterances in the character of Bridey Murphy as being simply revivals and dramatizations under hypnosis of buried memories of her own childhood and youth in Madison and Chicago.

Barker's "The Truth about Bridey Murphy" was an objective report both of the verifications he obtained and of those he did not succeed in getting during his three weeks in Ireland. In that report, he did not conclude either for or against the supposition that Bridey and Virginia are two different incarnations of one same individual, but let the reader draw his own conclusions, if any. Unlike Barker's, however, many of the other articles on the case in newspapers and periodicals are patently attempts to exorcise the demon which, in the shape of Bernstein's book, was then tempting the hundreds of thousands of its readers to belief in reincarnation—a doctrine unorthodox both in contemporary Christian theology and in contemporary psychology. Indeed, the *Denver Post's* staff writer points out in the article "Chicago Newspaper Charges Unproved" that the Rev. Wally White, whose name appears at the head of a number of the *Chicago American* articles, "stated clearly [that] his purpose was to debunk reincarnation because of its assault upon established religious doctrines."

The *American's* articles hardly mention most of the facts summarized by Barker in *CFBI*, on which the case, such as it is—for Bridey as an earlier "edition" of Virginia really rests. Rather, the *American* dismisses them wholesale with the allegation that Virginia was "regaled" with Irish stories by an aunt of hers who was "as Irish as the lakes of Killarney."

Virginia, however, states that the aunt so alluded to, Mrs. Marie Burns, was born in New York, was of Scotch-Irish descent, and spent most of her life in Chicago. Virginia adds (*HBCL*, part IV): "I didn't become really well acquainted with her until she came to live with us when I was 18. You'd think I would recall her having 'regaled' me with Irish tales if she had, at that tender age, wouldn't you?" Virginia further states that she does not remember anybody telling her anything about Ireland any time, and knows about Ireland only the few things everybody has heard.

But the article appears to regard the mere fact that Aunt Marie was living with Virginia at about the time the latter left Chicago as warranting the assertion that "it seems likely that some of the Irish references used by Bridey. . . . .stem from the tales of Aunt Marie" (*San Francisco Examiner*, June 5). The *American's* articles, thus virtually ignoring the real evidence for Bridey's existence, concentrate their attention instead on "parallels"—of which some samples will presently be cited—between incidents in Virginia's childhood and in Bridey's life; incidents, however, which, even if truly derived from Virginia's childhood, would leave wholly untouched the real case, based as we have seen on verifications of obscure Irish facts, for the contention that the Bridey statements represent genuine memories of Ireland.

As a sample of the *American's* "success" in tracing back to Virginia's childhood various items in Bridey's statements about Ireland, may be mentioned its "discoveries" in Madison relevant to the name of Father John Joseph Gorman who married Bridey, and to Bridey's address in Cork, "the Meadows." What the *American's* reporter discovered in Madison is that, less than 100 feet from the house on Blair St. where Virginia lived in Madison until age 3, Blair St. is crossed by *Gorham* St.; that a block and a half from the house is St. *John's* Lutheran Church; and that the pastor of the church attended by the parents of that three year old child was called *John* N. Walsted! But the reporter need not have gone so far to find persons called John. It is safe to say that on the very block of her house, or indeed on virtually any block of any city in the United States, half-a-dozen Johns could be found.

As regards "the Meadows," the *American's* discovery was that "less than two blocks from Ruth's house [i.e., Virginia's, in Madison] is a lake front park—a 'meadow' where she must have played many times."

But the *American's* prize discovery in Madison was that, like Bridey, "Ruth [i.e., Virginia]. . . . .did have a little brother who died," October 29, 1927, still-born. The fact, however, is that Virginia *never had a brother*, still-born or other. Indeed, reference to this mythical brother appeared only in the original June 14, 1956 article in Chicago; and was left out of the syndicated version of the article.

Another typical example of the "parallels" which the *American's* investigations brought to light refers to the fact that, in the fourth hypnotic session, Virginia suddenly sneezed hard. A friend of hers, referred to in the article merely as "Ann," is quoted as saying; "if anyone could sneeze hard, it was Ruth."

One may well ask, So what? for Bridey was not reporting at

the time some hard sneezing she might have done in Ireland. It was Virginia's nose that sneezed; just as it was Virginia's larynx and lips that were uttering Bridey's memories.

Bridey's then calling for "a linen" is accounted for in the article by the fact that the same "Ann" always called her white linen handkerchiefs "white linen handkerchiefs"!! Comment on these various "parallels" would be superfluous.

The Hearst *San Francisco Examiner,* which reproduces the May 28 article of the Hearst *Chicago American* by the Rev. Wally White, pastor of the Chicago Gospel Tabernacle, states that the *American's* investigation "was launched after it was learned that Mrs. Simmons [i.e., Virginia Tighe] had attended Sunday School as a girl in Rev. White's church."

The reader would naturally infer from this that the Rev. White had known Virginia as a girl in Chicago. It is therefore interesting to refer to what Virginia has to say when questioned by Barker on the subject. She states (*HBCL,* part V): I went to Sunday School at the Chicago Gospel Tabernacle from the time I was about four till I was thirteen or so." The Rev. Wally White "was not there when I was. The first time I met him was this summer [1956] when he suddenly appeared at our door here in Pueblo. . . . .he said he wanted to pray for me."

It would seem, then, that the featuring of this clergyman's name at the head of several of the *American's* articles was just psychological window-dressing for the benefit of pious but naive readers. For such readers, seeing articles under the by-line of a clergyman, and having been told that he is the pastor of the church Virginia attended in Chicago, would naturally assume that he has first hand knowledge of her childhood and youth; that his articles are based on that special knowledge; and therefore that, since clergymen are truthful, the articles bearing the Rev. White's by-line must be authoritative. But although the reader is likely to infer all this from the articles, they carefully refrain from actually asserting any of it.

The incident of the bed-scratching and the ensuing spanking, of which the *American* makes much, may indeed as we stated in our account of it belong to the life of Virginia in Chicago rather than to that of Bridey in Cork. But this is less likely in the case of Bridey's "uncle Plazz."

The *American* claims that he really is "a sixty-one year old retired city employe," to find whom its reporters "combed Chicago," and whose first name is Plezz. But the paper withholds his last name and address "in order to protect his privacy." It describes him and his wife, however, as old friends of the aunt who brought up Virginia in Chicago; stating that he and his wife would visit Virginia and her aunt and uncle two or three times a week and that the visits would be returned; and that he and two of his daughters would play with Virginia. He is said to remember her "very well from the time she was about three or four until she was in the eighth grade," which would be until she was thirteen or fourteen. This would mean a close association for some ten years.

But let the reader now ask himself how credible is such an "uncle Plezz" in Chicago, in the face of the fact that Virginia, at age 33, has "no conscious memory of any such person" nor even of the name, as she emphatically declares when questioned about it by Barker. (*HBCL,* part IV).

Again, the May 29, 1956 Chicago article states that Virginia "took her early lessons in forensics from a Mrs. H.S.M." (left otherwise unidentified.) Immediately after this, it prints long passages from stage-Irish dialect pieces, and states that Ruth [i.e., Virginia] memorized them.

This immediate juxtaposition would lead a hasty reader to assume that that teacher is the authority for the identification of the particular pieces of which passages are quoted, and for the statement that Virginia memorized them. Attentive reading, however, reveals that the article carefully refrains from so asserting. It only asserts, nakedly, that Virginia memorized those particular pieces.

What the lady teacher apparently alluded to actually taught was elocution, not forensics which has to do with argumentation or debate. And what Virginia herself has to say on the subject of that lady's lessons is this: "I took elocution lessons back in 1935 or 36. . . .there was a well-to-do woman. . . . .who offered that kind of training for small groups of youngsters. . . .When I was

12 or 13 I went to her after school on certain days. I'm afraid I wasn't much good—I can't remember anything specifically that she taught us" (*HBCL*, part VI).

Robert Byers, of the *Denver Post's* staff, located that teacher. She is Mrs. Harry G. Saulnier. She remembered that "Virginia was a pupil for a short time, but she must have been rather average or I would remember her better." Mrs. Saulnier said that "she had no recollection specifically of the pieces Mrs. Tighe memorized," and that she has anyway never heard of any entitled "Mr. Dooley on Archey Road," which the *American* asserted Virginia had learned *(CNCU)*.

So far as concerns the "Irish jigs," which the paper asserts Virginia learned to dance, Virginia identifies them as having been The Black Bottom, and the Charleston!

The climax, however, of the *Chicago American* series of articles was the discovery of a Mrs. Bridie Murphy Corkell in Chicago, who lived across the street from one of the places where Virginia and her foster parents had resided; whom Virginia knew; and on whose son John, Virginia is asserted to have had "a mad crush."

Virginia remembers John as "Buddy Corkell;" but as regards the alleged "mad crush," she says: "Heavens, he was 7 or 8 years older than I was. He was married by the time I was old enough to have any romantic interest in boys." She also remembers Mrs. Corkell, but although the article states that she "was in the Corkell home many times," Virginia never spoke with Mrs. Corkell—nor does the article assert that she ever did.

Further, Virginia never knew that Mrs. Corkell's first name was Bridie, and still less that her maiden name was Murphy, if indeed it was. For when the *Denver Post* tried to verify this, Mrs. Corkell was not taking telephone calls. And when its reporter Bob Byers inquired from her parish priest in Chicago, he confirmed her first name as Bridie, but was unable to verify her maiden name as Murphy (*HBCL*, p. VI); nor could the Rev. Wally White do so.

But the reader will hardly guess who this Mrs. Corkell, whom the *American* "discovered" turns out to be. By one more of the strange coincidences in the case, Mrs. Bridie (Murphy?) Corkell happens to be *the mother of the editor of the Sunday edition of the Chicago American* at the time the articles were published!

7. **The comments of psychiatrists on the Bridey Murphy case.** *Life's* first article *(OSAB)* states that "the psychiatrists who have considered the case have no doubt that if Ruth Simmons could completely reveal her life to them, preferably under hypnosis, they could end the search for Bridey Murphy abruptly."

What this opinion actually represents, however, is only their adhesion to the methodological principle that a phenomenon whose cause is not actually observed is to be presumed to arise from causes similar to those from which past phenomena more or less similar to it were observed to have arisen. This is good scientific procedure, of course; but only in so far as, in order to be able to follow it, one is not forced to ignore some patent dissimilarities between the new phenomenon and the old; or forced to postulate *ad hoc* similarities which are not in fact observed; or forced to stretch beyond the breaking point some of those which are observed. For were it not for these limits of applicability of that methodological principle, no as yet unknown laws of nature would ever be discovered; every new fact would be trimmed, bent, or stretched to fit into the Procrustean bed of the already discovered modes of explanation.

One would be guilty of doing just this if, for example, one were to claim that, in the "Rosemary" xenoglossy case, her ability while in trance to *converse* in ancient Egyptian language is scientifically explicable in a manner similar to that in which *is* scientifically explained the case of xenoglossy mentioned by Dr. Rosen in his introduction to the book, *A Scientific Report on "The Search for Bridey Murphy."* In the latter case, a hypnotized patient's ability to *recite* some ten words in the ancient language, Oscan, was scientifically explained by the discovery that once in the library while day-dreaming his eyes had rested on a book near him which happened to be open at a page where those words in Oscan were printed. The "Rosemary" case is similar to this *only* in that both are cases of xenoglossy. For, patently, nothing like what accounted for the ability of the patient to *recite* a certain ten words of an ancient language unknown to him would account for "Rosemary's" ability to *converse* in responsive phrases in an ancient language she had never studied.

Similarly, the emergence—whether spontaneously or under hypnosis—of personalities seemingly distinct from that of the individual concerned, but which actually are dissociated portions of his own total personality, is today a well known phenomenon. But as we saw in an earlier chapter, some cases of emergent new personalities stubbornly resist assimilation to cases of mere dissociation, either because, as in that of the "Watseka Wonder", the new personality is unmistakably identified as that of a particular other individual who has died; or because the new personality demonstrates knowledge which the individual through whose body it expresses itself certainly never had or which it is exceedingly improbable it could ever have had.

In such a case, to postulate as a number of psychiatrists have done in the Bridey Murphy case, that Virginia *must* some time have somehow learned in an ordinary manner the recondite Irish facts Bridey mentioned, is *not* scientific procedure, but is just piously conservative wishful thinking. The kind of statements it brings forth from some of the experts are what Dr. Jule Eisenbud, a keen and open minded Denver psychiatrist, was alluding to when he wrote in commenting on the Bridey Murphy case that "psychology and psychiatry experts. . . .were lured into talking more gibberish than Bridey at her worst" (*Tomorrow*, Vol. 4, No. 4, p. 48). And another psychiatrist, likewise gifted with a keen and open mind, Dr. Ian Stevenson, in his review mentioned earlier *(RIS)* justly charges the authors of *A Scientific Report on "The Search for Bridey Murphy"* with gratuitously assuming *ab initio* that memories of a past incarnation could not possibly be a valid explanation of Virginia's verified statements; with evident ignorance of some of the facts turned up by Barker in Ireland; and with resorting to the old trick of explaining away the data by "analyzing" Bernstein's motives.

Indeed, insistence on turning every puzzling *ad rem* question into a question *ad hominem* is the occupational disease to which psychiatrists are most susceptible! In psychiatrists whom it affects, it has a way of generating fantasies even more fantastic than those of their patients. Whether or not that self-styled "Scientific Report" reveals hidden motivations in Bernstein and in Virginia, it affords in any case an edifying exhibit of the emotional thinking which Bernstein's book let loose in the psyches of the supposedly coldly scientific experts who authored that report.

It is important in this general connection to bear in mind that psychiatrists are concerned with hypnotism essentially as an instrument of therapy; and that, even if the notions to which they have come as to what is a "true" hypnotic state or as to the "true" nature of the interrelation between subject and hypnotist are valid *for therapeutic purposes,* these notions are on the contrary myopic or parochial if supposed to apply automatically to hypnotism in general. For the status of those notions then becomes that of dogmas of a creed, which function somewhat as do side-blinders on a horse: they confine the attention and the hypotheses of the "wearers" of those dogmas to but one particular segment of the total range of the possible capacities of hypnotism, or of the possible meanings of some of the things which occur in hypnosis.

For instance Dr. Raginsky, in the paper on "Medical Hypnosis" which he contributes to that "Scientific Report" comments at one place on the fact that in the sixth of Bernstein's sessions, Bridey talks back to Bernstein and even asks him questions. This, Dr. Raginsky writes, is "hardly a true hypnotic state;" for she ceases to be "the passive receptive typical hypnotic subject" (p. 15).

Thus, because Dr. Raginsky's horizon is specifically that of *medical* hypnosis, and by a "true" hypnotic state he therefore automatically means a hypnotic state suitable for medical purposes, it never occurs to him that the subject's behavior on that occasion perhaps was evidence that hypnosis can sometimes be effective for certain purposes foreign to psychiatry—possibly in particular for that of awakening latent paranormal capacities in the subject, such as would be capacity to remember a life that really had preceded birth and conception; or the capacities for telepathy or clairvoyance which the early hypnotists did at times successfully awaken in their subjects. The success in this, of those "mesmerists" or "magnetizers," as compared with usual failure of hypnotists to achieve the same today, may indicate that the procedure of the former was shaped by dogmas which, even if like the present ones somewhat fanciful, were anyway different, and, as it happened, effective ones for the purpose of awakening latent paranormal capacities.

The field of hypnotism is peculiar in that, in it, any particular belief held by the hypnotists as to the relation of a hypnotized subject to his hypnotist—for instance belief that the relation is one in which the subject is passive and receptive and the hypnotist active and directive—is likely to generate automatically empirical proofs of its own correctness! For the hypnotist's belief as to the nature of the relation between subject and hypnotist automatically shapes the hypnotist's own attitude, the tone of his voice, his manner, and his particular procedure in the induction of hypnosis; and these characteristics of his behavior constitute powerful suggestions—additional to any which he may explicitly give to his subject— as to the particular role the subject is to enact. And the subject's faithful enactment of the role thus automatically handed to him, which the hypnotist believes is the subject's role in the "true" relationship between the two, is then taken by the hypnotist as evidence confirming the correctness of his conception of that relationship!

Medicine is not a science but a practical art; which, however, like other branches of engineering, draws so far as it can on the knowledge the sciences have so far won. In the case of medicine, the relevant sciences are chiefly physics, chemistry, and biology. Psychology, which in its behavioristic and physiological branches has recently though barely been admitted to the company of those adult sciences, has so far contributed but little to medicine. And psychiatry, which is as yet but an infant branch of medicine, has still less claim than have most of its older branches to the status of a science. The title of the book, *A Scientific Report on "The Search for Bridey Murphy,"* is therefore naively pretentious. The fact is that the more really scientific a psychiatrist is, the less is he likely to pontificate in the name of Science, as do at many places the authors of that book.

8. **What conclusions are and are not warranted about the case.** The outcome of our review and discussion of the Bridey

Murphy case may now be summarily stated. It is, on the one hand, that neither the articles in magazines and newspapers which we have mentioned and commented upon, nor the comments of the authors of the so-called "Scientific Report" and of other psychiattrists hostile to the reincarnation hypothesis, have succeeded in disproving, or even in establishing a strong case against, the possibility that many of the statements of the Bridey personality are genuinely memories of an earlier life of Virginia Tighe over a century ago in Ireland.

On the other hand, for reasons other than those which were advanced by those various hostile critics, and which will be set forth in the next chapter, the verifications summarized by Barker, of obscure points in Ireland mentioned in Bridey's six recorded conversations with Bernstein, do not prove that Virginia is a reincarnation of Bridey, nor do they establish a particularly strong case for it. They do, on the other hand, constitute fairly strong evidence that, in the hypnotic trances, *paranormal* knowledge of one or another of several possible kinds concerning those recondite facts of nineteenth century Ireland, became manifest. This brings us directly to the question of what sort of empirical evidence, if we had it, we would regard as constituting definite proof of reincarnation.

Chapter XXVI

HOW STANDS THE CASE FOR THE REALITY OF SURVIVAL AS REINCARNATION

The distinctions formulated in Secs. 2, 3, and 4 of Chapt. XIV make it possible to give to the expression "survival after death" a meaning which is precise but involves no assumption as to whether the life-after-death one has in view is life discarnate, or life reincarnate. In the present chapter, however, what we are concerned with is survival specifically as reincarnation of the mind, or of some part of the mind, of a deceased person in another human body. The question before us is therefore whether the facts we have reviewed, which seem to evidence reincarnation, admit of alternative interpretations perhaps more plausible.

1. **Mediumistic communications from minds surviving discarnate, vs. memories in a reincarnated mind.** If the possibility of life at all after death is assumed, then the most obvious of the alternative interpretations of the facts which suggest reincarnation is the one Spiritualists would ordinarily adopt; namely, that the person, through whose organs of expression true statements are uttered concerning the past life on earth of a deceased person, is not a reincarnation of the mind of the deceased, but is a *medium* through whose temporarily borrowed lips or hand the surviving discarnate mind of the deceased speaks or writes, mentioning facts of its past life it remembers, that are adequate to identify him.

This hypothesis concerning the source of true communications of past facts recommends itself especially when, as for instance in the case of Mrs. Piper, the true communications received appear to emanate from several quite different persons who were contemporaries of one another. On the other hand, the reincarnation hypothesis remains as plausible as the Spiritualistic when, as in the Bridey Murphy case, virtually only one personality manifests itself through the entranced organism, and does so steadily throughout a prolonged series of experiments; or, if several personalities appear, they present themselves as a series of incarnations of the same entity, memory including experiences of discarnate existence during the intervals between the several incarnations. In the Bridey Murphy case, there seemed to be memory of a brief and painful life as a sick baby in New Amsterdam at some time before the birth of Bridey; but because of its brevity, of the distress attaching to it, and of the unlikelihood that it could have contained memories of verifiable details, Bernstein did not push the attempt to explore it. There is no evidence, then, that this brief life as a sick baby actually occurred, nor that the scanty account of it Virginia gave represented a *memory* of some episode rather than only an invention to satisfy the hypnotist's demand for regression to a time before Bridey's birth.

2. **Reincarnation as "possession."** The best case on record of reincarnation as "possession" is that of the Watseka Wonder described in Sec. 4 of Chapt. XVII. In that case, the mind of a definitely identified person, Mary Roff deceased at age 18 some 12 years before, did to all intents and purposes reincarnate in the body not of a neonate but of a 13 year old girl, Lurancy Vennum, displacing altogether the latter's personality for a period of some 14 weeks.

Reincarnation in the sense this would illustrate is very rare, and is anyway not reincarnation as ordinarily conceived, which is not thus episodic but lasts through the whole time between the birth and death of the body concerned; and in which what is reincarnated is not a developed mind and therefore can be supposed to be only a set of latent aptitudes brought from one or more previous lives.

It should, however, be noted that aside from this, reincarnation in the "possession" sense illustrated by the Watseka Wonder case differs from the cases of *direct control* of a medium's body by the surviving mind of a deceased person only in two respects, which are a matter of degree rather than of kind.

One is that, in the mediumistic cases, the "possession," i.e., the direct control, is but momentary—usually a matter of minutes rather than of even as long as an hour—whereas Mary Roff's possession or "direct control" of Lurancy's body endured for more than three months.

The other difference is that the body Mary Roff "controlled" was not in trance like that of a medium used for communication by the surviving mind of a deceased person, but was as aware of and active upon its physical environment as that of a normal person. It is true that some mediums or automatists do not go into trance while giving communications purporting to emanate from the surviving mind of a deceased person. But in this case this means that they remain aware that they are functioning as an intermediary, while so functioning. That is, *only a part of their organism* is being "possessed"—only their organs of speech or of writing. Their body does not, even for the duration of the seance, proceed to behave and to occupy itself as it would if the "possessing" personality were controlling the whole body instead of only its organs of speech or its hand. In the Watseka case, on the other hand, the Mary Roff personality possessed the whole of Lurancy's body which, during 14 weeks, then did occupy itself and respond to its environment as Mary Roff's own body would have, had it been still alive and occupied by the mind of Mary Roff.

3. **Reincarnation and illusion of memory.** If the possibility of survival after death is *not*, as in the two preceding sections it was, assumed *ab initio*, then the verified memories that purport to be memories of an earlier life on earth of the person who has them are likely to be dismissed by the critic as being really illusions of memory similar to those cited in Sec. 2 of Chapt. XXII, of a man whose memories of incidents in the Harrison presidential campaign really were memories only of the images of those incidents he had formed as a child from descriptions of them by his uncles.

The difference would be only that the experient's verified memories, instead of being referred by him to an early part of his life, would be referred to an earlier life he imagined he had lived on earth; whereas the truth would be that the facts he really remembers are facts he learned in a normal manner during his present life and then forgot, but which the subconscious part of his mind retained, and which eventually emerged again into his consciousness in dramatized form as content of a so-called "progignomatic fantasy;" that is, of an imagination or day-dream which he does not realize to be this, of himself as living on earth a life anterior to his present one. The fantasy might be presenting itself spontaneously as an effect of repression of strong but unacknowledged impulses or cravings. Or it might be created under hypnosis, in compliance with the hypnotist's command to the subject to push back his consciousness to a time earlier than the birth or conception of his body.

Evidently, the acceptability or not in a given case, of this explanation of the fact that the incidents remembered and ascribed to an earlier life did really occur, though in the present life, turns on the probability or improbability or perhaps the certainty or impossibility—in the light of all we know about the person's contacts, his education, his available sources of information, etc.—that he should have learned normally during the course of his present life the past facts he now remembers but refers to an earlier life.

The probability that he did so learn them, however, depends in part on the "antecedent" improbability that the mind, or any part of the mind, of a deceased person survives after death; for if it does not, it could of course not remember anything. But in Part III it was shown that such survival is not antecedently either improbable or probable—the allegations to the contrary being based not on facts known, but only on gratuitous fideistic or scientistic assumptions.

4. **Extrasensory perceptions, vs. memories of an earlier life.** If one proceeds under the assumption that survival after death is not possible, and if it turns out to be highly improbable or impossible that some of the memories purportedly of an earlier life should really be memories of facts normally learned in the present life and then forgotten, then one might attempt to account for the correspondence of those purported memories to real facts by

supposing that the person concerned ascertained those facts not normally but *by extrasensory perception*—by telepathy, perhaps, from the minds of persons who know them, or by clairvoyance or retrocognition. The probabilities or improbabilities of this, however, are the same no matter whether the survival to which this supposition would provide an alternative be survival as reincarnation, or survival in a discarnate state. It will be recalled that in Chapt. XIX, we examined Prof. E. R. Dodds' contention that the identificatory information alleged by believers in survival to emanate from the surviving discarnate spirits of deceased persons is really obtained through unconscious exercise of telepathy or/and clairvoyance by the mediums or automatists who communicate it; and we concluded that although *some* of the *prima facie* evidence for survival may with some plausibility be explained away in this manner, nevertheless certain others of the evidential items cannot be so accounted for without postulating for extrasensory perception a scope far outranging that for which there is independent evidences; nor without depending even then on certain additional and unplausible postulations.

These conclusions apply with equal force when the form of survival under consideration is not discarnate survival specifically but is survival as reincarnation, whether immediately after death or after survival in a discarnate state for some time.

5. **What would be the best possible evidence of reincarnation.** That the mind of a now living person is *the same mind* as that of a person whose body died some time before means, according to the analysis offered in Sec. 4 of Chapt. XIV, that the mind of the person who died *has become* the mind present in the now living person. If they are in this sense the same mind, then automatically the history of the later one *includes* the history of the earlier one. Such knowledge, however, as a mind has of its own history consists of such *memories* as it has of its past experiences.

At this point, we need to distinguish between *memories* and *memory.* Memory is the capacity of a mind to "remember" past events that were its own subjective experiences, and objective events or facts that it experienced, i.e., perceived. According to the analysis of the notion of "capacity"—or "ability" or "disposition" or "power"—given in Sec. 2 of Chapt. VI, a capacity is an abiding causal connection between any event of a given kind C and some event of a given other kind E, occurring in any state of affairs of a given kind S. And *exercise* of a capacity—e.g., of the capacity designated "memory"—is what occurs when an event of kind C occurring in a state of affairs of kind S causes in it an event of kind E.—e.g., awareness of an event experienced in the past.

A memory, on the other hand, is the *present awareness* of an event or fact one experienced in the past, which *occurs* if something now causes *exercise* of one's capacity to remember that event or fact. *Memory*, then, is a capacity, not an occurrence; whereas a *memory* is an occurrence, not a capacity.

If now we ask how a given mind *knows itself to be the same mind* as one which existed earlier, the answer is as follows.

If a memory it has is of a *subjective* experience—e.g., of a thought, an emotion, an intention, a desire, etc., which it had—and it is a *genuine* memory of it, then the mind that has this memory is necessarily the same mind as the mind that had the subjective experience remembered; for nobody but oneself can remember his own subjective experiences. Another person could, at most, only remember such perceptible objective expressions, if any and whether candid or deceitful, as one gave to them; and anyway one gives no perceptible expression to many of them. This, however, brings up the question whether memory of any of one's subjective experiences can be illusory not genuine; and I submit that, if one distinguishes clearly between subjective experiences themselves, and such status—e.g., of "dream," or "hallucination," or "perception," or "sign of. . ." etc.—as one may ascribe to them, then it becomes evident that memory of one's subjective experiences, like presentness of them, cannot be illusory. For illusion is possible at all only where interpretation enters. And pastness of a subjective experience one remembers is not inferred but is just as direct an experience as is presentness of a subjective experience. Vacuousness of the supposition that one's memory of a subjective experience can be illusory (e.g., of a subjective experience one calls "pain," or "dizziness," or "fear," or "bitter taste," etc.) follows from the fact that any attempt one might make to prove either that it is or is not illusory would automatically presuppose that one *does remember* the subjective experience one designates by the particular one of those words one employed.

If, on the other hand, a memory is of some *objective* fact or event, then the only evidence there could be—which, however, would be adequate—that a mind whether incarnate or discarnate having that memory is the *same* mind as a certain mind that was incarnate at a given earlier time, would consist of the following three items together: (a) that the memories of objective facts or events the present mind has *include* memories of them which the earlier mind had; (b) that these included memories were *veridical*, i.e., are known to correspond to what those objective facts or events were; and (c) that those memories are known to be genuinely *memories* because the person having them is known *not* to have had opportunity to acquire his knowledge of those objective facts or events in any way other than personal observation of them.

Possession by a given mind of memories of subjective experiences of an earlier mind, or/and possession of memories of objective facts or events also remembered by that earlier mind, would thus mean that the earlier mind had eventually become the given mind and was thus an intrinsic early part of it.

This relation, however, is precisely the relation which, according to the accounts we have of the cases of Katsugoro, of Alexandrina Samona, and of Shanti Devi, did obtain between the whole of the memories each had, and the portion of these relating to a period anterior to the birth of their present body.

These cases, then—if the reports are accurate, which we have of them and of other cases where memory likewise *spontaneously* extends to a period earlier than the birth or conception of the present body—provide the best conceivable kind of evidence that the person having those memories is a reincarnation of one who had died earlier. Indeed, the account we have of each of these cases, if it is accurate, constitutes an account *of what it means,* to say that the *mind* of a given deceased person *reincarnated in* the body of a neonate who has now reached a certain age.

If, however, we wish to speak—as ordinarily—of reincarnation also in cases other than these; that is, in cases like that of each of the rest of us, where no such spontaneous memories of an earlier incarnation are possessed; then that which is supposed to be reincarnated in our body cannot be an earlier *mind*. It can be only the "seed" left by an earlier mind—a seed consisting of the set of what Prof. Broad would term its "supreme dispositions," and which we have described as the set of its *basic aptitudes;* that is, of its capacities to acquire under respectively appropriate circumstances various more determinate kinds of capacities.

It is conceivable, however, that one of those reincarnated basic aptitudes should be aptitude to regain, under appropriate stimulus, memories now latent that would satisfy requirements (a), (b), and (c) above, and would therefore *be* memories of an earlier incarnation. Moreover, the appropriate stimulus—or a sometimes adequate stimulus—for the regaining of them whether temporarily or enduringly, might consist of a demand to this effect made on a person under hypnosis by the hypnotist.

To have regained them in this manner would then mean that knowledge of the *sameness* of the mind of the deceased person and of the mind of the person who has been given that stimulus, has been temporarily or enduringly *achieved,* instead of having been spontaneous and native as in the cases of Katsugoro and of the other children cited.

INDEX

309

N A LIFE AFTER DEATH

DATE DUE

MAR 3 1987			
MAR 1 6 1987			
MAR 3 0 1987			
MAY 2 6 199			
MAY 2 7 133			
NOV 0 4 199			
NOV 2 0 1997			
JUL 0 9 1998			
MAR 2 6 1999			
OCT 1 0 2001			
OCT 3 1 2009			